ELEVATING *the* RACE

ELEVATING *the* RACE

THEOPHILUS G. STEWARD,

BLACK THEOLOGY,

AND THE MAKING OF

AN AFRICAN AMERICAN

CIVIL SOCIETY,

1865–1924

Albert G. Miller

THE UNIVERSITY OF TENNESSEE PRESS / Knoxville

Copyright © 2003 by The University of Tennessee Press / Knoxville.
All Rights Reserved. Manufactured in the United States of America.
First Edition.

This book is printed on acid-free paper.

Library of Congress Cataloging-in-Publication Data

Miller, Albert George, 1951–
Elevating the race: Theophilus G. Steward, Black theology, and the making
of an African American civil society, 1865–1924/Albert G. Miller.— 1st ed.
      p. cm.
Includes bibliographical references (p.   ) and index.
ISBN 1-57233-221-2 (cl.: alk. paper)
  1. Steward, T. G. (Theophilus Gould), 1843–1924.
  2. African Americans—Biography.
  3. African American political activists—Biography.
  4. African American theologians—Biography.
  5. African Methodist Episcopal Church—Clergy—Biography.
  6. Wilberforce University—Presidents—Biography.
  7. African Americans—Civil rights—History.
  8. African Americans—Social conditions—To 1964.
  9. Black theology—History.
 10. Civil society—United States—History.
  I. Title.

E185.97.S83 M55 2003
973.8'092—dc21   2002152527

To God be the glory

To my ancestors—my mother,
Ethel Mitchell Miller Jackson;
my father, Albert Leondas Miller;
my step-father, Frank James Jackson;
my aunt, Charlotte Miller; and my
mother-in-law, Hattie Grier Gilbo

To my family—Brenda, the love of
my life, and my four independent
and beautiful children!

Contents

Acknowledgments

T. G. Steward initially came to my attention in the summer of 1986, when I was starting my German language class at Princeton University. Moses Moore, now at Arizona State University, mentioned Steward as a topic to investigate while researching his dissertation on the nineteenth-century Yale-trained scholar Orishatukeh Faduma. I, at the time, was too engulfed in the conjugating of verbs to think about research topics. Steward came again to my attention in the spring of 1988 during Al Raboteau's African American religious history class. He used Steward's *End of the World* as an example of some nineteenth-century black Americans' response to theodicy resulting from the experience in the nadir period. Al was an excellent mentor and is a great friend. He along with Kathy Raboteau provided both my family and me with great support during my stay in Princeton, especially during some family medical emergencies. Al and John Wilson, now dean of the Graduate School at Princeton University, patiently guided me through the dissertation stage of this project.

While visiting Princeton for my graduation in 1994, I wandered into Nell Painter's office, and before I left she had committed to reading the dissertation. Nell responded at the end of that summer with four single-spaced pages of suggestions about how to turn the dissertation into a book. She also mentioned several publishers to contact. I will never forget her unsolicited support of my work, especially when I was not one of her students or even in the History Department.

Victor Anderson, Yvonne Chireau, Michael Dyson, Tim Fulop, William Hart, Obery Hendricks, Ian Straker, Linda Stromhier, and other graduate students tolerated my rambling on about my Steward findings. Judith Weisenfeld graciously read the manuscript over its various evolutions.

As Steward came alive for me, several scholars of American religious history were crucial. David Wills, Randall Burkett, Will Gravely, and the late James Washington took a special interest in my work. They opened their individual archives and research on black churches and church leaders and helped me to understand the connection between Steward and many of his contemporaries. Wills's unpublished dissertation on aspects of social thought in the African Methodist Episcopal Church found within the *A.M.E. Church Review* remains the best source on that journal as well as the history that surrounds it and that church. Peter Paris of Princeton Seminary was also a great support because of his wonderful work on the late-nineteenth-century understandings of the moral discourse of male leaders of the black church. Jualynne Dodson guided me regarding the role of black women in the AME Church. Most of the above people were actively involved in the Northeast Seminar for the Study of Black Religion. They and others who were present gently but rigorously prodded and explored many of my assumptions when I presented my early findings on Steward at one of their sessions at Union Theological Seminary in New York.

I met William Seraile, author of the fine biography on Steward, just as he was finishing the first draft of his book. He shared hard-to-find sources with me and encouraged me to pursue my own angle on Steward's life.

I have learned through this process that reference librarians are not only a breed of their own but worth their collective weight in gold. The assistance of Emily Belcher, Mary George, and the reference staff of the Firestone Library at Princeton was priceless as I began to unearth Steward's writings. Diana Lachatanere and the staff of the Schomburg Center for Research in Black Culture provided valuable help in researching Steward and accessing his papers. Ms. Jacqueline Y. Brown and the reference librarians in the Archives at Wilberforce University helped me to locate AME Church sources. The reference librarians in Mudd Library at Oberlin College, especially Cynthia Comer and Kerry Langan, provided valuable assistance as I finished the research for the dissertation.

Several at Oberlin College deserve mention as well. My colleagues in the Religion Department are owed a debt of gratitude for their patience and support of my work both at the dissertation stage and during its transition to a book. Their support, encouragement, and urgings helped me to maintain sanity while teaching, advising students, and carrying out the other service duties within the college community. Grover Zinn read several chapters and made comments. I am especially indebted to my colleague Paula Richman, as she, at several crucial points in the writing process, helped me think through the outline of several chapters. She also read much of the manuscript and made invaluable comments. I must thank Nancy Dye, president of Oberlin College, and Clayton Koppes, dean of the College of Arts and Sciences at Oberlin, for the generous support of their respective offices. Diana Roose, assistant to President Dye, also deserves mention. Sandy Zagarell of the English Department read the *Charleston Love Story* chapter and helped me to understand this novel's nineteenth-century literary context. The late Calvin Hernton of the African American Studies Department also made valuable comments on this chapter. Pam Brooks also made significant comments on the chapter on TGS and women. Erika Nalls Hodge, my former student advisee and first research assistant, suffered my lunacy in the last stages of completing the dissertation.

Several people were helpful at the stage of editing the manuscript. My longtime friend and comrade, the Rev. Ron Potter, assisted with my understanding of the nuances of nineteenth- and early twentieth-century American theology as well as Steward's place therein. The Rev. Mary Meadow and June Goodwin read and made valuable comments in the early part of editing process. Malcolm Cash, friend, writer, poet, educator and activist, read the latter stages of the manuscript. Many thanks go to Phyllis Yarber Hogan for her assistance with the indexing. This book would still be languishing in my head had Cynthia Eller not graciously taken over as my primary editor and turned the dissertation into what I hope is a coherent book. She was crucial in my ability to get the manuscript to press. I will be forever grateful for her swift and clear work.

Many have provided moral support throughout the years of my work on Steward. My national church family, the House of the Lord Pentecostal Church, especially the Reverend Doctors Herbert and Karen Daughtry, were at the core of that support with their faithfulness and commitment to my family and me. My two sisters, Cannie Briscoe and Mabel Harris, and their families were my biggest cheerleaders as I walked across the stage to pick up my degree from Princeton University.

Finally, no one made more sacrifices than my immediate family. My mostly grown children (Opuruiché, Imani, Caleb, and the now pre-teen Isoke) suffered through several missed summer vacations as I had to trek back to the office to finish the dissertation. My faithful and loving companion, Brenda LaVerne Grier-Miller, kept me on task and gave me the encouragement to finish as I took on too many other community activist projects and ministry activities.

A. G. Miller
Oberlin, Ohio

Introduction

At this juncture, while so many theories are being presented as model plans for the reformation of society with regard to our race, *it really becomes necessary to inquire minutely into the present position we occupy; the reasons why we inhabit this and not another; and into the position we desire to occupy; our fitness for it, and the obstacles in the way of our attaining it. . . . All we require is, that it be not based upon accidents, such as color, race, previous condition, but that manhood—moral and intellectual worth—be the basis of classification; and that without constraint, the mind be allowed to seek its own level and the man his associates. . . .* What Can Elevate Us? . . . *To elevate the blacks and place them beyond the reach of foul wrong, power, force, must be put into their hands. . . . The strength must be infused in the man. He must be made strong.* This will come only from labor, study, and thought. The only way to elevate is to increase the intrinsic worth.

Theophilus Gould Steward, c. 1867

Black theology had its modern beginning in the 1960s as African American ministers developed responses to the challenges of the civil rights and black power movements, as well as to racism in America. More specifically, the movement responded to the racist theological assumptions of white American churches. James Cone, the premiere spokesman of modern black theology, began the codification of the movement in his groundbreaking work, *Black Power and Black Theology,*[1] first published in 1969. Since then, many second-generation African American theologians and biblical scholars have come forth to broaden the discourse of this intellectual and theological movement, and it has emerged as a major wing of a larger liberation theology movement. But much of black theology is developed with a limited awareness of the African American thought that preceded it. Early in this modern movement— save for Gayraud Wilmore's work, *Black Religion and Black Radicalism*[2]— little acknowledgment was given to the fact that an earlier discourse dealing with similar issues had taken place among African Americans. It is only recently that the ideas of late-nineteenth- and early-twentieth- century thinkers and activists have been acknowledged and explored. Many historians have looked at these thinkers in terms of their contribu- tions to a secular discourse concerning notions of integration and black nationalism. But these figures must also be examined as the religious thinkers they were. They developed theological treatises challenging the prevailing racist ideologies of the day and were integral members in their religious communities.

One of the most prominent of these thinkers was Theophilus Gould Steward (1843–1924), an African Methodist Episcopal (AME) minister who actively constructed a theological discourse which challenged both black and white religious and secular institutions of his time. He joined in debate with his contemporaries regarding the best strategies to lift Afri- can Americans out of the quagmire of the post-Reconstruction period. The black theology movement today has yet to reach the vast majority of the leadership of the African American religious community and has remained largely an intellectual enterprise.[3] However, Steward occupied a somewhat different place in the social fabric. He was what Cornel West (drawing upon the work of early-twentieth-century Italian Marxist Antonio Gramsci) called an "organic intellectual," that is, one who linked the life of the mind to activism in public affairs.[4] Steward was in particular deeply committed to using his intellectual powers to challenge the church from within, to reshape its theological outlook, and in turn to join in the effort to establish institutions of civil society (such as educational institutions) for African Americans. Reverdy C. Ransom, a prominent contemporary of Steward, remarked of him, "I shall not say he was a proud and haughty man, but his moral and social standards were so high, and his sense of the proprieties so firmly held, he would neither bow nor cater to flattery and political trickery, or stoop to win the applause of the crowd, to win favor or gain promotion."[5] Although Steward's tenacious pursuit of high stan- dards led him into conflict with the very community he served, even when he was ostracized from the church he used his intellectual gifts in other arenas, ones he understood to be yet other facets of civil society.

If one individual epitomizes the postbellum endeavor to create an African American civil society, it would be Steward. A pastor in the AME Church for twenty-seven years, he began his ministry as a missionary in South Carolina and Georgia during the Reconstruction period. He later became a military chaplain, spending sixteen years in the Twenty-fifth Infantry of the U.S. military. After retiring from the military in 1906, he served as a professor of history, logic, and French at Wilberforce University in Wilberforce, Ohio, until his death eighteen years later.[6]

Steward was a contemporary of and acquainted with such notables as William E. B. Du Bois (author, educator, and social activist), the Reverend Alexander Crummell (famed clergyman, teacher, and missionary), Bishop James Theodore Holly (prelate of the Orthodox Apostolic Church of Haiti), Hallie Quinn Brown (educator and orator), Frederick Douglass (who attended Metropolitan AME Church in Washington, D.C., while Steward was pastor), Fannie Jackson Coppin (educator), and the Reverend Francis Grimké (pastor of the Fifteenth Street Presbyterian Church in Washington, D.C.). He was acquainted with several bishops of the AME Church, including Benjamin F. Lee, his cousin; his early mentor, Daniel Alexander Payne; his later protégé, Levi J. Coppin; Japez P. Campbell; Benjamin T. Tanner; Moses B. Salter; and W. J. Gaines. Within the larger African American community, Steward was clearly seen as a national figure. The author of more than fifteen books and lengthy pamphlets, and of more than eighty-five articles, Steward, in many ways, represents a host of well-published and highly intellectual African American scholars and leaders who have been almost completely overlooked in historical and theological scholarship.

Steward's work took him all over the United States and around the world, where he served a variety of populations, from parishioners to ministers to enlisted men and students. In all of these capacities, he never swerved from his central goal of developing strategies to equip African Americans with the necessary skills to enter American society as full participants. Like other African American leaders of the time, Steward worked toward empowering the African American community, making self-determination a possibility. At the same time, he challenged white American institutions and their intellectual discriminatory agendas, developing a vision of civilization and civil society that informed his seminal ideas about race elevation in the form of education, African American religious institutions, and theology. He was actively involved in creating and molding the various institutions that would meet the needs of the African American community and organize against the onslaught coming from the wider society.

Many thought that the emancipation of slaves during the Civil War would bring along the millennium, a time of peace and justice in the land for all people, including African Americans. Instead, what developed was another period of continued oppression and disenfranchisement under the constitutionally guaranteed rights of citizenship. Historian Rayford Logan calls this period "the Nadir" of African American history, lasting from 1877 to 1921, the exact period of Steward's work as a minister and thinker.[7] The increase in lynching, continued disfranchisement and discriminatory judicial interpretations by the Supreme Court, as well as the codification of legal discriminatory statutes characterized this period. But in spite of disfranchisement, Jim Crow laws, and the blighted hopes of the Reconstruction period, African Americans struggled during this period for both recognition and equal rights as American citizens. They also worked, through individual and institutional efforts, to make themselves ready to accept and participate in these citizenship rights, should they be granted. African Americans on the whole were in need of significant social uplift or elevation. At the same time, they wanted to maintain their distinctiveness as African Americans. W. E. B. Du Bois suggested in *The Souls of Black Folk* that the African American did not want to "bleach his Negro soul in a flood of white Americanism, for he knows that Negro blood has a message for the world."[8] Many nineteenth-century African Americans felt that out of their sojourn in America their people had something to contribute to the larger society. The best way for African Americans to both contribute their message to the world and to elevate themselves was through the development of institutions of civil society.

During the nadir period, African Americans developed a "civil society" made up of religious, educational, and social institutions that they saw as helping them to prepare for citizenship participation. In the main, these institutions served as vehicles that promoted a version of nineteenth-century, white, middle-class American cultural values: progress, civilization, and Christianity. But these same institutions also became a buffer for African Americans, absorbing the harsh blows of racism and oppression dealt by the larger society.

I define "civil society" as that network of institutions that exists between private individuals and the state, forming, in Evelyn Brooks Higginbotham's words, "an arena for the rational formation and functioning of information, in other words, public opinion."[9] But civil society does more: it provides space for the development of communal moral values, those virtues the community feels are necessary for group cohesion and for individual and corporate success. It also creates the social spaces for individuals and groups to build unity, nurture one another, and develop strategies to counteract various outside competing and hegemonic forces. The institutions of civil society can be understood as mediating structures that stand "between the individual in his private life and the larger institutions of public life."[10] Peter Berger and Richard Neuhaus argue that life is an ongoing struggle between the public and the private spheres, where the public institutions of government are overwhelming and alienating, and the private sphere is not powerful enough to restrain the public. I would add that a third force, that of capital developing institutions, significantly influences the way the private and public spheres interact with one another. This creates the need for mediating structures. As Berger and Neuhaus describe them, such structures "have a private face, giving private life a measure of stability, and they have a public face, transferring meaning and value to the megastructures. Thus, mediating structures alleviate each facet of the double crisis of modern society. Their strategic position derives from their reducing both the anomic precariousness of individual existence in isolation from society and the threat of alienation to the public order."[11] These are precisely the functions that civil society served within the nineteenth-century African American community. There were significant concerns as to how best to fend off racism, which had saturated every sector of society. At the same time African Americans were concerned about how best to participate in that society. From early on, African Americans began to build institutions, such as churches, the Free African Society, the Prince Hall Masons, literary societies, schools, and newspapers which were used both as buffers from white society and as tools of liberation. Foremost among these institutions was the church. Higginbotham has suggested that the black church be seen as "a social space for discussion of public concerns."[12] The church was the breeding ground for other institutions and strategies for survival and liberation. More than anything else, the church was able to provide the social space and security necessary for African Americans to develop their own collective identity, which was critical during the nadir period, when physical, mental, economic, and political attacks against African Americans were at their worst.

Steward and Race

Steward exemplified Cornel West's theory of the African American humanist tradition that highly affirms the distinctiveness of black culture and personality. In his *Prophesy Deliverance! An Afro-American Revolutionary Christianity,* West outlines four different responses to the dilemma of African Americans in American society: exceptionalist, assimilationalist, marginalist, and humanist traditions.[13] The African American humanist tradition, notes West,

> accents the universal human content of Afro-American cultural forms. It makes no ontological or sociological claims about Afro-American superiority or inferiority. Rather, it focuses on the ways in which creative Afro-American cultural modes of expression embody themes and motifs analogous to the vigorous cultural forms of other racial, ethnic, or national groups. This tradition affirms Afro-American membership in the human race, not above it or below it.[14]

Steward first and foremost saw himself and others as human beings with certain likes and dislikes. Although he was committed to the African American community and its progress, he did not privilege this or any other community with any ontological or sociological claims of superiority or inferiority:

> If a man finds any comfort in cultivating what he supposes is a "race prejudice," I have no quarrel with him; only he ought to treat his prejudices just as he would his curs—keep them on his own premises or muzzle them when he takes them in public. Personally I have never been conscious of anything signified by the term colored. I can feel my individuality and my responsibility, but my consciousness fails to give any response to the adjective that unreasoning prejudice attaches to my person.[15]

His upbringing and his family background shaped Steward's ideas, in part. At the core of his intellectual and spiritual life was his mixed racial family background, which must be placed within the historical context of a northern pre–Civil War America. Steward and his family members had light, near-white complexions, and as a result, they existed in an odd tension between the white and black communities. For example, Steward's brother William, like Steward himself, served in Georgia and Florida during Reconstruction. During this time, William wrote a letter to the American Missionary Association administration complaining that a former teacher "a lady formally, if not yet, under your auspices, circulates malicious fabrications, to my detriment among black and white, says (I am very fair skinned) I am a 'low down' Yankee passing off for a Negro."[16] Steward and his family, in spite of their sometimes marginal racial position, made a clear identification with the African American community.

Perhaps as a consequence of his mixed racial background, race as a biological distinction was of little importance for Steward. Steward saw race as a social and ideological construct, invented to make distinctions between peoples based on power relations. Historian Barbara Fields claims that in constructing the notion of race the first assumption is that race "is an observable physical fact, a thing, rather than a notion that is profoundly and in its very essence ideological."[17] For Steward, although he understood the social and political power placed on the idea of race, "color" was indeed a physical fact: a thing to be neither "ashamed of nor proud of; as of no more moral, intellectual or social worth than height or weight. It is physical, and that is all." He declared that "[a]s to all other ideas of whatever sort or kind that are sought to be pressed into the word 'colored,' as applied to people, I have all my life-long failed to find any verification of them either in my own consciousness, or in my actual intercourse with other human beings." If he could rid society of the term "colored," he said, particularly as it related negatively to Afro-Americans, he would gladly see it fall into disuse: "Would anything be lost if the custom of classing people as colored should be dropped? I do not think the colored people themselves care anything about it one way or the other; but would it not be better to allow all those words which make distinctions in our citizenship to fall into innocuous desuetude?" Nevertheless, he realized that the racist nature of America would not change in the near future and, therefore, these distinctions would remain. This attitude is

reflected in his comments on the adjective "African" in the name of the
AME Church: "It was the African Church; but it was open to all, of whatever race or clime. . . . He [Bishop Payne] was anxious, as many others
were at the time, to see some way open through which the prefix African
might give place to a broader term. Alas! Such a day has not come as yet,
nor does it appear likely to do so soon."[18]

In a more positive vein, Steward understood the importance of a distinctive group. There was a strong sense of pride and self-determination
in the Gould clan. At the same time, they hoped for a society that would
be more accepting of them as a people of mixed heritage without denigrating their African ancestry in the process. Steward was raised to believe
that there was no distinction between people, an idea reinforced by his
multicultural upbringing in Gouldtown.[19] The Goulds' mixed racial line-
age, unlike most others of that era, was not based on slavery, its sexual
brutalities, or concubinage, but on mutual consent and intermarriage.[20]
The family even claimed its ancestral connection to Lord Fenwick, though
Fenwick despised the relationship between his granddaughter and Gould,
the interracial founding couple of Gouldtown. Yet they chose to identify
with the African American community.[21]

Steward was considered a "Race Man": one who had a strong sense of
racial identity and who constantly fought for racial pride, elevation, and
self-determination. He was committed to racial pluralism and the integration of African Americans into American society as a socioethical ideal,
inspired by a Christian egalitarian faith. Steward agreed with W. E. B. Du
Bois, who explained that "[t]he problem of the twentieth century is the
problem of the color-line, —the relation of the darker to the lighter races
of men in Asia, Africa, in America and the islands of the sea."[22] By no
means, though, could Steward be considered a black nationalist, as were
some of his contemporaries, such as Bishop Henry M. Turner. He was
clearly committed to the notion of integration and consistently struggled
for a fair and equitable society for all races in America.

The principal means Steward advocated for that end was black self-
determination. Ironically, this placed him in the company of both black
nationalists and assimilationists. There has not been a clear differentiation
in the historiography of this period between black nationalist and assimilationist thought when it comes to strategies of self-determination.[23] Self-
determination was the foundation for both ideologies: it could be used as

a tool to gain the end of either a nationalist separation from American society or an assimilationist inclusion in American society.[24]

Black nationalism in its most developed form suggested that blacks should separate permanently from whites and establish a nation—whether in Africa, the Caribbean, or the continental United States—in which they would have complete control over every aspect of their religious, economic, social, and cultural lives without the interference of white racism. Black nationalism blossomed in Martin R. Delany's African Colonization Movement and Bishop James Theodore Holly's emigration-to-Haiti movement in the 1850s and early 1860s.[25] It was also central in the work and rhetoric of Bishop Henry M. Turner of the African Methodist Episcopal Church and others in the 1880s as hopes for equality and freedom were frustrated during the latter part of the Reconstruction period. It continued into the twentieth century in the ideology of Marcus Garvey and the Universal Negro Improvement Association, the largest black mass movement in American history before the civil rights movement. Elijah Muhammad and the Nation of Islam later developed these themes further.

An assimilationist ideology, on the other hand, had as its ultimate goal the full participation of black people in the rights and privileges guaranteed in the American Constitution and, more broadly, in the philosophy of the universal rights of humankind. Rather than separating themselves from America, assimilationists strove to make America live up to its democratic rhetoric. Frederick Douglass and Booker T. Washington represented this ideology throughout much of the nineteenth century. Civil rights activist Ralph Bunche and union organizer A. Philip Randolph espoused it during the 1930s, 1940s, and 1950s. And assimilationism would be vividly illustrated in the civil rights movement of the 1950s and 1960s, led by the Rev. Martin Luther King and others.

The strategy of black self-determination asserted that the ultimate goals of equality, freedom, and justice, whether of the nationalist or the assimilationist variety, would only be achieved for black Americans through their own efforts at racial unity, self-help, self-respect, and cooperation. These goals had to be accomplished through black people's own efforts rather than through dependency upon whites for leadership and support. Development of separate actions and institutions were thus a natural outcome of the strategy of black self-determination. Due to racism and slavery in American life, action that was separate and independent of whites was called for as the best way to struggle for inclusion in American society. Leonard I. Sweet, in *Black Images of America 1784–1870*, stated it this way: "At the same time that blacks recognized that separate demands seemed to contradict the ideal of equality which their ancestors had helped to establish in the American Revolution, they also realized that without their own independent actions to secure their emancipation, elevation, and equality; black identity, equality, and self-confidence would be no more than an artificial product of white abolitionist tutelage."[26] A self-determination strategy was a necessary foundation for the flowering of a black nationalist ideology of separation of the races as espoused by Henry M. Turner, Marcus Garvey, and others of later generations. Conversely, a black self-determination strategy was also the foundation for the assimilationist philosophies of Frederick Douglass, Booker T. Washington, and others. Black nationalism assumes a goal of disengagement from American society as much as humanly possibly. The assimilationist philosophy, while at times advocating radical means, always presupposed an overall commitment to that same society. Both could use the strategy of self-determination to achieve their goals. We find this strategy of self-determination active in the life and thought of Theophilus Gould Steward as he struggled for an integrated society and for the social elevation of African Americans.

Steward's Theology

Steward stood at the boundary between the African American experience of prophetic religion and the intellectual's response to the challenge of modernity by the mainstream churches. On the one hand, Steward's development was shaped by the evangelical Christian theology that permeated American culture through its revival fervor and various church structures.[27] For Steward, evangelicalism was shaped by the Christian egalitarian ideal, which was central to the African American religious tradition in general and the AME Church in particular. The AME official motto, "God our Father; Christ our Redeemer; Man our Brother," was a primary example of this ideal within the African American Protestant evangelical tradition. This egalitarian principle, which Steward attempted to articulate throughout his career, was crucial in shaping his life.

Steward responded theologically to the challenge of nineteenth-century modernity with its new advances in industrialization, science, evolution, and biblical criticism.[28] He was, first and foremost, a theologian, committed to what Paul Griffin has called a "rational orthodox theology":

> Rational orthodox theology was a religious orientation that affirmed the unity of truth in a divine and rational universe. Its proponents held that while revelation stood above reason in so far as human reason alone could never unilaterally [have] deduced the truths of Christian Scripture, true reason or "sanctified reason" and revelation never contradicted each other. On the contrary, its advocates contended that the two were divinely instituted and divinely harmonious. For them, it took both reason and revelation to comprehend what constituted genuine Christianity.[29]

Steward was committed to the affirmation of the "unity of truth in a divine and rational universe,"[30] but he went beyond most of his peers and took seriously the more liberal theological leanings of his time. In his book *Genesis Re-Read,* Steward attempted to harmonize—to both reconcile and hold them in creative tension—the theory of evolution (as articulated by Thomas Huxley, "Darwin's Bulldog") and biblical criticism with the evangelical spirit of America.

At various points in his life, Steward acted in what seemed to be contradictory fashions. In *The End of the World,* for example, he was extremely critical of the imperialist vision for a Christian America proposed by white Americans such as Josiah Strong.[31] He nonetheless accepted a commission as chaplain in the U.S. military during the end of the conflict with Native Americans and during the Spanish-American War. He seemingly participated in these enterprises without any ethical difficulties. At other times, Steward's divine egalitarian doctrine led him to stand against popular opinion, as when he argued for a very unpopular proposal for an integrated school system in Delaware.

In addition to assessing Steward's intellectual life and professional religious experience, this book will also analyze his institutional participation and leadership in the church of the late nineteenth and early twentieth centuries. Steward's experience in the African American context did not develop in a vacuum. He was influenced by and contributed to the larger American religious experience. Thus, his life will be compared and contrasted with his contemporaries: Bishops Henry M. Turner, Daniel A. Payne, and James T. Holly, as well as Alexander Crummell and other African

American intellectuals. Steward's thought will also be set within movements such as evangelicalism, the social gospel, and the nineteenth-century rhetoric of Manifest Destiny, which provided the larger social context for his life and thought.

Steward's emphasis on "rational orthodox religion," and the tension which it created for his career within the AME Church, evinces his particular position of marginality as a figure standing between the African American and the white mainstream American churches. The following chapters focus on the themes that dominated Steward's life. Chapter 1 gives a biographical sketch of Steward's life. Steward's notion of the interaction between education and civil society and his attempt to establish an educated and rational culture for the African American is studied in chapter 2. Chapter 3 centers on Steward's attempt to reconcile the two theological worlds within which he interacted: black evangelical revival religion and the newly emerging reconciliation between theology and modern science. Chapter 4 returns to Steward's evolving understanding of rational theology and its intersection with personal moral virtues. He adjusted his in the writing of a Victorian novel titled *A Charleston Love Story; or, Hortense Vanross.* Chapter 5 explores tension between Steward's vision for a nonracial, democratic, and Christian America as a model for world civilization and the contradictions of race as both an American and worldwide concern. Steward's changing views of the role of women in his developing notion of African American civil society is examined in chapter 6. Finally, chapter 7 focuses on the vital role that Steward saw the military playing on behalf of African Americans as a civil societal institution and looks at his maturing view of imperialism and race.

Biographical Sketch

Theophilus Gould Steward was born on April 23, 1843, in Gould-town, New Jersey, a racially mixed community. He was the fourth of six children born to James and Rebecca Steward. James was an orphan; his parents emigrated to Haiti during the Boyer expedition of 1824 and never returned. James was left in the care of Elijah Gould, Rebecca's uncle, who raised him until James and Rebecca married.[1] Rebecca was a descendant of the founders of Gouldtown, a black man named Gould (no other name given),[2] and the British-born Elizabeth Adams, granddaughter of John Fenwick, who in 1675 was the lord proprietor of Fenwick Colony, which is in modern-day southern New Jersey. Upon their union, Lord Fenwick cut Elizabeth off from any share of his estate "unless the Lord open her eyes to see her abominable transgression against him, me and her father, by giving her true repentance and forsaking that Black that hath been the ruin of her and becoming penitent for her sins."[3] The son of this union, Benjamin, married a Finnish immigrant woman named Ann, and some of their descendants continued to intermarry with whites, Native Americans, others of mixed race, and Africans, creating a "mulatto" community at Gouldtown.[4] It was into this community that Steward was born, but as the larger American society demanded that one be either black or white, Steward chose black. That it was a choice can be seen in Steward's comment that some earlier members of his family "intermarried with whites, and members of their immediate offspring went away and lost their identity, they and their descendants becoming white."[5]

Steward named his mother as the paramount influence on his early educational and spiritual formation. While he claimed that both his father and mother were committed to providing "a practical education" for their children, it was his mother, he believed, who bore more of this responsibility because she was "better informed" than his father. Steward praised his mother's influence on his education, recalling that "she . . . examined and encouraged the children even when in school, and kept the love of learning burning briskly at the time."[6]

A triangle consisting of home, Sunday school, and church defined Steward's early youth, but his mother's influence was definitive at every point.[7] Rebecca took the lead in joining the AME Church in Gouldtown, while her husband and children followed. Steward's mother also had a significant influence on others in this farming community. All accounts in the *Memoirs of Mrs. Rebecca Steward,* edited and written by T. G. Steward in 1877, evidenced that she was a spiritual mother and leader in the community.

Steward's older brother, William, it is worth noting, perceived the spiritual formative process differently. He thought that both his mother and father shared credit in their moral upbringing. William, in a 1917 letter to Theophilus, responded to the query why neither him nor his brothers and sisters had become "addicted to profane drinking or Sabbath breaking." William suggested that both his father and mother were responsible: "Mother's teaching of reverence for the 'good man' [God,] father's upright example, steady employment, avoidance of rowdyism, careful selection of our associates, were among the causes of our not acquiring habits of profanity, drinking and Sabbath breaking."[8]

Early in his career and ministry, Steward came under the mentorship of the powerful bishop of the AME Church, Daniel Alexander Payne, who ordained Steward in 1865 at age twenty-one.[9] Relations between Payne and Steward would later become strained.

Steward was licensed to exhort in Trinity AME Church in April 1862 and was admitted on probation to the traveling connection of the AME Church in June 1864. He remained there until his first assignment, at the age of twenty, to Macedonia AME Church in South Camden, New Jersey. After serving as pastor at Macedonia for a year while teaching in a normal school, he was summoned by Bishop Payne to accompany him south as a missionary in Reconstruction South Carolina.

At the first Annual Conference of the AME Church in the South, Steward was among the first group of clergy to be ordained as both deacon and elder by Bishop Payne on May 15, 1865, in Charleston, South

Carolina. He was commissioned to mission work in several rural communities in South Carolina, including areas around Georgetown, Beaufort, Summerville, and Marion. Steward was also appointed pastor of Morris Brown Church, which was organized in the fall of 1866 in Charleston. He taught school in both Marion and Charleston.[10]

It was in Charleston that he met his future wife, Elizabeth Gadsden, the daughter of Charles Gadsden and Martha Gadsden, a well-known free black family in the Methodist circles of Charleston.[11] They married on January 1, 1866. To this union were born eight sons: James (1868), Charles (1870), Frank Randolph (1872), Stephen Hunter (1874), Benjamin Gadsden (1877), Theophilus Bolden (c. 1879), Gustavus Adolphus (1881), and Walter (1886).[12]

In June 1867, Steward, reassigned to the Georgia Conference, took the first church in that conference in Lumpkin, Georgia. Then in March 1868, Steward replaced Henry McNeal Turner as pastor of the AME Church in Macon, Georgia (Turner had been elected to the Georgia House of Representatives).[13] During his three-year pastorate in Macon, the church was embroiled in a legal battle with the Methodist Episcopal Church, South over the church property. Steward oversaw the rebuilding of the church in this period after it was mysteriously burned down (arson was suspected but never proved). Steward was also active in Georgia politics and was the cashier in the Freedman's Bank in Macon during this time. While he did not organize schools in Macon, he did tutor a young parishioner named William Sanders Scarborough,[14] who went on to receive a degree from Atlanta University and bachelor's and master's degrees in classics from Oberlin College, becoming a Greek scholar. Scarborough later reconnected with Steward at Wilberforce University, where he taught for many years and eventually became president.

In 1871, Steward was transferred north to Wilmington, Delaware, and was appointed pastor of Bethel AME Church for two years. He was actively involved in the Delaware Republican Party and in Reconstruction Delaware politics, especially as they affected education. There he also met and was a mentor to the young Levi J. Coppin, who later to became an AME bishop. In 1873, Steward set sail for Haiti in for a short-lived and unsuccessful six-month mission effort. In anticipation for this missionary trip, Steward began to learn French in Wilmington, a skill that served him in later years.[15]

Steward returned from Haiti to pastor rural AME churches in Sussex County, Delaware. After an unproductive experience there, he was transferred to Bridge Street AME Church in Brooklyn, New York. In Brooklyn, he began his long publishing career. Throughout his life, Steward wrote dozens of articles for the AME Church's weekly newspaper, the *Christian Recorder,* as well as other local newspapers. During his time in Brooklyn, he also wrote a volume on his early ministry, *My First Four Years in the Itinerary of the African Methodist Episcopal Church,* and a tribute to his recently deceased mother, *Memoirs of Mrs. Rebecca Steward.*[16] It was during this time that Steward encountered Thomas Huxley, an advocate for Charles Darwin, when Huxley was giving a series of lectures on evolution. Steward reviewed the lectures in a Sunday evening address before a packed house. This was the inspiration for his *Genesis Re-Read,* published ten years later. While in Brooklyn, Steward also continued his language study, furthering his mastery of French and took up the study of Hebrew, Latin, and Greek.[17] Steward's Greek teacher was the Rev. Rufus L. Perry, the renowned black Baptist pastor, educator, editor of several black Baptist newspapers (including the *National Monitor*) and author of *The Cushites.*[18]

In 1877, Steward was transferred to Philadelphia to pastor Zion Mission AME Church. He took this opportunity to attend the Episcopal Divinity School of Philadelphia, from which he graduated in 1880 at the top of his class.[19] During his seminary years, Steward began to show his appreciation for the other Protestant traditions. He indicated that he "found the professors men advanced in years, ripe in scholarship, and profoundly Christian. . . . In a word, I found genuine religion, among the Episcopalians." This newfound ecumenism would prove to be useful later, when Steward joined the military.

In 1880–81, Steward served as pastor of the AME Church in the Frankford section of Philadelphia. He was then returned to Bethel AME Church in Wilmington, Delaware, where he had a turbulent experience with his congregation owing to his activism in the Republican Party and his views surrounding issues of equal and integrated education.

Steward had a much better experience with his congregation at Philadelphia's Union AME Church from 1883 to 1886. The congregation recognized him for "his strict integrity of character, his broad intellectual acquirements and his fearless devotion to the right as it presents itself to him."[20] He was also very productive in his writing, completing his three theological works: *Death, Hades, and Resurrection, The Divine Attributes,* and *Genesis Re-Read.*[21]

Following this period, Steward transferred to Washington, D.C., as pastor of the newly built Metropolitan AME Church, a leading congregation in Washington. This church was attended by such distinguished individuals as Frederick Douglass, John W. Cromwell, John Mercer Langston, Blanche Kelso Bruce, John R. Lynch, and P. B. S. Pinchback. While in Washington, Steward became actively involved in Washington society and led the Minister's Union, an organization that represented all of the black ministers in the city. The union praised him as being "a felt power in the community in every good word and work."[22] While at Metropolitan, he wrote and published *The End of the World,* which countered Josiah Strong's *Our Country.*[23] Strong had argued that it was Anglo-Saxons' responsibility to evangelize people of color with their brand of postmillennial Christianity. Steward challenged Strong's racist and paternalistic version of Christianity and suggested that people of color would exhibit a truer form of Christianity in the next millennial age.

When Steward was transferred to Bethel AME Church in Baltimore in 1888, he again advocated the cause of public education for African American youth and again found himself embroiled in controversy. Up to this time, he had been elected to every quarterly, annual, and general conference in every district where he had been stationed.[24] He was the recording secretary for many of the quarterly and annual conferences in which he participated and was responsible for the publication and distribution of the conference proceedings. The 1888 conference marked the last to which Steward would be elected a delegate. His demise in the church's political structure was due largely to his conflict with some of the more powerful bishops in the church over various theological and polity issues, including his support of a slate of candidates from the South for the office of bishop, his opposition to a standardized denominational liturgy, and his desire to limit the power of the office of bishop.

Steward actively supported the election of indigenous leaders from the South. He especially supported the candidacy of Wesley J. Gaines. Steward had known Gaines since his ministry in Georgia. Gaines followed Steward as pastor of the Macon church, which was later renamed in honor of Steward. They remained lifelong friends. By the 1800s, the AME church was largely a southern church, most of its growth occurring in the southern states after the Civil War. Many church members, especially from the South, called for church leadership to reflect this shift in membership. The 1880 General Conference elected Henry McNeal Turner and Richard H. Cain, both free-born southerners from South Carolina and Virginia, respectively, as bishops. Both had affiliated with the church in the North as free men and then returned to the South, where they served as powerful ministers in the period of Reconstruction. As Steward put it, "It was now time that some of the real sons of that section, some of the new men themselves, who had developed power and leadership should be elevated to the bishopric."[25] Four bishops were elected at the 1888 General Conference, including W. J. Gaines of Georgia and Abraham Grant of Texas.

The next major issue with which Steward became involved was the question of liturgy. Steward opposed the adoption of a prescribed liturgy, developed by J. C. Embry, which included the reading of the Decalogue every Sunday and the recitation of the Apostles' Creed. In *Fifty Years,* Steward stated that his opposition was not based on his resistance to a particular order of service but rather on what he perceived as inconsistency:

> I knew our whole trend had been in the line of free and simple methods, and that this attempt to convert the church into the cathedral type could but result in confusion. Men standing up with surplice and gown calling people to come to the table and put their money thereon, employing jests, provoking laughter: people sitting stock still in their seats, lazily and listlessly singing the "Gloria Patri," drawling over the Commandments, grouping three or four of them together to make one response cover all—these are some of the events I foresaw, and some that I have seen. And as to the reading of the Psalter, it fared so badly that it soon dropped out altogether.[26]

Steward and his former mentor, Bishop Payne, clashed over this motion. The *Indianapolis News* reported that Payne attacked Steward, "referring to him several times 'such a man as Steward' in a tone of contempt. Thus the discussion was allowed to fall into personalities which aroused much ill-feeling."[27]

The other major issue that Steward championed was that of the status of the general officers in the general conference. Steward, along with others, argued for the removal of the general officers as voting members in the general conference. The *Indianapolis News* noted that "the discussion and reception or rejection of the reports of these officers by the conference is always to some extent modified and biased by they themselves being present to work and vote in their own favor." The debate became heated (as did many of the issues at this conference) and "grew personal."[28] Steward and Bishop Turner were at odds over this issue, and even though the amendment passed 101 to 55, the battle did not end; Turner did not end the fight and later changed the tide of opinion to his side. As Steward recalled, "The Bishop added to the work of his pen that of his voice in making fiery, denunciatory speeches before the Conferences during which I came in for a good share of open attacks. . . . Before the General Conference of 1892 assembled those of the Conference of 1888 had figuratively repented in sackcloth and ashes, and as for me, the Baltimore Conference in 1891 decided that my views and connection with this subject and others, rendered me unavailable as a delegate."[29]

After the 1888 conference, Steward's visibility diminished, probably due to his debate with Turner and the negative fallout that it generated. He suffered an illness between 1889 and 1891, though he continued to pastor, first at Mount Pisgah Church in Washington and then at Water's Chapel in Baltimore. In the summer of 1891, with the support of John R. Lynch and Blanche K. Bruce and at the urging of Francis Grimké, Steward was nominated for the chaplaincy to the U.S. Senate by President Benjamin Harrison. Steward procured a letter of recommendation from his friend and Philadelphia businessman Postmaster General John Wanamaker. With the Senate confirmation, Steward was appointed chaplain of the Twenty-fifth Infantry, a black regiment in the regular army.[30] Steward claimed that his illness affected his duties, but even in his illness he accepted a difficult commission in the military. Possibly the move was prompted more by his diminished role in the AME Church hierarchy than by any illness.

Steward was stationed at Fort Missoula, Montana, for most of eight years with his family. In 1893, both his son James and his beloved wife Elizabeth died. Three years later, in November 1896, he married Susan Maria Smith McKinney, M.D., a person of note in her own right. Steward knew McKinney from the time of his pastorate at Bridge Street AME Church in the 1870s, where she was also an accomplished musician serving as organist and choirmaster.[31] She was the widow of the Reverend

William S. McKinney, a black Episcopal priest from South Carolina, and was the first black woman to graduate from a medical school in New York (the New York Medical College for Women, where she was the valedictorian). She was a successful physician, active in the Temperance movement and the Negro women's club movement.[32]

Steward's military experience was deeply ingrained in him. "I had become so inured to the uniform," he recalled, "and as I found here a military organization, I found it convenient to keep up the life of the garrison in my own surroundings for some time." While in the West, Steward immersed himself in military life, becoming "possessed of the army spirit" and identifying "with its discipline and training as well as with its out-door life."[33] He was critically aware of the realities of racism in America, yet he saw in the army the discipline needed for the uplift of African Americans. The army, he declared, was nothing more than a force to carry out the will of the state: "The army must be purely executive, carrying out the mandates of the State. The moral and political questions must be resolved by men to other professions. The soldier has all that he can do to attend to the exigencies of the battle."[34] But Steward believed that the army was perhaps the one institution in America in which African Americans had a better chance for equality:[35]

> The Army, by the very aristocracy of its constitution, contributes much to make effective the doctrines of equality. The black soldier and the white soldier carry the same rations, serve under the same laws, participate in the same experience, wear the same uniforms, are nursed in the same hospitals, and buried in the same cemeteries. . . . So . . . the Army of our Republic, by its aristocracy of commission, has proven itself the most effectual barrier against the inundating waves of race discrimination that the country has as yet produced.[36]

Steward challenged the black soldiers to live a moral life and constantly defended them in public for their morals and heroism. He also challenged the United States toward a peaceful benevolence in the way it ruled the countries of Cuba and Puerto Rico after the Spanish-American War. Steward's concern was that these peoples, who had experienced domination by Spain—and, he suggested, had not experienced racism America-style—would not stand for racial mistreatment by whites and would act as malcontents and plot revolution. His desire was that these countries would choose American citizenship based on the benevolent action of the U.S. military.[37]

During his time in Montana, Steward experienced another burst of literary productivity. He wrote for a wide variety of journals, newspapers, and magazines, including the *Arena, Cleveland Gazette, Indianapolis Freeman, Independent, A.M.E. Church Review, Colored American Magazine, Harper's Weekly,* and *Colored American.* Many of his articles focused on aspects of military life, including the role of the black soldier within the military, and on race in general.[38] Steward also published two books during this time, a novel titled *A Charleston Love Story; or, Hortense Vanross* and a history, *The Colored Regulars in the United States Army.*[39] He also edited a volume of short articles by sixteen chaplains, *Active Service: or Religious Work Among U.S. Soldiers,* which defined and defended the necessity for religious work in the military.[40]

From 1899 to 1901, Steward was stationed in the Philippines, where he served both as chaplain and organizer of educational institutions on behalf of Filipino people. During this time he wrote several articles related to life in the Philippines and African American soldiers' participation in garrisoning the island. Steward spent his last five years in the military stationed in Fort Niobrara, Nebraska.

Upon retirement from the military at age sixty-three, Steward became a professor of history, logic, and French at the AME school, Wilberforce University. Within a year he became the vice president under his old friend, President William S. Scarborough. Steward was very active in assisting in the transformation of Wilberforce from a normal school to a university with college-level curriculum. He also continued his literary production with the writing of *The Haitian Revolution* and, with his brother William, *Gouldtown.*[41] He resigned as vice president of Wilberforce in 1918, the same year his second wife died. He continued to teach and was active as a preacher and lecturer up to his own death on January 11, 1924.

Steward's long and active life can be broken down into three distinct professional careers: pastor, chaplain, and educator. In each of these segments of his life, he was committed to the development of an African American civil society through a variety of religious, educational, and social institutions. He hoped that these institutions would be the vehicles to carry African Americans to a level of self-sufficiency.

The Struggle for an African American Civil Society: The AME Church, Education, and Social Life

T heophilus Steward's early vision for the African American community was clearly oriented toward late-nineteenth-century, middle-class American values. He envisioned education as the major vehicle for African Americans to create a civil society, which in turn would lead to the social uplift of his people. His conception of education evolved throughout his lifetime as his idea of civil society developed into a broader notion of what he called civilization. His view of education was shaped by his egalitarian theological orientation, which was in turn grounded in the AME Church's tradition of Christian egalitarianism.[1]

Most of Steward's energies were directed toward establishing an educated and rational culture for African Americans. He worked to develop a culture which would be respected in the larger society and stand equal with the great cultures of the world, a vision vividly captured in this 1885 editorial:

> For the colored race the era of Mumbo Jumbo, of fetichism, and Voudouism has passed away, and the African has now asserted with the true logic of a true premise, the rights to an equal recognition among the Caucasian races. He has accomplished it at last, not by any pitiful bending of the knees and supplication for the inherent rights of his race, but has for the last few decades been silently and industrially working, until as was exemplified

in this recent conference, colored men stood up as leaders. In all things that go to show scholarship, ready oratory, words to the point, clothing the most practical and progressive theories in language, which for beauty of expression and vigorous, scintillating oratory, it would be difficult to find anything superior throughout the land.[2]

Steward was committed to the notion of education as a tool for social uplift. The Reverend Reverdy C. Ransom, who wrote the introduction to Steward's autobiography, *Fifty Years of Gospel Ministry,* compared Steward's notion of civil society to that of Booker T. Washington. "Here we have an American of African descent who is not struggling, 'Up from Slavery,'" Ransom stated, "but a Christian scholar who met the freedmen on the very threshold of their emancipation, and who since with singleness of devotion has been guiding them and their descendants in the paths of *knowledge, character and virtue*" (emphasis added).[3]

As shall be shown, Ransom's characterization of Steward as a Christian scholar proselytizing his version of knowledge, character, and virtue to the African American community was most appropriate. At times, these three aspects of his educational philosophy converged, and at times they diverged. Steward combined focuses on acquisition of knowledge—that is, the expansion of the mind through classical liberal arts training—and the development of character and virtue. He felt that a delicate balance of classical liberal education and moral training was necessary for the creation of a strong African American culture. He always believed in the link between education, morality, and the well-being of the African American community, but his views on precisely how the educational process was carried out would change over the course of his life. The major distinction was between his views on liberal education, which took the forefront during his role as a pastor, and his views regarding moral development, which developed full bloom during his role as army chaplain. In his role as pastor and educator, Steward advocated the expansion of schooling and intellectual opportunities for African Americans. At the governmental level, he challenged city and state policies that resulted in inadequate funding of public education for African Americans, and he argued for integrated schools at a time when it went against the grain of both the white and black communities. As a chaplain, Steward provided education for the enlisted men. His work as a professor and administrator at Wilberforce University also reflected his vision of a literate African American culture. Clearly, Steward lived out his concern for a "civilized" black society, one that clearly looked for white society's approval and yet struggled for a sense of self-determination.

Education

Throughout his life, Steward demonstrated had a strong propensity toward the life of the mind. In the areas of religious education and classical training, his mother, Rebecca, established a strong impetus for his zest of learning. Rebecca was an unusual woman who delighted in reading and writing poetry, short stories, and theological treatises. She enjoyed "good preaching" and listed as a pleasure the attendance at classic lectures on Gothic architecture by Dr. Lord. Her nephew, prominent AME minister Theodore Gould, observed that Rebecca was such an informed student on biblical doctrine and the "current or popular questions of the day" that it caused a "very eminent and learned bishop" to state after a visit with her, "No one can possibly spend five minutes in conversation with Sister Steward without being edified." Gould further indicated that another "intelligent" minister affirmed that she was "one of the best read women [he] ever had the favor of conversing with."[4]

One example of Rebecca Steward's theological and intellectual independence—which rubbed off on Steward—was her refusal to commit her children to infant baptism. She was obstinate in this view, even though the AME Church advocated infant baptism. She was so convinced of its unbiblical nature that "she hesitated to give her children to God and the church in this ordinance." Steward indicated that, "of her six children not one was baptised [sic] in infancy, nor did she teach them to 'say prayers.' It required great faith to depart from so general a custom, but being taught of God, she dared to do it."[5] Rebecca had a strong effect on all of her children, but especially on Theophilus.

Little is known about Steward's early education, and even Steward's own statements regarding his education contain contradictions. In his *Memoirs,* he implied that he was enrolled in a local school in Gouldtown.[6] In his book *My First Four Years,* he clearly stated that he and his other siblings went to the local "district school" where they were taught "to read, write, and according to the old expression, 'to cipher.' . . . Upon the whole we attended a good public school generally taught by very proficient teachers."[7] Yet in his later book, *Fifty Years*, he seemingly exaggerated his educational deficit to heighten the contrasts between himself and his fellow classmates at the Divinity School of the Protestant Episcopal Church in West Philadelphia, where he matriculated at the Divinity School in 1877 and graduated with highest honors in 1880. "The class I entered was composed wholly of college men, excepting myself," Steward wrote. "I had never attended even a graded school; never entered a high school as student; [and] never approached a college."[8]

Steward was a motivated thinker who was largely self-taught and widely read in the classical theological and philosophical literature of the times. Eventually he developed command of several languages, including French, German, Spanish, Hebrew, and Greek. While stationed in Montana as chaplain of the Twenty-fifth Infantry, Steward studied Arabic in a summer course,[9] and while pursuing his seminary education, he took a course in the evenings in "elocution [at] the National School of Elocution and Oratory." During his military career, his own academic interests had evolved to the study of the social sciences, with a focus on "anthropology with a special reference of the Afro-American race."[10]

Early Teaching Experience

It was during Steward's early teaching experience that he developed his view of education as an important factor in religious development. Although moral training was an important feature in his educational philosophy, during this phase of his career Steward focused more on the importance of the development of the mind and classical training.

Steward's missionary responsibilities, from 1865 to 1872, were those of building and gathering AME congregations throughout South Carolina and Georgia. He was also responsible for the development of schools for the newly freed slaves. In South Carolina, Steward organized schools in Beaufort, Marion, and Charleston in conjunction with the American Missionary Association (AMA) and the New England Freedman's Aid Society (NEFAS) at different times in his missionary experience.[11] Much of this school development advanced with less-than-consistent support from the AMA. Steward complained several times of what he perceived

as a breach of contract between Bishop Payne and the AMA in not supply-
ing half of Steward's support.[12] This was particularly true of his experience
in Beaufort.[13] As a result, Steward's relationship with the AMA lasted less
than one year. After he left, the NEFAS employed both Steward and his new
wife, Elizabeth Gadsden-Steward, as missionary teachers in Charleston.[14]

Steward's shift from the AMA to NEFAS might have reflected more
than just a dispute over financial support. There was a clear difference in
educational philosophy between the two organizations, and this affected
Steward's thinking about education. The AMA was an advocate of both
"the instruction of youth in letters" and instruction in "evangelical religion." Their policy was to employ only teachers who were "members of
evangelical churches."[15]

The NEFAS was the more liberal and nonsectarian wing of the freedman's associations, reflecting "the secular reformism of the Garrisonians
and . . . Universalism, Rationalism, and Unitarianism."[16] Octavius Brooks
Frothingham, a leading Unitarian preacher and a NEFAS board member,
provided an example of this philosophical and theological debate in his
1866 letter written to the *Independent*. He argued that teachers were less
able to fulfill their primary function of teaching literacy when combined
with religious instruction or "if the teaching of divinity or the Word of God
crowd[ed] out, [took] precedence of limit[ed], [defined], or [colored] the
instruction in letters and the wisdom of men."[17]

Frothingham's remedy was to suggest that religious instruction should
remain in the church or denomination and be taught separately there:

> The religious denominations may undertake the double work.
> They may plant the parochial school by the side of the church;
> they may teach at once the rules of arithmetic, and the lessons
> of the catechism, the laws of grammar, and the doctrines of the-
> ology. . . . Such a system gives parochial schools. On the other
> hand, the various religious denominations may assume as their
> peculiar province, the work of religious instruction. To that they
> may confine themselves, while the whole community unites in a
> common effort for the education of the masses, not only in sec-
> ular knowledge, but in those precepts of morality and teaching
> of the Christian religion in which all agree. This system gives the
> common school. It is the almost universal system of Protestant
> Republicanism.[18]

The AMA countered this argument in an article in the *Boston Recorder,* charging that the common schools began under evangelical influence and owed their origin to evangelical religion. Referring to the newly freed slaves, the writer asked, "Is there one colored man or woman in a thousand among the Freedmen who objects to having their children taught all the religion that an evangelical teacher would wish to impart?" Further, the AMA declared, "blacks themselves ask for such instruction; the whites do not object to it. Evangelical men at the North, and those who act with them in the support of evangelical churches, desire it. The only men who object to it are those who wish to exclude evangelical religion from the community."[19] Reconstruction historian Ronald E. Butchart has persuasively argued that at stake in this debate was the evangelicals' preference for denominationally controlled schools that separated children by race: "Black children were not to attend a school in common with white children, nor were they to share a common curriculum. They had, according to the evangelicals, a special nature that called for a special curriculum in special schools. The traits imputed to the blacks concerned their moral and religious character; therefore, their education had to be specifically moral and religious and particularly evangelical." Since, according to the AMA, "it is their [black children's] moral natures that most require culture, and these need not mere education, but the sanction of religion," evangelicals sought education in an environment that did not assume racial equality, at least at the present time.[20]

Given these differences in educational philosophy between the AMA and NEFAS, it is highly likely that Steward was aware of these conflicts and was influenced by the northern liberal argument. He may well have felt as comfortable with NEFAS as with the AMA, or possibly more so, since he was an early advocate of racially integrated education.[21] Clearly, he would have defended NEFAS in supporting the equality of the newly freedpersons. He rejected the common stereotype that former slaves were more one thing than another—that they were overly religious, devoid of morals and/or intellect, smarter or more ignorant than their white southern neighbors. He outlined his early thoughts in a letter to Reverend Michael Strieby and George Whipple, corresponding secretaries of the AMA. He was aware of what had been written by northern missionaries, superintendents, and agents on the condition of the newly freed masses. He suggested that opinions varied as widely as the condition of the former slaves themselves. Some went south expecting to find slaves "degraded to nearly a level with the domestic animals," while others thought of them "only as a very religious and intelligent class of men." Steward indicated that some thought that former slaves were "uncommonly dull . . . lazy, indolent and careless of the things that make for their present or future welfare." Contrary to these various myths and stereotypes, he argued, there was a great variety among former slaves:

> They are men, moral and intellectual beings, and in almost every possible stage of intellectual and moral development. Some whose intellectual faculties have long lain dormant, struggle into life very slowly. Others who have been house servants . . . start on the intellectual march far in advance of their more unfortunate comrades. Some have had such rigid training and extensive practice under their gentlemanly owners in the fine arts of "fibbing and picking" that all must allow them to be fully equal to "white men" in that respect.[22]

Without a doubt the liberal philosophy of NEFAS significantly affected Steward, without lessening his commitment to revival or evangelical religion, since he also showed constant concern for religious development among the former slaves. In the same correspondence, Steward spoke about the slow progress of religious revival within the churches under his charge. Yet he was clear to make a distinction between the two spheres.

He outlined his convictions about education in a lecture given during his missionary work in South Carolina between 1865 and 1867 titled "The Centre of Power in the Work of Social Reform." He began the lecture by agreeing with the general scientific notion of natural selection and its implications for the social ordering of society:

> As in the great work of nature there seems to be a regular gradation from the lowest form of unorganized matter to the tallest archangel of uncreated light, based upon "essential differences," so in society will there ever remain the high and the low, the small and the great—to which arrangement we have no objection. All we require is, that it be not based upon accident, such as color, race, previous condition, but that manhood—moral and intellectual worth—be the basis of classification: and that without constraint, the mind be allowed to seek its own level and the man his associates.[23]

He contended that class distinction still existed in this country, even though there were fewer legal restrictions and more "equal rights" than in other countries. "[T]here still exists social grades—a top and a bottom of society," he wrote.[24]

Steward was under no illusion about the existence of de facto and de jure racism, yet he was able to identify the notion of class within race: "Though all white men who have not forfeited that privilege are permitted to enjoy the emoluments of citizenship, and all black men in some states are deprived of that right, still there exists on both sides, among blacks and among whites, upper and lower classes."[25]

Steward sets up his argument to suggest that if race or "accidental differences" were not a factor, humans would organize naturally around class interests. What is critical to Steward is the notion of "culture." He argued that as birds of a feather flock together, "so do men of equal and similar culture gravitate to each other." He privileged the power of intelligence and moral character that defined his understanding of "culture": "Opinions, professions, purposes, and even interests fail to reduce differences and to make men equal in the same sense that equality in intelligence and sameness in character do." There are, he noted, lower and higher classes, the lower classes "doomed to eke out a miserable existence by hard toil" while the wealthy "revel in luxury." The most "outcast, proscribed and despised class" was the newly freed slave, who was "denied the commonest rights, shut out from the commonest privileges," and "pronounced incapable of thinking and acting as men." The African American's wretched condition was due to the law of the strong over the weak, a condition that had not changed even with the Civil War. Public sentiment and laws did not save former slaves from this degradation, nor had the Freedmen's Bureau. Even with public sentiment and laws on their side, society still defrauded former slaves. Giving the critical assessment of Reconstruction legislation, Steward indicated that "so far no great change for the better has taken place in our condition since the breaking up of slavery."[26]

Steward asserted that elective franchise, laws, and wealth would not ultimately protect and elevate the African American or "raise us one step higher in the order of society, nor change our lot": "For let this be maintained as a truth: That it is by developed strength, by conquest, that a people rises from lower to a higher condition. Individual examples in support of this might be gathered from the wrestler's ring, to the latest discovery in science."²⁷ While coming close to sounding as though he was espousing the "survival of the fittest" rhetoric of the social Darwinists, Steward argued that the strength of which he spoke was that of knowledge combined with character, and was thus something that could be developed and learned. Quoting both the biblical Solomon ("wisdom is strength") and the modern Bacon ("knowledge is power"),²⁸ he argued that throughout history, intelligence had overpowered ignorance, and that those who rose to power were those who developed their intellect. Using England and America as examples, he noted that

> [b]arbarous peoples have been civilized, the waste country made the home of a mighty nation, the oppressed elevated, by infusing into them the power of education. . . . And education diffused among our people in this state [South Carolina] and others, is the thing needed to change their condition.
>
> I would have every one that hears me to-night transfer a part of that care for wealth, and apply it to personal improvement. To get that key which will unlock the door to every privilege, and that will furnish happiness in every circumstance. Exercise the mind; let it grow strong and what can resist its power?²⁹

While education did not supersede the importance of evangelical religion as a moral force for Steward, he nevertheless placed a strong focus on liberal education as a way to elevate his people and develop a civil society. Indeed, Steward viewed "culture" as a combination of intelligence and character which would grant African Americans the power to control their destiny and command respect from other peoples, especially white Americans.

Steward further elaborated his views regarding the importance of intellectual development as distinct but not separate from religious development in a sermon titled "The Bible and Education."³⁰ Highlighting the text of I Corinthians 14:20 ("Brethren be not children in understanding. Howbeit in malice be ye children; but in understanding be ye men"), this sermon argued that the Bible, correctly interpreted, encouraged and promoted the development of the intellect as valuable in its own right.

Steward argued that Christians should imitate children in being innocent of malice, dependence on God, obedience to God, and desire of divine things,³¹ but that Christians should not imitate children in the way of ignorance. He challenged former slaves to throw off the stereotypically affixed label of "childish character" through the development of the mind:

> The Bible, though sent from God to teach us expressly what we must do to be saved, does not condemn secular learning, but rather encourages it. No excuse can be put in plea for ignorance. The philosophy of the case is about this: as we have increased in stature and gained in strength and possessions, as we have ceased to be children in size, innocence and dependence, and are not free and responsible beings, so we should cease to be children in understanding. Becoming men, we must put away childish things.[32]

Here one gets a broader sense of Steward's understanding of the role of education and its connection to the Christian faith. His vision of education had a clear religious foundation but went beyond religion to embrace a secular function. Education was ultimately to improve one's intellect, broaden one's notion of cultured society, and prepare one for self-determined action. Drawing again upon the science of evolution, Steward argued that though "there are hereditary defects of the mind" and children take after their parents, it is nevertheless the responsibility of individuals to struggle for improvement wherever they find themselves. "A man is therefore to be judged by society and God, concerning the improvement and growth of his mind," he stated, "and is not accountable for its original cast. . . . Society and God, the world and heaven, time and eternity, demand of each man a cultivated and developed mind." Typical for the times, Steward drew upon the language of dichotomy between the "primitive" and the "civilized": "No one expects from the bushman what he does from the man of civilization; and God does not demand of the heathen what he demands of the Christian."[33] Furthermore,

> [to]-day the best intellectual food is served up in books and newspapers, and if we cannot feed upon them, we must remain pigmies among giants; and a natural law will assign us an inferior position. But we must not only read and take in knowledge, but digest and employ it: think, speak, and write. We must by teaching gain other talents with those bestowed. Be not children in the poverty, or imbecility of mind. Be children in wickedness, but not in the power to know and judge.[34]

Steward again connected education with his developing notion of civil society in this sermon by challenging the congregation not to be "fickle-minded as children, tossed to and fro by every wind of doctrine," but to have a clear purpose in life and give all of its efforts and focus to that goal. "And," he added, "this is consistent with the teaching of the Bible which every where advises us to consistency; so 'let our light shine' to be living epistles, and etc. Now, this position cannot be attained without the steady and constant exercise of the moral powers. . . . It requires education, mental, moral, and physical, to make a successful and consistent character."[35]

Steward drew upon the popular idiom of "manhood" to articulate his notion of African Americans' participation in the development of a civil and cultured society. For Steward, the ingredients of manhood were moral character and technical skill undergirded by intellectual acumen, all of which were developed by discipline and study. The development of manhood was not the result of an "accident" of birth, as the racial theorist of the day contended, or due to the "fortuitous" circumstances of one's class status: "Such manhood as was attained by Hugh Miller, who started out as a stone cutter and without significant training, who by dint of industry and study placed his name in the front rank of men of science, and made it an ornament to his native land. He was a man in investigation. . . . It is not distinction which is often the result of accident or mere fortuitous circumstances that we demand, but real solid character, and real useful possessions."[36]

Even with its heavily masculine language and tone, historian William H. Becker argued that the notion of "manhood" was a common term and theme within late-nineteenth- and early-twentieth-century African American church leadership. Becker argued that manhood was intimately connected to the theme of missions, which was a major motif in the black church.[37] (In this case, Becker is referencing foreign missions to Africans on the continent and in the diaspora.)

For Steward, "manhood" was clearly the nexus for themes of leadership, self-assertion, independence, black identity, and vocation:

> It [manhood] may be superior in trade or business transactions. It is, on the whole, that thing which makes society more productive, more steady and more holy. Such manhood as gives life to business by the increase of production and the diversity of industry, and that makes the wheels of manufacture whirl more

lively; that catches and harnesses the great forces of nature and causes them to work for our comfort. Such manhood as unclogs the operations of commerce by its foresightedness, probity and integrity, and causes the machinery of Government to move steadily on by its patrotism [*sic*] and statesmanship. A manhood capable of self-government, with strong arms, true hearts, and wise heads, is the demand of the day, especially among the colored people. Oh! that all this congregation were men of understanding, capable of choosing what is best, and of subjecting appetites and passions to the dictates of the better sense. It can be. We may be, in regard to human affairs, self-supporting and consequently self-controlling. Our conversation may improve to such as becomes men. All childishness can be put away, and we may become industrious, sober, intelligent and virtuous citizens. Men in the American and scriptural sense.[38]

By calling upon the congregation's religious and African nationalist sentiments, Steward further solidified the connection between manhood and civil society. Quoting Psalms 68:31—"Princes shall come out of Egypt; Ethiopia shall soon stretch out her hands unto God" (which African American religious historian Albert J. Raboteau has suggested was "the most quoted verse in black religious history")—[39] Steward commented, "Ethiopia is stretching out her hands to God. The Negro as a bondman no longer dwells among us, and the Western shore of Africa is cheered with the thrifty Republic of Liberia. The imaginary curse is flying home to roost, and the field of enterprise and effort is thrown open to the Anglo-African. The light is come. The glory of God is arisen; Who will not come forth and help complete the victory?"[40]

Steward understood this notion of manhood as a process of self-determination, which would provide a philosophical underpinning for the practical steps of uplift. He would carry these ideas with him as he returned north, particularly as he grappled with the issue of black education.

The Struggle for Northern Educational Equality

After leaving the Deep South, Steward shifted his focus on education to the level of public policy. While pastoring the Bethel AME Church in Wilmington, he became a major voice in the political arena advocating for equal rights and education for blacks.[41] The social condition of African Americans in Delaware, the most northern slave state prior to the Civil War and a border state during the conflict, was inferior. In 1866, Democrats controlled the state and initially rejected the Thirteenth, Fourteenth, and Fifteenth Amendments to the Bill of Rights, which ended slavery and ensured suffrage and equal treatment before the law to former slaves.[42] Opponents of these amendments enacted several laws that limited the participation of blacks in political and educational spheres.[43] The will of the state legislature was clearly expressed in one of a series of resolutions passed by the state that declared, "The immutable laws of the Creator have affixed upon the brow of the white races the ineffaceable stamps of superiority and that all attempts to elevate the negro to the social or political equality of the white man is the result either of an unwise and wicked fanaticism or of a blind and perverse infidelity, subversive of the ends for which this government was established, and contrary to the doctrines and teachings of our fathers."[44] Even after the passage of the Fifteenth Amendment in 1870 by the Delaware legislature, the Assessment Law of 1873 was enacted, linking suffrage to proof of taxation payment. This legislation was a major blow to black male suffrage in the state and for the most part discouraged black men from voting for about twenty-five years (at which time the new state constitution removed its requirement).[45] As late as 1872, blacks recognized that the effects of the U.S. constitutional changes had no effect on African American life in Delaware: "Whereas, the power which was overthrown still lives in this State, in its opposition to civil rights, in its opposition to the Fifteenth Amendment of the United States constitution, in opposition to the Educational bill, which was intended to do us justice, in its opposition to the repeal of the Black Laws of our State in the attempts, sometimes by violence, to keep us from voting, and in opposition to our enrollment in the assessment lists of the counties [in] which we reside."[46]

It is within the above context that African Americans in Delaware raised their concerns for education. The attitude of white Delawareans toward African American education was one of "indifference rather than of interference." According to the 1870 census, the black population of Delaware was 22,794, roughly one-fifth of the total population. About half of this population was counted as being able to read and write.[47] Nevertheless, in 1866 there were only seven schools for African Americans in Delaware.

Due to the combined efforts of some Quakers and the black community, the wretched educational situation for the African American in Delaware began to see improvement. Between 1867 and 1876 the number of schools for blacks had risen to thirty-nine.[48] Still, there was no support from the state in these efforts. The Delaware Association for the Education of Colored People, a white Quaker-influenced organization,[49] said in its 1870 annual report that given the climate and the limited resources, "reliance must be placed for the funds for the present year on a large increase of individual contributions, on the part of the friends of the cause, and especially on the increasing ability and willingness of the colored people themselves to bear a larger share of their own [brethren] in the future." Black citizens had already contributed ten cents per week per pupil to the cause.[50] But most blacks were day laborers, received the lowest wages, were the least able to adequately fund the education of their children, and had already "shown a spirit of self-sacrifice that merit[ed] the highest praise and commendation." Up to 1875, the schools for African Americans run by the association were supported by donations. In fact, African Americans supplied more than one-third of the total $10,483.24 budget in 1870.[51] But the amount raised was not nearly enough to educate all the eligible black youth in the state. More formal support was needed from the state of Delaware.

The association had contributed significantly to the educational development of the African American community, yet its demeanor was one of "disinterested" service and "quiet and unobtrusive methods."[52] The organization's non-engagement posture was consistent with the pacifist nature of the Quaker movement. It may have also reflected the general Quaker attitude toward social and political elevation of African Americans beyond the educational arena.[53] But this posture limited the association's abilities to challenge the state legislature to provide the equal financial support necessary to provide quality education for Delaware's black citizens.

Steward was active as a leader of his church in protesting the state's indifference toward education for African Americans. "Rural schools for white children were mere excuses, while for colored children no provision was made by the State," he recalled. "The ideas upon which school legislation was based, what little there was in operation, was, that the taxes paid by whites for education should be applied to the support of schools for white children, and colored people should be taxed to support of schools for their own children. Against this principle, I protested at once."[54]

When Steward arrived in Delaware from Georgia, he immediately became active within the Republican Party. Like other African American leaders, he felt that their unyielding loyalty might increase African Americans' political leverage in the state Republican Party, especially in relation to their concerns regarding education. During his time in Delaware, Steward served on the State Central Committee of the Republican Party, wrote campaign literature, and "stumped the entire State in the interest of [Ulysses S.] Grant and [Henry] Wilson."[55] In September 1872, black Republicans met in Camden, Delaware, in a convention to show their support for the Republican Party and to raise their concerns regarding the education of black youth. William Howard Day[56] was elected president of the convention, and Steward, despite his short time in the state, had already developed enough influence to be elected vice president. The major resolution of the convention stated the demand for equal citizenship rights in the state as was mandated by national legislation. The convention also resolved that

> colored people have a legal right to the same free and full education for their children as their white fellow citizens, and duly appreciating the fact that on such an education depends in a very great degree their future standing and usefulness as citizens and having long and patiently waited and appealed in vain for a recognition of those rights, we think the time has now come for us to take some steps toward obtaining them, and well knowing the worth of the ancient proverb that "The Gods help those alone who help themselves," that we shall now cease being supplicants, and demand through the courts those rights of which we have been so long deprived.[57]

The Republican Party was relatively successful in the 1872 national election; Grant won by a landslide. In Delaware, Republicans were able to elect one person to Congress and to secure three electoral votes.[58] But although Republicans made some gains in the state elections, they were still in the minority by fourteen to seven seats in the state house of representatives and by eight to one in the state senate.[59] Nevertheless, Steward and others decided to press forward with their campaign for black education, arguing that "the opportuneness of this convention will appear when we recall that the State would be represented in Congress by a Republican member, and that the Legislature of the State would also have within it Republican representatives who owed their election very largely to the colored voters who had stood by the party to a man."[60] On December 2, 1872, Steward took the lead in calling for an education convention to be held in Dover on January 9, 1873. "Our rights as citizens are not respected in Democratic Delaware," he argued in an advertisement for the convention. He backed up this assertion with three points: black children were "excluded from the schools provisions made by the State ... [and] do not go to the public schools"; black citizens were "excluded from the juries of the State and Federal Courts within the State"; and blacks were discriminated against by the legal authorities, who excluded them "from professions and the mechanic arts, and doom[ed them] inevitably to the hardest work and the lowest wages."[61]

Opposition to the black education convention came quickly, including from within the African American community. Major opposition came from William Howard Day, editor of *Our Mutual Progress*,[62] in the form of several editorials printed in several periodicals,[63] which sarcastically asked why the circular distributed by Steward was signed only "T. G. Steward," not followed by any of Steward's titles:

> The Circular is signed by T. G. Steward, not T. G. Steward, member of the State Central Committee; not T. G. Steward, a Vice President of the late Colored Men's State Convention, which inaugurated the work for school and other rights, and whose officers and committees ought to have been consulted and put forward as the movers in and supports of this one, *if it be best to hold a State Convention* at this time named; not T. G. Steward, Pastor of Bethel Church, in Wilmington, or as the designated Missionary of the Bethel Connection to the West Indies; to go as soon as the money is raised; but simply and solely T. G. Steward.[64]

Day charged that the call for a convention was a "one-sided movement" with the intent of promoting Steward's leadership. He claimed that Steward had sidestepped the educational committee established by the September convention because most likely the convention would not have gained their support or, if endorsed, might have promoted some person other than Steward. Day implied that Steward was a short-lived, fly-by-night charlatan who was more interested in promoting himself than in education, particularly compared to some others in the state, who prior to Steward's arrival had made significant sacrifices on behalf of black education. Day highlighted two individuals in particular: Daniel B. Anderson (whose name, the editorial noted, should have appeared on the circular) and himself, who "four years ago went to Dover, and carried the memorials of the whole people to a Democratic Legislature, when it demanded courage not only to present memorials, but even to go to Dover, when the Legislature was in session." Day argued that instead of a convention, what was needed was "Hundred [a subdivision of a county] and County meetings," and "[t]he sooner Mr. Steward begins these the better. But that would be work; cost money; and would not make certain third rate selfish men so immediately prominent." Day further stated that where every means should be used to "protect rights and secure schools," it should be done "in the right spirit, with no sectarian or selfish object in view—and the people will respond."[65]

Steward's almost immediate response was less accusatory but at times equally biting. In responding to "simply and solely" signing his circular T. G. Steward, he stated that it was "rather remarkable in these days of assumption and brass that one should put his name in print without a high-sounding title associated with it, but certainly it is not an unpardonable offense to do so."[66] Regarding the education convention itself, Steward contended that the call for a convention did not blot the work done at the September gathering. That meeting, he argued, was in the context of an uncertain political campaign, and since then the Republican Party had secured seats in both state houses, thus setting the stage for new action:

> The convention is called by the necessities of the situation, as it seems to me every right thinking man must admit.
>
> Twenty thousand people excluded from school privileges, subject to the law's severest penalties, doomed inevitably to poverty and overlooked by the Church, cannot be kept silent. Does Mr. Day know that the present facilities of education and religion among the colored people of Delaware do not meet the demand, and that without their increase the proportion of ignorance and vice must increase among them?[67]

Steward maintained that "the stern voice of necessity and the relentless hand of duty" dictated the organization of the convention. He claimed

that people would respond to the call of the convention "not as a compli-
ment to T. G. Steward, nor simply in obedience to party managers, but as
freemen, justly comprehending the value of the sacred right, and raising
up in the dignity of earnest manhood to secure it." Finally, he quipped,
"Not wishing to trespass on your space, I will only add that T. G. Steward
seeks no cheap popularity in this movement, nor does he care who is glo-
rified so the work is done; nor is he careful at what 'rate' he shall be
classed by *Our National Progress* or its distinguished editor."[68]

It is not clear just how much sympathy the general populous had for
the sentiments espoused by Day. It is interesting to note Steward's interjection of church and religion in his response to Day. Day was an African
Methodist Episcopal Zion Church (AMEZ) minister and, as we know,
Steward was an African Methodist Episcopal minister. There was a long
history of antagonism between the two ecclesiastical bodies.[69] This fric-
tion was probably exacerbated by the strong egos of both men. Both were
rising stars from rival denominations attempting to stake out and control
territory for their denominations. Day, who later became a bishop in the
AMEZ Church, insinuated that Steward would soon be off on his missionary trek to Haiti (which was true) and therefore did not have the
long-term interests of the black community at heart. The truth is that both
men's tenure in Delaware would be short-lived. Within a month of this
controversy, Day had moved to Harrisburg, Pennsylvania, and Steward
left for his Haitian missionary journey in June 1873.[70]

The convention did take place, on January 9, 1873, in Dover, Delaware, at Whatcoat Methodist Episcopal Chapel. Steward must have been
very sensitive to Day's criticism, because he declined appointment to the
top leadership positions of president, vice president, or either of two secretaries (of which his protégé, Levi Coppin, was one). Yet Steward as a
dominant force in the convention, sitting on the credentials committee,
the committee on permanent organization, and the committee on the
address. Historian Ronald L. Lewis was on target in his comment that
"the Republican detractors were essentially correct in their observation
that it was a T. G. Steward program."[71]

The convention adopted a resolution put forth by Steward, which recognized the fact that the state government had ignored their previous pleas
for assistance in education. It called for blacks to pledge themselves to "ask
and agitate until the same rights are accorded to us as are enjoyed by other

citizens of the State." The convention adopted another resolution that stopped short of petitioning the state legislature for funds. It gave praise and appreciation for the "humane and christian [*sic*] efforts" in education which had been carried out on behalf of the Delaware black community by the Delaware Association for the Moral and Mental Improvement of Colored People and the black teachers under their employ.[72]

Steward also offered a resolution concerning corporal punishment: "Resolved that we hereby utter our abhorrence of the present penal code so far as it inflicts corporal punishment upon citizens convicted of crimes, regard the whipping post and pillory as blots upon our civilization, and a standing reproach to our State." He connected the lack of education with the increase of crime in a systemic way, arguing that Delaware would either have to build more schools or more jails.[73]

Toward the end of the convention, Steward's address committee issued a public statement that was drafted by Steward:

> Believing in the sovereignty of the people, and also believing that the people are in the main right upon all questions of justice and patriotism, your Committee beg leave to offer the following address to the people without regard to party or politics . . . .
>
> On behalf of the colored people whom we represent, we feel it our duty again to speak. We know this subject is often pushed before the public, but the evils complained of are not remedied; the wrongs are not *redressed,* and as long as they exist we must continue "in season and out of season," and by every honorable means to enforce our rights.
>
> We specially ask now that equal school rights be afforded us. This we do not ask merely as a matter of right, but as a crying necessity—a necessity without which the future of our race appears almost utterly hopeless. This appeal is not only addressed to the sense of justice, but to the higher sentiments of generosity and christian [*sic*] philanthropy. It is well known that as a people we are not able to sustain schools among ourselves sufficient to well educate our children. To impose upon us specially this burden, is as unfair as unwise. . . .
>
> We say against the spirit of the age, because non progressive in its character and in the interests of ignorance; because tending to perpetuate poverty, multiply crime, and aid human degradation.

Insulting to the laws of Congress, because directly against the express provisions of the Fourteenth and Fifteenth Amendments; laws of the highest authority known in the land. Detrimental to the public good, or to the best interests of the State, because entailing upon the State a burden of ignorance and discontent. For as long as a portion of citizens are thus excluded and restricted in their rights, it is folly to expect that portion to be contented, they must of necessity be a disturbing element, and will not cease to agitate the body politic. Again, it puts upon the State and yet which must be the most expensive to govern. Intelligence, it is well known, is much cheaper to the State than ignorance. To foster education then, is the noblest work of the State; to oppose it among any class of citizens is to oppose the State's highest interest.

But this discrimination is outrageous to the colored people because it is sullen opposition against their rights as citizens. It is founded upon no principle, backed by no argument, but sustained entirely by a prejudice founded upon a long course of false education. We therefore, in the name of all that is good to the State, and on behalf of the dearest interests of the colored people, do again urge upon our white fellow citizens to assist us in educating ourselves so that we may become a people of which the State itself may be proud.

We appeal not now alone to christian philanthropy, but we appeal to the sense of fairness and right. By the laws of the State we are entirely ignored in all school privileges, we are not taxed it is true as other citizens are taxed, but the school tax as any other tax. Let it be levied and collected, and we will find no fault. We will share in common with all other citizens all the burdens of civil government, and only ask an equal share in its benefits. More than this we do not desire; less than this we dare not ask.

In our efforts to secure the right from the State we invite the cooperation of all good citizens, feeling sure that the good we seek will be to the advantage of all.[74]

Three months after the convention Steward was asked to speak to a white Methodist preacher's meeting regarding the "Religious and Social Condition of the Colored People of Delaware."[75] Concerning education, he reviewed the recent history of unresponsiveness of the state toward

black education and the valiant efforts of the Delaware Association for
the Moral and Mental Improvement of the Colored People. He attributed
the poor economic and educational state of African Americans to the lack
of financial support by the state and to the passiveness of poor parents.
Here Steward began to develop a critical assessment as to how poverty
and apathy toward education became a vicious cycle for the African American community:

> Two things contribute to this result. First the expense, which
> ranges from ten to twenty cents a week for each child, is some-
> times more than the parent can pay; secondly it is often more than
> he is willing to pay. People uneducated do not generally appreci-
> ate education. The sad dereliction of the state, the poverty and
> indifference of parents are dooming us to a mental darkness that
> must retard the church and hinder the gospel of Christ. If there
> can be no improvement in our educational facilities, I fear the
> proportion in ignorance must increase. Bad as our condition
> now is, it seems actually growing worse.[76]

Steward again pointed out the social costs of neglecting education. This
time, knowing his audience, he focused on vice and intemperance. He suggested that limited education would create a good ground for "the rumseller
and policy holder" to "ply their vocations among them without fear." But he
"regarded education and religion as its antidote. With these a people may
stand ever against rum. Without them their destruction is easily wrought."[77]

Steward asserted that as a matter of course he had seen wicked white
men, "a detached flame of hell—standing in human form briskly engaged
in coining black men's souls into money by selling them a drink unfit to
moisten the palate of a decent devil": "We say a great deal about race prejudice. If Satan can employ white men with success, why may not God? If
white men can hand out to black men the double extract of damnation,
why may not white men give to them water and bread and salvation?" He
declared that white Methodists' Christian duty was to "demand a public
school system that shall afford the best possible advantages, and to all the
people in the State alike."[78]

Steward began to advocate mixed public schools when he returned to
Delaware for another pastorate in 1881–83. Not much had changed concerning the plight of education in the state or in the city of Wilmington
since his last pastorate. The 1873 convention had little effect.

By 1875, the Wilmington Board of Education had taken the black schools under its control. The *Daily Commercial* of Wilmington supported the black community's request to the state legislature to be taxed to support black schools across the state. The paper published a series of editorials advocating the collection of funds universally among blacks in support of their schools.[79] According to historian Ronald L. Lewis, the legislation became law in part because the Democrats "opted for the more acceptable alternative of a segregated school system even if the state recognized blacks as full citizens by assuming the responsibility for collecting the requisite tax revenues from them."[80] The amount collected and given to the Delaware association was never enough to adequately finance black public education; it was only sufficient to meet about a third of the expenses. Thus, African Americans continued to raise the rest among them.[81] Added to this, by 1880 the Democrats controlled the Wilmington city government as well as the state legislature due to perceived Republican governmental corruption.

The Democrats continued to implement the property Assessment Law of 1873 to freeze out blacks from voting, and a major race riot in Wilmington had erupted.[82] In 1881, the state legislature passed an act making "an annual State appropriation of $2400 to be distributed *pro rata* among the schools of each county." The amount increased in 1883 to five thousand dollars. Still, for most black schools in the state the average length of the school year was five months, with four months in the rural areas and eight months in the cities.[83]

Steward found this environment upon his return to Wilmington in 1881. Again as a member of the State Central Committee of the Republican Party, he used his position as a platform to advocate parity with white schools. The Democratic Party used this as an opportunity to stoke the fears of white citizens by suggesting that he was advocating "mixed schools." To this Steward responded, "Our contention was for schools supported from public money. The Democrats taking advantage of the Republican Party's expressed willingness to aid in the education of colored children, charged that party with having the purpose to establish 'mixed' public schools. This charge so frightened our candidates that they came out in most cowardly denials and denounced the idea of the so-called 'mixed schools.'"[84]

Even though the black community did not in fact advocate mixed schools, Steward clearly supported the idea in principle. When the

Republicans reneged on their support, he resigned from the Republican committee. Some members of Steward's congregation were agitated by his advocacy of mixed schools. "Blacks themselves, including members of his own congregation," historian Lewis suggests, "were disgruntled by Steward's integrationist position, probably because they believed that their most immediate chance for uplift rested with a Republican victory at the polls." Lewis further states that Steward may have been disingenuous when he dismissed as "a plain lie" the Frankford newspaper's statement that he advocated mixed schools from his pulpit.[85] Rather than being disingenuous, it would appear that Steward, for the sake of party unity, supported the party line. Yet when the Republican Party began to back away from its commitment to parity in public education due to Democrat-inspired rumors concerning their support of mixed schools, Steward began to speak his true feelings regarding racially mixed schools.

Once unencumbered by political loyalties, Steward spoke out in favor of integrated schools in speech and print, even at the risk of alienating his own congregation.[86] He argued that the use of the "mixed schools" term was a smoke screen: "encouragement of such a prejudice is an attempt to organize and arm the whole community against the colored child, an inhuman and senseless persecution."

Public schools, Steward argued, were just that: public. He maintained that since blacks paid taxes to the state as whites did, the schools which were held by the state were for everyone. "All the people are joint stock owners in the common schools," he said. "The colored people are equal owners with the whites; all are beneficiaries." Religion, science, and philosophy proved there was "no distinguishment [*sic*] possible to the eye of the soul between the races; all mankind being children of one common Father, God—all possessed of the same qualities and powers of emotion and expression and of intelligent capabilities found nowhere else except among men." He admonished his congregation, declaring, "There is no religion in a passive giving up to opposing influences. Let there be a continuous struggle for your rights. Education is such a boon that it must be accepted even under the stigma of colored schools, a half loaf being better than none. But if we must accept colored schools, then what shall be the color? And shall there not be a school for every shade? How absurd to make any distinction." He challenged them to "appreciate their own manhood and defend it" and claimed that self-respect and self-defense "must come before the outside public can be expected to appreciate it."[87]

Steward quoted Charles Sumner's speech before the Supreme Court in 1849 in favor of mixed, or common, schools. He called upon African Americans' sense of self-esteem, exhorting his hearers to "respect their rights as men and citizens before God and before the law, and not to be contented with less than their full rights. Let the struggle be longer or shorter, more or less severe, with God and the right upon their side victory is sure to come."[88]

Steward's views gained wide attention and commentary. Henry C. Conrad, the actuary of the Delaware Association for the Education of Colored People, felt obligated to state his opposition to mixed schools in his August 21, 1883 report, *A Glimpse at the Colored Schools of Delaware,* some months after Steward's departure to pastor a congregation in Philadelphia. Conrad said that he had "never found any disposition among the colored people to desire their children educated in the same school buildings with white children, or to claim 'mixed schools' as has so often been asserted." He argued that on the contrary he believed that the "overwhelming and practically unanimous sentiment among colored people is emphatically in favor of separate and distinct schools for their own children. Personally, I desire to be understood as radically opposed to the education of the two races in the same school buildings."[89]

During the time of this conflict several newspapers had indicated that Steward had been "semi-officially notified by the trustees of his church that they would learn with pleasure of his acceptance of a call in some other locality." In his autobiography, Steward attempted to minimize the negative feeling toward him in the congregation due to his outspokenness on the subject of mixed schools: "This action naturally caused some feeling in the church, although nothing like a rupture. Conference would come on in May and I expected to leave at that time."[90] Yet before the annual conference at which Steward was reassigned, several papers published reports of conflict between Steward and his congregation regarding their opposition to his position concerning mixed schools.[91]

Steward gave one last fiery shot concerning his views in a letter to the editor published in the local newspaper:

> Sir: You report a fact when you say that some of my congregation have been made dissatisfied with me because I advocate the equal rights of the people. I believe that in this country there ought to be one set of public schools in which all the children

should be educated. These have been my views publicly expressed
for the past ten years. I see no reason to change them. That unprin-
cipled politicians induce my people to oppose me on this account
in order to increase their own value in the political market is a fact
which I regret, but cannot alter and am not responsible for. The
crime of maintaining genuine Republican doctrine—the doctrine
that Sumner, the acknowledged idol of the colored people, maintained—has become an offense to the pious colored people of this
city, according to the statements of those who claim to represent
them, by the side of which theft, adultery and drunkenness are
mere peccadilloes. I wish to say that I have a better opinion of the
colored people of Wilmington than this. I believe that they have
been misled, and are misrepresented by trading politicians—
politicians who would sell me for old rags if thereby they could
increase the value of their political charms.[92]

After Steward was transferred to Bethel Church in Baltimore in June
1888, he again involved himself with efforts to improve schools for
African American children. The question of mixed schools did not arise
in Baltimore; instead, Steward lobbied for hiring African American teachers in the black schools. It is interesting to note the contrast between his
demand in Wilmington for integrated schools and his push for black teachers in the Baltimore school system. It is highly possible that the teaching
staff in Wilmington was integrated. This was obviously not the case in
Baltimore. The confluence of issues in Wilmington forced Steward to
show his true hand on pupil integration, but not so in Baltimore.
Throughout his early years in the ministry, Steward consistently focused
on the importance of a liberal education for African Americans. He did
not utterly neglect the role education could play in children's moral formation, the proof being his belief that education would reduce crime
rates in the black community. But overall during the late nineteenth century Steward was far more concerned to impart the basics of literacy to
black children to ensure that their opportunities and training would
match those of white children. His focus was to change later in his life,
however, as he became involved with the military chaplaincy and began to
speak more about education's role in forming moral character. This may
have been due to the very nature of the army, with its emphasis on discipline. It could also be related to the shift in class status of the individuals
with whom Steward worked.

Education and the Military

As a chaplain with the Twenty-fifth Infantry of the U.S. Army between 1891 and 1906,[93] Steward's primary responsibility with his black regiment was teaching or giving oversight to the educational process among the soldiers. According to the Revised Statute of the United States Army, section 1124, "The duty of chaplains of regiments of colored troops and of post-chaplains shall include the instruction of enlisted men in the common English branches of education."[94] Earl F. Stover, a historian of the U.S. military chaplaincy, has suggested that when it came to appointing black chaplains, no thought was initially given to black soldiers' religious orientation or to the appointment of a black chaplain who understood black religious worship traditions.[95] In fact, much of the chaplain's time was absorbed with educational responsibilities, mainly supervising post schools for children, working with enlisted men, and teaching. Many African American soldiers could not read or write. Significant numbers of white soldiers were also illiterate. Due to the influx of European immigrants, many soldiers did not speak English.[96]

While most chaplains had primary responsibilities for education of the troops, they also discharged religious duties such as the performance of marriages and burials and leading worship services and Bible studies.[97] The chaplains made significant efforts at evangelization and moral reform, which yielded reductions in intemperance and sometimes resulted in religious conversions among the soldiers. This work was generally performed without the encouragement or support of the army officers, although there were officers who supported the chaplain's work and professed Christianity.[98]

In Steward's case, his early years of chaplaincy were greatly supported by Col. George Andrews of Fort Missoula, Montana.[99] Later, however, he was to be hampered by a different colonel who was not concerned at all about his religious and educational duties.[100]

During Steward's tenure as chaplain, his educational work with black soldiers began to develop a two-track approach: one for the poor and uneducated soldier and the second for the upwardly aspiring middle-class African American. He wrote an article, six months into his appointment, titled "The Morals of the Army" and published in the *Independent,* which attempted to offset what Steward felt was the prevailing view that the military was a "school for vice; and that drunkenness, licentiousness, gambling, and profanity have almost universal sway."[101] He argued that, contrary to general opinion, the strictness of military discipline militated against such debauchery. He admitted that there were some difficulties and suggested prescriptions for their remedy. In defending the military, Steward concluded his article with this assessment:

> Military training, and the schools that are established at the post, as well as the special religious work of the chaplains, all bears directly against the prominent vices, as well as in favor of a general harmonious development of mind and body in a soldierly direction. Faithfulness, truthfulness, a sense of responsibility and carefulness form the basis of soldier character; and these qualities are not against good morals. The soldier is trained to be firm and strong in body, to be careful in receiving an order, to be faithful and exact in executing it. Duty, duty, duty, is the ever-recurring watchword. Hence it is my opinion that the Army, notwithstanding the drawbacks I have mentioned, is by no means a school of vice. In a special and limited sense it may be said to train men to virtue.[102]

Later Steward became convinced that the military was the one place where black men could develop the "virtues" which were essential for the development of an African American civil society. Further, he became convinced that the military was able to instill moral values in a population when other civil society institutions had proved ineffective.

Steward's work within the military provided a reflective lens through which he could review other nonmilitary civil society institutions. He saw that the military was more efficient in accomplishing the work of education. He became concerned that with all the efforts of the church, the press, and the school in the black community, illiteracy was on the rise, along with vice and immorality. He articulated these views in an 1898 article titled "Washington and Crummell."[103]

The article was an analysis of philosophy and methods regarding racial uplift. Steward was inspired to write it by an American Negro Academy (ANA) paper, "Civilization, the Primal Need of the Race" by the recently deceased Alexander Crummell. (Both Steward and Crummell were founding members of the ANA.)[104] Crummell had engaged in ongoing debates with Booker T. Washington, the founder of Tuskeegee Institute, over methods for racial uplift. Steward summarized Crummell's view of racial uplift through education, which focused on the development of civilization through the shaping of the mind through studying the classics, books, art, and refined culture. He saw Crummell as idealistic and subjective, suggesting that his approach was to "let civilization be brought down to them from her Olympian heights." On the other hand, Washington, Steward said, found racial uplift through the development of the hands, with practical skills such as farming, technology, and business. Washington wanted to build civilization "from the bottom up," a "practical and objective" philosophy in Steward's opinion.[105] Showing his general preference for Crummell's view, Steward indicated that the world would grow away from Washington's philosophy and toward Crummell's, stating that "one is the just complement of the other, and the two make a remarkable, symphonic whole":[106]

> The civilization lacking and desired has within it two great elements; or rather we may say is composed of two wide hemispheres. One of these is conservative, the other creative or constructive. Civilization produces, and saves; and is unquestionably a mental or soul condition. Things are not civilization, and so not civilize; they are instruments by which the mind may be aided. They are as necessary as pencil and paper to the study of mathematics; and as useless as these without the intellectual principles involved. For the evolution of the race we need the teaching and the inspiring example of both Washington and Crummell, the injunction of deep philosophy with daring enterprise, and more.[107]

Steward then gave a critique of the three civil institutions that African Americans depended upon: the church, the press, and the school. The church, he argued, enjoyed an "absolute monopoly, and hence has more to do with the vital forces of the race than all other agencies combined." But he charged, with great disappointment and displeasure, that the church had become lax to the point that it "was not helping as it should, and in some cases is not helping at all, the cause of Afro-American civilization." Giving the press a lesser role, he nevertheless indicated that it was "feeble, indefinite, and often half-starved." The black press was generally pushed out by its larger and more powerful white counterpart and "unappreciated by those it seeks to serve." Steward summarized: "Outside of politics and the church, the Negro press in this country is without significance, and without merit."[108]

In so far as schools were concerned, Steward charged—in an extremely cynical tone—that if the estimated "30,000 colored school teachers were all that their position requires of them, we would soon have a reading and writing people, to say the least." But he noted that this was not the case and that illiteracy within the African American community seemed to be growing. Furthermore, he claimed that "the education obtained in vast numbers of colored schools appears to be not only very slight, but often pernicious."[109] (Here he might have had in mind some of the negative educational experiences his children were subjected to by white teachers in Baltimore and other places.)[110] Students were given the illusion that they were provided with knowledge and training, he asserted, but in reality were given neither. The student was thus "injured as he sets out to assail the real issues in life. Church, press, and school, have up to this hour, failed to lay even a good foundation for the wholesale civilization of the race."[111]

Seeming to give up on these civil societal institutions, Steward indicated that he did not feel that they had the "conservative and producing power sufficient to hold their relative position in the midst of the common American people." Nor did he feel that they could overcome racism—what he called "the unfriendly attitude of a large percentage of the whites"—and accelerate "their productive capacity as to advance at [a] more rapid rate than their white competitors and thus improve their relative as well as their actual condition." He suggested that the African American's physical prowess and ability to develop capital (which he saw as positive attributes) would not outweigh the negatives working against their success, namely, "idleness, crime, vice, illiteracy, wretched female character, and the weakness and worthlessness of the so-called educated classes [within the black community]." He lamented that "[t]he few bright minds are torches only shining out in the almost total gloom of a special low colored level."[112]

It is not clear what spurred this lament, except that perhaps Steward's association with poor and illiterate blacks in the military had put him in touch with a class of African Americans different from the upwardly mobile parishioners of his earlier mid-Atlantic pastoral years. In any case, he indicated that he did not believe that blacks would ever rise to "civilization by evolution." He rejected both "Crummellism" and "Washingtonism" either separately or combined as able to "civilize the American Negro."[113] Steward had earlier in his life challenged the newly freed slaves to pursue education over money, elective franchise, and political power. Now, almost thirty years later, he seemed to be questioning the viability of classical education as a legitimate option for all classes of people. He even seemed to hint with the use of the phrase "The weakness and worthlessness of the so-called educated classes in our older communities" that inferior education had created a false middle class within the black community, which was the shell of what he felt was a true representative of civilized culture. He proposed a solution growing out of his observations and experience from the military.

For Steward, what was missing in the Crummell and Washington dichotomy was development of moral fiber and force, which he believed would to be the glue to make a cohesive unit in the black community. He was persuaded that "nothing will do for the Negro race in this land what the rifle will do for him. War will win-now [*sic*] out his chaff; war will steady his nerves; toughen his fibre, assure him his limitations, harden his virtue, and lay the foundation for his character." If fifty thousand or more black Americans were to enlist into the military over the course of twenty-five years, he calculated, "the race would be carried forward many centuries." He claimed that "the general Negro," a euphemism for poor blacks, needed to be "taught respect for law, order, and authority." Inner character became more foundational for Steward than acquired knowledge, and the army was the place to develop this: "This, the church cannot teach; this, the press can only point to; this, the school but fairly inculcates; this the army teaches and enforces." He noted that he had seen young men who prior to enlistment had defied the authority of home and school but now, in the military, had become "models of obedience, and finally [took] pride in observing military rule." Steward observed, "In the army each soldier is a part of the closely interlocked machine and he feels the part he plays. There is no greater civilizing agency for the Negro, whether we look upon the conservative [Washington] or advancing side [Crummell], than the army; and it is through this instrumentality amid the strife and blood soon to engulph [*sic*] more or less of the civilized world, that I look for the American Negro to emerge from his present lot."[114]

As it turned out, Steward did not choose the military so much as the opportunity to join the military chose him. But once in the army, he took on the military spirit completely. Outside the pale of the civilian societal institutions of church, press, and school, Steward critically assessed their

usefulness in creating "civilization." This was especially true for the institution he loved so much but from which he felt he had been ostracized:
the black church, and the AME Church in particular. He dared to com-
municate his changing views to the church directly, delivering an address,
"The Army as a Trained Force," to the General Conference of the AME
Church in Chicago in 1904. This was the first time in Steward's clerical
career that he had the opportunity to give a plenary address at a general
conference. It was also his first time attending a general conference since
his infamous participation at the 1888 general conference. His tone
regarding the failure of the church to effectuate change among the black
poor had softened since his "Crummell and Washington" article of six
years earlier, but it is clear that Steward still viewed the military as a training ground for more than martial readiness. The military, he believed, was
able to instill the moral force that was the basis for the development of any
civilization. In particular it produced a commitment to duty and obedience. "This sentiment of duty is the moral force in the army that gives dignity to its obedience," he said. "The army develops, strengthens, and
educates this sense of duty, until it becomes supreme. It is this sense of
duty which produces endurance to undergo privations, and leads men to
be patient under the greatest sacrifices. The physical force which we see in
the army depends upon the moral or spiritual which we do not see."[115]

Steward acknowledged that the primary function of the military was
destruction. Yet he defended this notion of physical devastation by defending the presence of might in the military, because it was the ground upon
which democracy and government were built. He warned his listeners that
one must not expect too much from the army: "It is not a Church, not a
Sunday-school, not a Missionary Society. Its code of morals is very short,
very narrow, but it enforces what it has." Here it seems that Steward had
softened his earlier critique, perhaps fearing ostracism from the church.

Through his army life Steward had come to realize that at the base of
the civil society which he was attempting to promote in the African
American community was a need for structure and discipline, that is,
moral force. This was true for both religious and secular education. The
notion of moral force was to be the base upon which education was to be
built. Once the moral foundation was laid, one could then pursue the
various options toward the development of civil society.

Education at Wilberforce University

Even as Steward's educational emphasis changed during his tenure in the military, he did not give up on the importance of the cultural and intellectual aspects of civil society, which included a focus on the importance of the contributions of people of African descent to the development of civilization, both historical and modern. These interests came to the fore during Steward's tenure at Wilberforce University[116] in Ohio, during which he became a professor of history, logic, and French and, after his first year, became vice president under the university's president, William Sanders Scarborough, Steward's longtime friend.[117] Steward held this administrative position until 1918.

Steward had long been acquainted with Wilberforce. In 1883 he had received an honorary doctoral degree from the university. When his cousin, Benjamin F. Lee resigned, as president of Wilberforce in 1884, Steward was nominated, unsuccessfully it turned out, for the presidency.[118] That same year Steward was elected to the university's chair of theology, but he declined the position. He spoke frequently at the university, however, and while an active chaplain in the army, he was stationed at Wilberforce and while there wrote *The Colored Regulars in the U. S Army*.[119]

When Steward arrived at Wilberforce in 1906, much of what was called a university was in fact equivalent to a grade school. This was also true of most historically black institutions of higher education during this era.[120] By 1918 the university had organized itself into several units: Payne Theological Seminary, the Normal and Industrial Department, the Military Department, the High School Academy, and the College Department.[121] Steward was placed in charge of the History Department and began to build a foundation of courses that moved from a general history of Western civilization through English history to American history and ended with a history of African Americans. The structure of these courses fleshed out the picture of African American civil society that Steward was still trying to build at this late stage of his life.

Steward's course on "General History" began with a focus on "the oriental peoples, that is, Asians and Africans, that have contributed most to western civilization," then examined early Greek and Roman history before turning to the rise of modern European nations.[122] This sequence is important because it illuminates Steward's commitment to highlight ancient African and Asian contributions to European civilization. Perhaps here Steward was influenced of his early Greek language teacher and colleague, Rufus Perry. Perry wrote *The Cushite; or, The Descendants of Ham as Found in the Sacred Scriptures and in the Writings of Ancient Historians and Poets from Noah to the Christian Era* in 1893, which highlighted the contributions of Africans to ancient classical civilization.[123]

Steward's other courses also focused on Africans and African Americans and their place in world and American history. His course "Civil War and Reconstruction" paid special attention to the "problems and struggles of the freedmen in the first years of their enfranchisement." Steward's purpose was to provide a coherent challenge to the prevailing revisionist view of Reconstruction during the time period. He also taught a course called "The History of African Peoples in the Western World." As with his civil war study, his goal was to challenge the accepted negative view of African Americans. One of his primary texts was *History of the Negro Race*, by African American pastor, politician, lawyer, and scholar George Washington Williams (1849–1891).[124] He also used his own *Haitian Revolution* as a textbook.[125] Each of these books highlighted what Steward felt were the significant contributions of Africans and African Americans to civilization. His stress on non-Western ancient history and African American history and culture can not be downplayed, considering the limited exposure that black people's history received in most American colleges and universities, even historically black ones, at that time. The white trustees at Howard University at this same time did not allow courses to be taught on "interracial relations" or on the "negro problem."[126] Steward's course at Wilberforce was expressly unique during the time period.

Steward showed his concern for the development of a cultured African American society in other ways as well. Along with other professors, he organized several debate clubs in order to encourage extracurricular intellectual life on the Wilberforce University campus.[127] His ongoing concern for the development of a cultured society within the African American can be seen in a letter dated March 3, 1923, just a year prior to his death, in which he praised some of the students who were in his junior class. The letter also hinted at what he saw as the connection between culture, race, and education:

In my junior class here I have some remarkably talented men; one fine artist; two [professional] musicians; one stage singer. One man from Alliance Ohio, has been the conductor or owner of a white orchestra for years—a fine violinist. Negroes are fast taking front places in the more refined parts of civilization. They are yet worshipping whites under the delusion of white superiority, but that will pass before long. Negroes have better taste than the whites of the same degree of development.[128]

Here at the end of Steward's life we see that he remained consistent to his vision of education that would both highlight the importance of classical liberal education and moral training to create a strong African American culture. At different phase of his life, Steward used the various civil society institutions (the church, military, and higher education) within which he found himself to experiment with his evolving ideas about how to bring about this grand African American civil society. Yet education was not the only part of Steward's vision for an African American civil society, though it was a uniquely important one. There were other arenas that he felt were crucially important to establishing this vision, especially black theology, that is, how black people understood their faith and notions about God. It is to this that the next chapter will turn.

Chapter 3

Evangelical Theology:
Striving for a Rational
Religious Orthodoxy

A frican American religion was in transition in the nineteenth century. Emotional and ecstatic spirituality, strongly influenced by slaves' religious practices, characterized much of early-nineteenth-century African American religious experience. Richard Allen, the first bishop of the AME Church, positively characterized this "plain and simple gospel":

> I was confident that there was no religious sect or denomination [that] would suit the capacity of the colored people as well as the Methodist; for the plain and simple gospel suits best for any people; for the unlearned can understand, and the learned are sure to understand; and the reason that the Methodist is so successful in the awakening and conversion of the colored people, the plain doctrine and having a good discipline. . . . We are beholden to the Methodists, under God, for the light of the Gospel we enjoy; for all other denominations preached so high-flown that we were not able to comprehend their doctrine. Sure am I that reading sermons will never prove so beneficial to the colored people as spiritual or extempore preaching.[1]

By the mid-1870s, the movement for a theologically trained ministry influenced a small portion of African American clergy, in particular AME Church clerics. This educated clergy was committed to preaching a "rational orthodox Christianity." As religious historian Paul Griffin describes it, rational orthodox theology was a religious orientation that affirmed the unity of truth in a divine and rational universe. Its proponents held that while revelation stood above reason in so far as human reason alone could never unilaterally deduce the truths of Christian Scripture, true reason or "sanctified reason" and revelation never contradicted each other. On the contrary, its advocates contended that the two were divinely instituted and divinely harmonious. For them, it took both reason and revelation to comprehend what constituted genuine Christianity.[2]

Bishop Daniel Payne, Steward's early mentor, led this movement in the AME Church, and Steward later came to epitomize it.

The AME Church's Early History in Theological Education

The early history of the AME Church, like that of other African American denominations, was one of enthusiastic revivalism. Born of the spirit of the Great Awakening, the church was committed to the evangelization of the African American masses. It discarded high form and traditions, including that of an educated clergy. Religious historian Nathan Hatch has suggested that African American preachers were recognized as natural leaders of their communities based on their demonstrated leadership and spiritual gifts. This was "a telling inversion of the Puritan legacy that had linked spiritual perception to common literacy and 'natural' leadership to virtues gained through classical education. Just as the black spiritual severed the intimate ties between church music and high culture . . . so black preaching treated sacred subjects with a 'strange familiarity' . . . almost profane."[3]

"Profane" may not be the most accurate description of African American preaching, but clearly the AME Church was committed to preaching a gospel that was understandable to the common person, especially Africans, both slave and free. Most of the early leaders of the AME Church were uneducated.[4] What is generally assumed is that these men were uneducated because they did not value education, but this is not the case. The average AME minister found himself in a difficult situation, as Bishop Payne recognized at the time.[5] Most ministers were adult men who had had little opportunity for even rudimentary education in their youth. Besides the daily religious responsibilities for their flock, these ministers had to earn their own livelihood and that of their families, usually via manual labor. Thus education was a luxury that most of them could not afford. In addition, only a limited number of higher educational institutions would admit African Americans during this period.[6] As Payne noted, education in those states

> in which the majority of the members of the African Methodist Church were located was strictly forbidden. The laws framed by the various state legislatures were so stringent, and the penalties so severe that we at this present day can only look back at them and shudder. Herein lies the chief cause of the lack of effort upon the part of the Church to increase it members. No one who has given these laws even the most cursory glance can blame the Church for shrinking from the pursuit of this cause; besides, any such efforts as might lead to the spread of education among the colored people, the great proportion of whom were slaves, offenders, but even . . . have endangered the very existence of the Church itself.[7]

One historian of the AME Church has suggested that the concern for education in the church began with Payne.[8] Given his passion for liberal arts education and his expertise as an educator (common school founder and headmaster, purchaser and president of Wilberforce University), his role as a prime advocate of education in the AME Church was understandable.

In general, Payne and other advocates of an educated clergy were more concerned about the development of a liberal arts education for ministers than they were about a particular, correct, theological orientation. Given the basic predicament of the African American community, their concerns focused on "the yoke of oppression" identified as slavery and "the unholy and cruel prejudice identified as unjust and unequal legislation."[9] The members of the northern, free African American community were concerned about not only their enslaved relatives in the South but also their own lack of suffrage, livelihood, and education in the North. Many African Americans in this pre– and post–Civil War period felt that their elevation as a race and their acceptance by white society could be obtained if they acted in acceptable and moral ways, that is, in a "civilized" fashion. Civilized traits included such virtues as temperance, punctuality, cleanliness, thriftiness, industriousness, and especially education. Education in this sense included all the above mentioned attributes as well as a broad liberal arts education. Thus Daniel Payne focused on "the three R's" (reading, writing, and arithmetic), geography, and Latin and Greek.[10]

When it came to the education of the clergy, the AME Church encouraged its ministers to obtain an education wherever they could matriculate. The clergy based their decisions not so much on the theological orientation of the various institutions, as on the posture of the institution toward slavery and its openness to accepting African Americans.[11] Of those clergy who were formally trained, educational affiliations included the Episcopalian, Presbyterian, Unitarian, and Lutheran denominational traditions. One of the resolutions of the 1841 Philadelphia Annual Conference challenged all of its elders and deacons to use "all means in [their] power from henceforth to cultivate [their] minds and increase [their] store of knowledge." The resolution also stated that all elders and deacons, licensed preachers and exhorters were to study, diligently and indefatigably, "English, Grammar, Geography, Arithmetic, Rollin's Ancient History, Modern History, Ecclesiastical History, Natural and Revealed Theology."[12] A glance at the rationale for these resolutions suggested that the church's leadership was more concerned about the advancement of an educated laity than a theologically focused clergy:

> Whereas, The great literary advantages which the rising generation enjoys require more than ordinary intelligence in the ministry that may be called to instruct them; and, whereas, our excellent discipline cannot be fully executed, nor our present plans of improvement fully consummated without an intelligent ministry; and still more, whereas, the word of God requires that the priest's lips should keep knowledge, and they (the people) should seek the law at his mouth, for he is the messenger of the Lord of Hosts; therefore.[13]

Unfortunately, even if there were opportunities for exposure to the liberal arts and theological training for AME ministers, the demand for missions and itinerancy, especially in the South among newly freed persons with significantly fewer educational opportunities, was most pressing. Much of the church leadership brought young men of talent into the mission field without significant training. Even Bishop Payne, with his keen interest in education, participated in this movement. He sent nine AME Church men as missionaries to the South, supported by the American Missionary Association. Steward was one of the nine. Of these nine, five had limited or no education. In a letter of request for support, Payne apologized for the limited education of those five:

> [William] Bentley and [William] Gaines are natives of Georgia. Though not regularly educated, they are intelligent men of sound judgment, and unquestionable piety. John Graham and Richard Vanderhorst are natives of South Carolina, what are true of Bentley and Gaines are also of them. . . . If I could have found men thoroughly educated, I should have preferred them provided their education was sustained by a deep toned piety, guided by *common sense.* May the omnipotent Lord of the Church say unto them what He said unto Saint Paul, "My grace is sufficient for thee, for my strength is made perfect in weakness."[14]

Steward was similarly undereducated, having attended only district or common schools, and having no high school education.[15] He was licensed in his local church as an exhorter on his nineteenth birthday and licensed to preach at twenty. At twenty-one, Steward, not yet baptized, was already appointed as pastor of a small church.[16] Despite his limited educational background, he nevertheless had an extraordinary zeal for theological education. Even as a young missionary in Georgia he took time to study the current historical and theological texts.

From May 27, 1868, to April 8, 1869, Steward kept a daily diary as "a faithful record of all things worth noting." In 1870, the journal entries included random church records for the year, while 1871 entries reflected random notes, sermons, and sermon outlines along with church records. Steward's entries in the journal included his almost daily meditation and study schedule in the early morning. He outlined the various duties of a pastor in the reconstruction of Georgia as well as the usual busy pastoral schedule of marriages, burials, and community organizing around the many needs of freed persons. The diary indicated his efforts in education, bank organizing, political work with the Republican Party, legal cases, and protection against the active Ku Klux Klan. All this was in addition to his activities in daily church life: texts for sermons preached, various preaching engagements in Macon and the surrounding area, revivals and camp meetings, Sunday school teaching, and school tutorials.

In the midst of all this, Steward made annotations in his journal regarding several books that he had found the time to read. They included Daniel D. Whedon, *The Freedom of the Will as a Basis of Human Responsibility and a Divine Government;* William Paley, *Natural Theology;* and Philip Schaff, *The Person of Christ: The Miracle of History with a Reply to Strauss and Renan and a Collection of Testimonies of Unbelievers.* Two other books Steward read were Myers's *God's Word Written*[17] and Abercrombie's *Intellectual Philosophy.*[18]

Many in Steward's congregation from 1871 to 1873 did not like his preaching style, characterizing him as a "Presbyterian" and "lecturer."[19] His unemotional and reasoned style was indicative of his emerging theological stance. Toward the latter part of his stay in Macon, Steward, at about twenty-seven years old, expressed his concern for the lack of theological preparation for young clergy. In this journal, he outlined in four handwritten pages the content of what he called a "Hand Book of Theology, designed for Young Ministers of the African M. E. Church Who have not had the Benefit of a Theological Training and as a Pocket Manual for All Ministers." This handbook defined theology as "discourse about God. . . . All knowledge whether classified or not which relates to God and the relations of intelligent creatures to him[.] All that information which gives a description of the nature and character of God, of the nature and power of angels, of the moral relations, duties and destines of men and which points out the faith and conduct necessary to secure Divine approbation is comprehended in the term Theology as used in the present day by divines." Steward defined the criterion for the use of the Bible and reason to distinguish between "false and true" religion. The Bible was the ultimate standard, and where the Bible did not speak, reason became the only practical criterion. He further briefly outlined sections on revealed theology and the Bible as divine revelation.[20]

Steward's journal entries are very important because they show that even in the midst of his pastoral responsibilities in the South, he assumed the challenge of developing himself theologically. His private meditations and reflections demonstrated that he was already leaning toward a rational orthodoxy which took full root during his three-year course of study at the Divinity School of the Protestant Episcopal Church (during his pastorate at Zion Mission AME Church in Philadelphia).

By this time, Steward had become involved in issues of theological training at the denominational level and participated in an increasing trend toward theological education for AME ministers. There was no consensus among the AME hierarchy regarding the best means to pursue the difficult task of preparing young men for ministry.

One example of this lack of consensus was the "Report of Committee on Education" adopted by the 1881 Philadelphia Annual Conference. The Committee on Education included Bishop J. M. Brown, Rev. C. E. Herbert, Rev. B. T. Tanner, and Steward. Their report suggested that even though the *Book of Discipline* had specified books in a course of study and most ministers had passed the examination, it was unclear how successful this had been in educating and training for ministry. The unspoken sentiment was that the local examining committees were passing people along without the candidates having satisfactorily internalized the material. This inadequacy seemed to effect the whole church, from doctrine to polity:

> We feel there is more need, if not of learning, at least of train-
> ing. The Methodist minister needs more accurate and technical
> instruction in the matter of the doctrine, the history and the polity
> of his church. It is unquestionably true, that the present condi-
> tion of our ministry suggests the necessity of special literature
> and special training; special literature that shall define the religion
> and ecclesiastical doctrines of our church, and special training in
> the administration of our discipline and worship. That while the
> hearts of our people and ministry are in the right place, their
> minds are in the wildest confusion on matters of church order, is
> too evident to be doubted; and the demand for well-defined
> doctrine and settled and established usage is becoming every day
> more urgent. The enlightened ministry of the church must furnish
> to the minds of our people this repose, being careful, at the same
> time, as they adjust the altar in its proper place, not to extin-
> guish the revival-fire kindled upon it by the illiterate but heaven-
> endowed fathers of a past generation.[21]

The report seemed to acquiesce in the difficulty of the clergy's inability to critically deal with theological texts. The committee conceded that they needed to do something to challenge the clergy to look more seriously at the impact of this education crisis on issues such as polity, liturgy, and revival.

As late as September 1884, Bishop Henry McNeal Turner forcefully stated his opinion regarding the education of the clergy. By this time the bishops had begun to recommend various books on theology to ministers to prepare them for admission to the clerical ranks. Prior to 1880 the main volumes were Richard Watson's *Theological Institutes* and Thomas N. Ralston's *Elements of Divinity.*[22] Turner indicated that these two works were "entirely too costly and heavy for the ordinary preacher, and too cumbersome for the circuit-rider to carry with him." The 1880 general conference ordered the bishops to take over the task of recommending study materials for entering clergy. The bishops formed a subcommittee that recommended a bulky and expensive three-volume set, Miner Raymond's *Systematic Theology.* This recommendation surprised and displeased Turner, who commented that the three volumes were "[a]ll bones and no meat—well, scarcely any meat. The result was, it drove theology out of the church. Not one applicant for admission in a hundred ever saw it, and not one committee in fifty was able to examine a candidate in it, even if the applicant had read it, hence no theology proper has been in the AME Church for years."[23]

Turner continued his lament: "How often has my heart burned with disgust when I was compelled to receive men in our ministry who knew no more about theology than a Hottentot knows about logarithm." He praised the action of the bishops in recommending Samuel Wakefield's *Complete System of Christian Theology,* a single volume that was much less expensive. "Here is a body of Divinity," he said, "sufficiently complete to answer all demands and enables our preachers to convert the world if they will."[24] He insisted that all potential ministerial candidates in his episcopal district read Wakefield's book as preparation for admittance to the ministry:

> Now, let every preacher who expects to apply for admission into any of my conferences get this book, unless you have studied Raymond; for as the Lord liveth, and my soul liveth, I shall not admit any preacher on trial in the future, nor ordain any deacon or elder who has not studied Wakefield or Raymond. I do not care if forty committees recommend them. Presiding elders who expect to offer brethren for any of these positions had better arm them with Wakefield at once, otherwise I positively will not regard them, for there is no excuse; none. . . . While I am not authorized to tell news out of school, I will say to all the young men who are candidates for admission and orders, you had better arm yourselves with Wakefield at once, judging from the way I heard the

Bishops talking to-day, for I think there is to be a new dispensation of things on the theological line. Let a hint suffice. Examining committees will need this book also, otherwise how can they
examine others?[25]

Steward played a key role in this new dispensation as the author of the
theological texts intended for use in the training of young AME minister.
The "Hand Book of Theology" Steward had conceived of during his pastorate in Georgia was finally brought to life as a series of texts developed
in relation to these new efforts at a consistent curriculum for AME ministers. Steward was a natural for this role. After his graduation with high
honors from the Divinity School of the Protestant Episcopal Church in
Philadelphia in 1880, he became one of the denomination's few seminary
trained ministers.

In July 1883, the AME Church embarked upon the task of providing
a theological education for its local and itinerant preachers, exhorters, and
Sunday school teachers. This effort at enlightenment was organized as
part of a larger and more ambitious plan called the Tawawa Sunday School
Assembly and Theological, Scientific and Literary Circle. The organization was designed to promote reading and study in arts and sciences, both
sacred and secular, to the AME Church constituency nationwide. It was
to provide a general enrichment in the areas of

> nature, art, science, and in secular and sacred literature, in connec-
> tion with the routine of daily life (especially among those whose
> educational advantages have been limited) so as to secure them the
> College student's general outlook upon the world and life; and to
> develop the habit of close, connected, persistent thinking; utilize the
> "Chimney-Corner" so as to make every home a school and church;
> in fact to organize in every community a band—those who desire
> to elevate the race and increase their knowledge and usefulness.[26]

The organization was to be structured into branches, each with its own
dean to oversee the division. Each of these deans was to supervise the
development of textbooks and literature that would be distributed at a
minimal cost to the registered members. They were also responsible for
the testing process and distribution of certificates.

By November 1883, the circle had developed an extension branch in
theology; its first dean was Steward.[27] This organization, called the Tawawa

Theological, Scientific and Literary Association (TTSLA), was designed as a correspondence course to provide theological education to its members, particularly its lay and ordained leadership. They were to be tested annually at a gathering at Wilberforce University, and if they passed the examination, the students would be given a certificate indicating their completion of the prescribed course of study. Those who could not attend Wilberforce could take the test at home and return it to the dean for marking.[28]

Steward's first theological work, *Death, Hades and Resurrection,* was listed as a "special essay to be read"[29] for the TTSLA. Although there are no extant copies of this volume, it was apparently a controversial work. Daniel R. Goodwin, Steward's former systematic divinity professor at the Divinity School of the Protestant Episcopal Church in Philadelphia, commented that the book was "a well-conceived, well-considered and well-written production" and that it "contained many very sticky and important thoughts" regarding topics of death, hell, and resurrection. While Goodwin felt that the subject could not be "dogmatized with certainty," he felt that Steward's views "on most points will be found sound and correct. Of course they might [cause] conflict, but in the mean time they are a contribution looking in the right direction."[30] Goodwin's comments were a forewarning for Steward within his own church. Steward indicated in a letter that Benjamin Tucker Tanner, later an AME Church bishop and major critic of Steward's work, pronounced the book "contradicting and absurd, but scholars of all grades[,] some of them utter strangers to me pronounced it otherwise[.]" On the other hand, Benjamin F. Lee, also later an AME Church bishop, remarked that Steward had "been most successful in soothing human feelings without insulting human reason, has accomplished much in aiding mankind in right development and noble efforts."[31]

Later, Steward was charged with writing the textbooks for the association. Three of his titles were required for the course on theology: *Incarnation and Atonement, Christian Evidence,*[32] and *Divine Attributes.*[33] *Divine Attributes* was the introductory text for the Tawawa Theological series. The text focused on defining the nature of God as found both in the biblical text and through reason. The foundation for the use of "reason" or rational discourse came from Scottish common sense philosophy. Although this philosophical tradition was generally associated with the Presbyterian tradition, other British and American denominational traditions utilized it widely.[34] One component of the Scottish common sense philosophical tradition was the idea that moral notions of good and bad, right and wrong, and justice and injustice were universal and innate. This went against the notion that moral ideas were an extension of belief in God received by humanity from the divine. As Steward explains,

> The view of one set of philosophers, the minority set, is that we have only to clearly establish the relation of the action or command to God and the righteousness follows. They make the righteousness inhere in the relation. They take this view in order to get rid of the ghost of innate ideas. The majority set of philosophers, who admit the doctrine of a common sense, believe in an inherent notion of truth and falsehood, right and wrong. This is the view unhesitatingly held by the writer of this book. He believes that neither sensation nor reflection give us the ideas of right and wrong, or truth and falsehood, but that observation and reflection can greatly enlarge the application of the ideas and make them more clear in some particulars. Dr. Paley says moral obligation depends upon the will of God, and right, which is correlative to it, must depend upon the same. This I do not believe. [Anthony Ashley Cooper, Earl of] Shaftsbury, as quoted by Stewart, says: "Whoever thinks that there is a God and pretends formally to believe that he is just and good, must suppose that there is independently such a thing as justice and injustice, truth and falsehood, right and wrong, according to which eternal and immutable standards he pronounces that God is just, righteous and true. If the mere will, decree, or law of God be said absolutely to constitute right and wrong, then are these latter words of no signification at all when applied to Him."[35]

The philosophical sophistication of Steward's argument reveals that theological and philosophical discourse had by that time evolved a considerable distance within the AME Church, but not without controversy. Indeed, Steward's theological views alienated him from his former mentor, Daniel Payne, as well as from others in the AME Church hierarchy. He was effectively eliminated from consideration for the bishopric and was ultimately forced out of active ecclesiastic life.

But Steward's fall from grace with the bishops was in the future. For now, the AME bishops unanimously recommended Steward's *Divine Attributes* as a text for aspiring and practicing AME ministers, though

Bishop Turner relegated it to the category of "helps," recommending Samuel Wakefield's *Complete System of Christian Theology* as the main text.[36] Nevertheless, Steward's *Divine Attributes* was formally protested by the annual conference held in Florida in late 1884.[37] The actual "Protest" read,

> To the Rt. Rev. Daniel A. Payne D.D.LL.D. Presiding Bishop of the 7th Episcopal district of the A.M.E. church, and members of the Florida Annual Conference.
>
> Whereas the book steward has received several pamphlets of the Tawawa series in systimatic [*sic*] Divinity by Rev. T. G. Steward D.D. and whereas, the doctrine contained in it, contradicts the scripture or word of God, as found on page 110 and 111 in said pamphlet, therefore be it resolved, that we most sadly protest against its circulation, among us, believing as we do, that the doctrine it contains is mischievous and dangerous to our connection.[38]

The powerful but aging Bishop Payne undoubtedly influenced the sentiments of Florida resolution. In his published memoir, *Recollections of Seventy Years*, Payne opined that Steward's theology was heretical. Speaking of *Divine Attributes* (which he mistakenly titled "First Lessons in Theology") and Steward's later work, *Genesis Re-Read*, Payne wrote, "These two productions of Dr. Theophilus Steward place him in a bright light as a scholarly writer, and do honor to his natural talents and literary acquirement. But as theological and religious efforts they are to be cautiously read, because of the heresy contained in them, which the discriminating judgment perceives, but which untrained intellect does not recognize."[39] Furthermore, Payne was not alone in raising concerns regarding Steward's theological orientation.

Divine Attributes

Steward wrote *Divine Attributes* in Philadelphia while he was the pastor of Union AME Church and published it through the denomination's publishing arm the Christian Recorder Print in 1884. "The book is designed to be elementary and suggestive," he noted. "Those who study it and go no further, it is believed, will obtain fair ideas of the subjects upon which it treats; those who desire to pursue the topic further will find suggestions in it."[40] Through *Divine Attributes,* Steward, relatively fresh from his seminary, developed a theology that was compatible with nineteenth-century American evangelicalism. The tension between his commitment to an evangelical ministry and his attraction to a rational philosophical tradition is evident throughout the text.

In keeping with its roots in American Evangelicalism, *Divine Attributes* was not designed to establish the existence of God but started from the presumption of God's existence. "Granting that the Bible is from God," Steward declared, "it affords at once presumptive proof that the existence of God was already quite universally known, since it surely assumes this much on man's part." Assuming that the "God-idea" was universal to humanity, Steward started his work by accounting for the existence of the idea of God in the human mind. He suggested that his theory had three constituent parts. The first part, called "traditional," argued that the God-idea passed down from "generation to generation preceding" over years to the point that its original revelation had faded "from human memory." Because this idea could not stand by itself, a second, supporting part was necessary. This component suggested that the idea of God was "constitutional," innate to the human psycho-social makeup. "There is in man . . . a tendency toward such an idea and a capacity to embrace and hold such an idea almost as a first truth," Steward contended.[41] The third constituent part of this theory, "sensational," suggested that laws and the experience of nature resonated with the traditional and constitutional. As in Rudolf Otto's idea of the numinous,[42] Steward indicated that nature called forth the need to worship God. The capacity of the God-idea as developed in the traditional and constitutional harmonized with the senses in an encounter with the natural elements, and "cause men to awake, under its inspiring music, to the thought of God." Steward went on to muse that "[t]he untutored savage, traversing his wild domain of mountain, wood and prairie, scanning with revered eye the heaven above and the world around," early learns to "see God in clouds and hear Him in the wind."[43]

On the basis of this triadic theory, Steward set out to delineate twelve attributes of God. These attributes were divided equally between the natural and the moral. The natural attributes were eternity, immutability, spirituality, omnipresence, omniscience, and omnipotence; the moral attributes were wisdom, truth, holiness, love, justice, and righteousness. He indicated that Scripture and reason affirmed these divine attributes.[44]

Steward tried to strike a balance between those who did not trust reason and philosophical discourse to support evangelical religion, and those who did not hold the Bible as revealed. He indicated that the Scriptures were "in accord with reason although they [went] beyond its inferences." In the presentation of his theology, however, he seemed to emphasize reason over Scripture. He argued for and justified this work by referring to numerous European philosophers and scientists, including Immanuel Kant, John Locke, Hugh Miller, Ormsby M. Mitchel, Dugold Stewart, Sir William Hamilton, Bishop Joseph Butler, and John Abercrombie.

The section of Steward's *Divine Attributes* on natural attributes was straightforward philosophical theology and created no problems for his readers. But the section on moral attributes inspired significant opposition from within certain corners of the church. Besides the warning of Payne and the resolution of the Florida Annual Conference, the editor of the *Christian Recorder,* Benjamin Tanner, critically reviewed *Divine Attributes.* Tanner began his review with pride as he praised the work:

> We have seldom perused anything with more real pleasure. And the thought that it came from within our ranks brought to light what we regard as a fact that the African Methodist Episcopal Church is beginning the production of a home literature on a plane quite as high, if not higher, than has ever been the case with a church before. Even the Patristic literature of our common Christianity can boast of no such book on Systematic Divinity, or the study of Divinity systematized, as the one before us.[45]

Tanner argued that Steward's work was the equal of, if not superior to, any of the theological productions in the larger Wesleyan movement in America. Yet he stopped short of a full endorsement. "We dissent," he said, "in toto from what he says on page 65, and have to acknowledge ourselves as of those sharing the 'notion' that the act of God determines all moral qualities. We have no idea of exalting man to the high seat of judgment on the divine conduct."[46]

Steward, following the lead of those advocates of common sense philosophy, especially Bishop Joseph Butler, had argued that "[t]he fact then appears to be that we are constituted so as to condemn falsehood, unprovoked violence, injustice, and to approve of benevolence to some preferably to others, abstracted from all considerations, which conduct is likeliest to

produce an overbalance of happiness or misery."[47] Steward not only suggested that the idea of God was innate to the constitution of humans but
also put forth the idea that "certain fundamental principles are stamped in
the constitution, and among these are to be found the idea of justice more
or less developed."[48] Thus women and men had the internal capacity to discern good and evil without the assistance or guidance of God or God's laws.
Steward's proposal came close to suggesting that humanity was ultimately
independent of God. His critics felt this proposition left too much room for
the atheistic view that humans could build a moral philosophy without need
for God. Payne and Tanner were quick to raise issue with the liberal tone and
potential dangers to orthodoxy that Steward promoted in his attempt to
be credible to his religious and ecclesiastical peers in the world outside the
AME Church. *Divine Attributes* was traditional in many of its views, yet
many felt it stretched the boundaries of orthodox evangelicalism.[49] This tendency toward a liberal interpretation of theology and the Scriptures became
even more evident in Steward's later work, *Genesis Re-Read*.

Genesis Re-Read

Steward can be thought of as representing the African American wing of
the "liberal evangelical" tradition, which was critically involved with developing scientific theories.[50] By the latter part of the nineteenth century, the
theory of evolution was making its impact on biblical studies. Darwin's
theory was gaining attention in America and around the world. In 1876,
Thomas Huxley lectured in the United States on evolution and in the
process attacked the validity of the creation story found in the first book
of the Bible, Genesis. Though historians have discussed the impact of
modernism on the Protestant Christian tradition, they have completely
ignored the impact of this movement on the African American church.[51]
Steward was wrestling with the significance of science at this time, especially the theory of evolution as espoused by Huxley. While admitting the
importance of these theoretical breakthroughs, he challenged their pre-
sumed inability to harmonize with the biblical story.

    The seed for *Genesis Re-Read* germinated some nine years before its
publication in 1885. Huxley's controversial lectures delivered in New York
were widely publicized. As testament to their impact, the *New York Times*
published the full texts of his lectures.[52]

These lectures heightened the existing debate within the scientific and clerical communities over the validity of the Darwinian theory of evolution.[53] There were three general reactions to Darwin's theory. There were those, mostly in the scientific community, who were committed to evolutionary theory and saw no place for a biblical emphasis on creation. Then there were those who held to the biblical version of creation and saw no validity in the new theory of species development. Finally, there were those who tried to bridge the gap between the two extremes and hold in tension a belief in both evolution and creation. This bifurcated belief could not be successful without developing a strong apologetic on behalf of the Bible, especially the book of Genesis.

In the African American community, only a few rejected the religious option altogether, though one of those who did was Frederick Douglass. He lamented that African Americans put more value in the Scriptures than in science, and that they "pursued what cannot be known [rather] than that which may be known."[54] He went on to say that "one sweep of the telescope around the heavens converts Gen[e]s[i]s into a m[y]th. The commonest stone on the earth does the work for the six days story. But one would be stoned if he said so in the presence of the religious crowd of colored people, yet all intelligent white men know this and know it none the less because they still cling to the Bible."[55] While Douglass admitted that he was not sure whether he was an evolutionist, he affirmed a leaning in that direction: "I do not know that I am an evolutionist, but to this extent I am one. I certainly have more patience with those who trace mankind upward from a low condition, even from the lower animals, than with those who start him at a high point of perfection and conduct him to a level with the brutes."[56]

Most African Americans, as Douglass claimed, held to a more conservative view that rejected evolution altogether in favor of biblical creation. As an example, a short editorial in the *Christian Recorder* published two years before Huxley's visit criticized those "good and learned men, pious but not wise" who straddled the fence by holding onto both evolution and creation, trying "hard to make it appear that the modern theory of 'Evolution' is consistent with belief in the Christian idea of a Creator, a great First Cause." While quoting Herbert Spencer's statement that evolution and creation were "mutually exclusive," the editor sarcastically thanked Spencer for his clarity and upheld it as a virtue that the Christian community should follow: "That is honest and intelligible and Christians can take their choice. If Evolution is God; worship it. If the Creator is God; worship him. We believe in the Creator and thank Mr. Spencer for stating the case so clearly and fairly. There are no two ways about it, and we heartily agree with Mr. Spencer in saying that Evolution and Creation are mutually exclusive."[57] The *Christian Recorder* also excerpted and published critical reviews of Huxley's doctrine by the white Methodist Episcopal preacher William Taylor. Taylor was a well-known preacher and proponent of the conservative movement of the holiness camp meetings and would later become bishop.[58] James A. Handy, co-contributor of an auxiliary chapter in Steward's later book, *The End of the World* and later an AME bishop, also argued against evolution in his article "The Mystery of Man":

> We cannot state how long a period may be necessary for the purpose of converting an infusorial animalcule into a man, as such a transformation has never been observed in progress. On the contrary, however, it is to be said that geology, ethnology and the natural history of man bear ample testimony of the truth of the Mosaic statement as recorded in the book of Genesis. The first man, the man of earth, was fashioned and conformed from the materials of this objective world, in bodily keeping from the order of the elements from which he was to derive the sustentation of his physical life. Raised erect from the ground as if by the hand that formed his body from the dust, the breath of the Almighty Creator kindled in every fibre of his frame and constituted within his body a distinct selfhood, a living soul, a full, a complete man.[59]

There were a few individuals who, in company with Steward, defied the religious conservatism within the black religious community concerning evolution and attempted to harmonize these two theories. Steward's first discussion of Huxley and evolutionary theory was at a public lecture at his Brooklyn, New York, church, the Bridge Street AME Church, several weeks after Huxley's lectures. He lectured to a full house. The *National Monitor,* a Brooklyn black Baptist weekly edited by the Reverend Rufus Perry, covered the lecture,[60] and the *Christian Recorder* reprinted excerpts. Perry stated that the manifest effect of the lectures "was to impress upon the minds of the hearers a higher regard for the Bible as of divine authority, and alone able to make us wise unto salvation." The *National Monitor's* editor went on to indicate that "[t]he character of the lecture, for substance and manner, was such as to suggest the thought that our people should improve the opportunity which pastors of the unquestioned ability and culture of Mr. Steward most signally afford." Two things are evident from this newspaper report. First, the black religious community clearly expressed some interest in the issue of evolutionary theory and its impact upon the Christian faith; and second, a small but significant portion of African American clergy was concerned with the issue of the intellectual abilities of African American clergy to engage the various theological and social trends of the day.

The two extant versions of the lecture, found in the *Christian Recorder* and in Steward's autobiography, *Fifty Years of Gospel Ministry,* are similar, but not identical.[61] Yet between the two versions, one gets a clear picture of the line of argument which Steward articulated to his audience. At the start of his lecture, Steward described science as "bold, disrespectful, aggressive, respecting neither opinions or men. It fears naught beside. *What is,* is the divinity before which it bows with intense devotion."[62] He contended that the same could not always be said about the scientist. Pointing to Huxley, Steward argued that the evolutionist, in his lecture, used a straw man in the form of John Milton and his poem *Paradise Lost* to attack Moses, the assumed author of the book of Genesis. Steward asserted that Huxley used this literary ploy in order not to directly confront what Steward called "Huxley's superior," the biblical text.

Huxley, in his lectures, claimed that he exchanged what he called the "Milton hypothesis" for the doctrine of creation. By the "Milton hypothesis," Huxley meant that "[t]he present conditions of things had endured for a comparatively moderate time, and then at the commencement of that time [it] came into existence, within the course of six days." His "present business," Huxley stated, "is not with the question how nature has originated or to the causes which have led to her origination, but as to the manner and order of her origination. Our present inquiry is not why the objects that constitute nature came into existence, but when they came into existence and in what order."[63] He further suggested that he used this "Milton hypothesis" because it was the common belief regarding creation among all Christians, both Protestants and Catholics. He avoided labeling it as a the biblical doctrine because, as he satirically stated, in the first place to say what the Hebrew text contains, and what is does not; and in the second place, were I to say that this is the Biblical hypothesis, I should be met by the authority of many an eminent scholar, to say nothing of men of science, who in recent times have absolutely denied that this doctrine is to be found in Genesis at all. If we are to listen to them we must believe that what seems so clearly spoken of as days of creation that we could make no mistake on that subject are not days at all, but periods of time which you may make just as long as convenience may require. And again, if we are to listen to them, we are to believe that when the verse says that God made the beast of the field, it is perfectly consistent with the phraseology to believe that they may have been evolved by natural processes lasting for millions of years. A person who is not a critic and is not a Hebrew scholar can only stand up and admire the marvelous flexibility of the language which admits of such diverse interpretations.

Huxley continued with his rationale for not using the Mosaic doctrine by stating, "[W]e are now assured, upon the authority of the highest critics, and even of dignitaries of the Church, that there is no evidence whatever that Moses wrote this particular chapter or knew anything about it." He indicated that he should avoid, as a lay person, being entangled in such a vexed debate: "So, as . . . happily, Milton leaves us in no ambiguity as to what he means, I will still continue to speak of it as the Miltonic hypothesis."[64] This gained Huxley a round of applause from his audience.

Steward, in his counterlecture, indicated that a scientist starts his investigation with a theory, or "constructs an imaginary plan, and investigates with enthusiasm because he is devoted to it. If this is true, all investigation must be more or less partial, and subject to criticism and review." Given that the scientist starts his theory from imagination, pointing toward Huxley, Steward argued that there "appears to be a tendency in man: To predict according to his wishes and to investigate with enthusiasm over a pet theory, a theory in which he delights, and upon which he is ever ready to argue. . . . Scientific men are sometimes cowards. Science is bold, but scientists are not always so." Steward respected Huxley's "years of patient investigation" and his "careful consultation of the views of others who have searched over this vast field of science" and indicated that he examined his work with a feeling of great respect and would retreat from his critique of Huxley's work were it not for the Bible, which he held in even higher esteem. With all of his greatness of stature and intellectual ability, Steward declared that Huxley, ultimately, was no demigod but "a man—and only a man": "And what is man? Let us have the Professor's own definition. He says: 'A man is little more than a mathematical point in duration—but a fleeting shadow' and then, quoting a Scriptural phrase, he says man 'is a reed shaken by the wind' of forms. Of course the Professor is no exception. He may be a tall reed, but is nevertheless a reed. He may make a great shadow, but it is a shadow nevertheless."[65]

Steward went on to challenge Huxley's notions of circumstantial evidence, to which he appealed to verify the evolutionary hypothesis. Huxley had argued in his first lecture that in attempting to ascertain how the universe came into existence, circumstantial evidence was a reliable source of knowledge:

> Suppose that a man tells you that he saw a person strike another and kill him. That is testimonial evidence of the fact of murder. But it is possible to have circumstantial evidence of the fact of murder—that is to say, you may find a man dying, with a wound upon his head having exactly the form and character of a wound which is made by an axe; and, with due precaution, you may conclude with the utmost certainty that the man has been murdered, and is dying in consequence of the violence inflicted by that implement.[66]

Huxley admitted the dangers and uncertainties of using circumstantial evidence but maintained that it was a "great deal better than testimonial evidence." He felt that circumstantial evidence was not open to doubt and falsification and one could be assured that the axe was the implement that murdered the person. On the other hand, testimonial evidence was "open to multitudinous errors; he [the witness] may have been actuated by malice; and it is possible, and constantly has happened that even a number of persons have declared that a thing has happened in this or that or the other way, when a careful analysis of the circumstantial evidence has shown that it did not happen that way, but in some other, which cases are clear of the value of circumstantial evidence of the highest weight and of the highest authority."[67] This notion of testimonial evidence was for Huxley an allusion to the biblical account of creation, now superseded by the circumstantial evidence offered by Darwin's evolutionary theory.

Steward confronted Huxley's notion of circumstantial evidence by giving a counterexample. Following Huxley's logic, Steward argued that one could assume that a fruit tree is a peach tree by its "leaves, its bark, its general appearance, and its fruit. How came it here? It grew from a peach seed. I know, because I have planted peach seeds and have seen peach trees grow from them. It was planted say, five years ago as I judge by the size of its trunk, and is of a given variety." Steward argued that this type of logic was faulty. Continuing with this example, he developed his argument in favor of testimonial evidence:

> But here comes the nursery-man. Let us consult him: Did you plant a peach seed here five years ago? No; I planted an apricot seed here six years ago. And this one remark of Revelation [*sic*] throws down the whole theory respecting that peach tree. Appearances are sometimes deceptive, no matter whether they are outside or inside. To us there are no other kind than outside. If we get beyond the outside it must be by reasoning, or by revelation. In the case before us, reasoning brings us to a peach seed; revelation brings us to an apricot seed, and no man would hesitate a moment to throw away his reasoning, and accept the statement. In a word the circumstantial evidence would vanish like a dissolving picture before the convincing light of testimonial evidence.[68]

Steward went on to challenge Huxley's antagonism toward the notion of creation as a gradual process. He argued that geology, the science on which Huxley based much of his lecture, was a new and inconclusive science and was subject to change. Various discrepancies between geology and creation theory could be explained, he said. Where the Bible indicated that plants were created first, geology showed no record. Huxley indicated that the two records of geology and creation could not be reconciled. Drawing upon the work of astronomer Ormsby MacKnight Mitchel, Steward, on the other hand, maintained that "[t]he most that can be derived from geologic discoveries is that animal and vegetable life were introduced at the same time. No vegetable life is found earlier than animal. Geology does show us, however, in the upper or latest strata the remains of animals that are now extinct and of animals that are still living."[69] Steward finished the lecture by showing what he felt was the purpose of the Bible, and he argued that the existence of discrepancies might be the result of biblical omission. There were also contradictions in science, he pointed out: "It was not yet proven that the records furnished by nature had been read with infallibility. No one doubted the truthfulness of nature, but the readers of nature did not, and do not claim inspiration, and we are not bound to grant to them the dogma of infallibility."[70]

Nine years after his public lecture, in *Genesis Re-Read*, Steward further developed his defense of the Bible, his challenge to scientific infallibility, and his call to harmonize the Mosaic and evolutionary theories. The book received several complimentary readings published in the *Christian Recorder*. The responses came from a variety of individuals. Frederick Douglass wrote, "With the millions of your countrymen who have African blood, I own myself a debtor to you for that production. It is a credit to the mind and heart of our whole people and a killing condemnation of our alleged mental inferiority. I have seldom read a book more elevated in style, more lucid and logical in argument, more rich in research, more profound in thought, or that gave evidence of more earnestness, industry and candor in its production. I rejoice that you were able to write it."[71] Bishop Turner also added his congratulatory note. He indicated that the volume was a major contribution to the church's literature. "It is one of the few books now before our ministry that will bear study," he wrote. "A casual reading will not enable the ordinary student of the Bible to grasp the theologico-scientific cast which is necessary to a thorough understanding of its contents; profound and protracted study will therefore be indispensable. I am sure it will be in great demand by the progressive men of our Church and of our day."[72] Susan S. McKinney (who later became Steward's second wife) also responded to the volume. She indicated that the book was thorough, carefully researched, and showed a wide grasp of language and physical science. "The argument adduced in defense of our precious Bible against the assaults of its scientific enemies are logically forcible and beyond successful contradiction," she commented. "Your book has proven a clincher to my faith in that Book which has been my guide from my youth up."[73]

In *Genesis Re-Read*, Steward's first step was to modify the conservative interpretation of the first seven days of creation as literal twenty-four hour days. He argued instead that "[t]o apply *a posteriori* reasoning to show that these days were great periods is very largely a waste of time, because it may at once be frankly admitted and the remark added, that neither Moses nor any human being could have been present to determine the length of these days. Nothing is insisted upon with regard to the length of these periods here."[74] From there Steward reiterated his earlier argument that while one must take science seriously, it was not infallible. He noted that the order of creation located in Genesis was of the same developmental progression as in the theory of evolution, and that the two must not therefore be regarded as antithetical. Instead, they could by viewed as complementary. Science for Steward could not be elevated over the Genesis story:

> How will we account for that given condition upon which evolution begins? Whence came those first elements and how came they possessed of those exact possibilities which are evolved from them? Evolution cannot tell, and we may reassert with increased boldness that for all evolution has as yet shown, Moses may have spoken the exact truth when he said, "In the beginning God created the heavens and the earth." Evolutionists say we do not know how the universe began; Genesis gives a direct statement of this beginning and there is nothing in evolution to interrupt our confidence in this statement.[75]

Despite this welcome, *Genesis Re-Read* did not escape without criticism. Benjamin Tanner, editor of the *A.M.E. Church Review*, raised several concerns that struck at the heart of Payne's and others' concern about Steward's "heretical" theological views.

Like the other reviewers, Tanner gave the volume high praise as a literary product, noting that Steward held "a leading position among the rising scholars of the race, whose name is already legion. His is among the first of the literary productions of the normal condition of things now happily existing in our land; and judging from what he has given us, the future promises to be immensely creditable."[76] But then he leveled his critique against Steward's broad use of liberal biblical interpretation. First, Tanner questioned Steward's use of "the method of a Mosaic illumination" in which "Steward suggested that Moses may have received the information contained in Genesis from several possible sources." Indeed, Steward went beyond the general belief that Moses wrote Genesis based on divine inspiration. He proposed that "it is probable that all the Jewish history which has been noted down by antediluvian patriarchs and Abraham and his descendants was well known to Moses, and the events of that period were so striking that they could hardly fail of being recorded." The logical conclusion from this proposition was that the writing of Genesis was not divinely inspired and handed down from God to Moses, but that Moses constructed it based on previously written texts. Later in *Genesis Re-Read,* Steward concluded that Moses redacted Genesis with the use of two different documents. Agreeing with the contemporary biblical criticism of his time, Steward proposed that Moses used "E" and "J" documents as sources of information to construct or edit Genesis: "A quite fair representative supposition is that Moses compiled two traditions or blended two documents,—the one Elohistic (from Elohim) the other Yahvistic (from Jehovah). This would indicate two shades of early religion, a Yahvistic and an Elohistic, and of these, the Elohistic would appear to be the earlier."[77]

Steward allowed that some of Genesis may have contained some errors in translation, but this did not, in his view, negate the text: "Errors may have occurred also in unimportant matters in transcribing, thus adding verbal difficulties to the unavoidable omissions. . . . The mere existence of difficulties, even should they be beyond our power to explication, should not throw discredit over the whole book."[78]

Steward had further postulated that the only person who witnessed the creation was the "Creator Himself" and that Moses received the information from God "directly or indirectly." Thus if one found inaccuracy, "it does not necessarily vitiate the testimony of the historian with regard to the ordinary events recorded within the periods already treated of [*sic*]." He further provided room for the sake of his argument that Moses could have been wrong or even misinformed about the creation story. He argued that if Genesis was part wrong, it did not have to be completely wrong. "Should it therefore result that the cosmogony of Moses is disproved by fact, we need only give up so much of the record as is overthrown," he argued. "It does not follow, I repeat, that we must give up all of Genesis, all of the Pentateuch, all of the Scriptures of the Old and New Testament, and all of the Jewish and Christian religions even should the story of creation fail."[79] Steward admitted the mythical nature of the creation story. The histories of all "branches of the human race" were constructed on the foundation of fables and myth, he noted. "We do not discard that which is probable and which is confirmed, because we find it connected necessarily with a recital of what is absurd and unsupported." Steward confessed that he did not know finally if the Genesis creation story was true, but declared, "I desire to have the reader consider that all that is urged here is that this matter is worthy of belief; not that we can really know it to be true."[80]

Tanner was uncomfortable with the use of three different methods of interpretation. "Of course the author does not present them as original with him; but the peculiar feature in the matter is he endorses them all, or at least, declares each as probable," Tanner stated.[81] He felt that this type of hedging on the construction of Genesis only made it more difficult to defend the Bible from its scientific detractors. Steward, in Tanner's view, conceded too much ground to the scientific critics.

Tanner took a hard line on Steward's postulations, quoting the maxim "False in part, false in whole." He maintained that it was necessary to hold to the inerrancy of the Scripture throughout. If Moses was not divinely inspired when he wrote one part of the text, he was not divinely inspired when he wrote other parts. Tanner argued that it would not do, for "Christian writers even when essaying to fight unbelievers on their own ground to so lightly surrender this all necessary out post. The only possible result will be to reduce Moses to the common rank of a secular historian. And Moses reduced to-day, Joshua and Samuel and the prophets will be reduced to-morrow."[82]

Steward's scholarship, up to this point in his life, had served as a vehicle to challenge the AME Church to broaden its theological views to accommodate the developing scientific and biblical theories of the times. Yet many in the church perceived Steward's liberal interpretation of the Scripture as dangerous and heretical. This was especially true for Daniel Payne and Benjamin Tanner. Steward's push for a rational theology came at a time in the life of the AME Church in which many members were leaning toward a more conservative mode. David Wills has suggested that there were no major denominational battles between conservatives and liberals during this period, but rather a steady shift toward conservatism: "What occurred instead was a gradual reduction in the vitality and sophistication of theological debate and a general failure to develop further the creative links between theology and blackness that had been explored by men like Steward and Tanner. Conservative voices continued to predominate, but they spoke with less erudition and frequently with less self-confidence."[83] Steward thus found himself at theological odds with the predominant leaders of the church. This conflict spilled over into Steward's involvement in the polity of the church. Continued tensions with Payne, along with the conflict of personalities between Steward, Henry M. Turner, and others, led to Steward's ultimate demise as a significant leader in the church hierarchy. As will be shown in chapter 4, Steward's liberal tendencies would be clearly articulated in his later book, *The End of the World*, as he takes on the racist writings of Congregationalist missionary Josiah Strong. Steward would later be more sensitive to the liberal label and attempt to balance his views in the writing of his one and only novel, *A Charleston Love Story; or, Hortense Vanross.*

Chapter 4

Civilization, America, and Race

T heophilus Steward lived in conflict between his vision for a Christian civilization in America and the reality which he was forced to see. He envisioned a democratized and nonracialized society in which all people would be recognized as equal participants and contributors to this vision. The reality, Steward believed, was very different: America was a society of class privilege, sexual inequality, and racial injustice which did not allow all of its participants to contribute. For African Americans, race was clearly the defining factor that prohibited that participation. Throughout Steward's life and thought, there was a tension between his belief in an evolving civilization, which would continue to be inclusive and widening, and his realization that racism had saturated most sectors of American life. Steward's answer was to take a middle-road position between full-blown black nationalism and integration.

Steward was cautious about supporting a back-to-Africa movement, as can be seen in the response of Steward and others on the Committee on African Migration of the South Carolina Annual Conference of the AME Church to the 1878 Liberian emigration plan by South Carolina African Americans under the auspices of the Liberian Exodus Joint Stock Steamship Company. Without denigrating the plan overtly, the committee raised concerns about its soundness.[1] And the members of the committee expressed their "unqualified disapprobation of any organized effort to expatriate us from the country dear to us by every memory of our life."[2] Soon-to-be-bishop Henry Turner gave his support to the emigration attempt and later became the quintessential symbol of black nationalism and the back-to-Africa movement.[3]

While countering the back-to-Africa movement, Steward never supported the assimilation policy advocated by Booker T. Washington. In fact, Steward felt that Washington's social philosophy was pernicious.[4] Yet between these two extremes, Steward was committed to identifying and providing a critique of racism as he saw it. He was also committed to highlighting those areas in which African Americans proved themselves able to function and surpass their white counterparts in civil society. All this was done in the attempt to reconcile his vision of America with its reality. What we see in Steward is a vacillation between his black self-determinationist rhetoric and his concern for universal humanity. Much of this tension between particularism and universalism can be seen in a comparison of two of Steward's works, *The End of the World* and *Our Civilization*. The tension is also seen in the wide-ranging and sometimes conflicting views Steward expressed regarding the U.S. military, African American soldiers, and American foreign policy.

The End of the World

Steward was acutely aware of the racism in every stratum of American society. Through his chaplaincy, he also became more intensely cognizant that racism had taken on an international character with the continued expansion of the United States' role as imperial protector of the Western Hemisphere. The philosophy of Manifest Destiny became increasingly troubling to Steward in the mid-1880s and into the twentieth century, especially as it influenced the American church. Much of Euro-American Christianity was based on a postmillennialist vision that followed the thinking of social Darwinism. In this vision, Manifest Destiny was seen as the last great hope of ushering in a new society, a society that was to be the crowning glory of Anglo-Saxon achievement as well as the harbinger of the kingdom of God. This argument was reflected in Josiah Strong's *Our Country*, first published in 1886.[5]

Steward, using a modified postmillennialist, biblical interpretation of Daniel, Matthew, and Revelation, challenged the evangelical imperialism of Josiah Strong in his theological work *The End of the World*.[6] In this work, published in 1888, Steward asserts that the "Anglo-Saxon" race will lead itself to self-destruction and that people of color will rise to create a more equitable and just world.

To better understand Steward's discussion of Manifest Destiny, it is important to know more about the book that precipitated it—Josiah Strong's *Our Country*.[7] Strong was a Congregational minister and the secretary for the Congregational Home Missionary Society in Ohio, Kentucky, West Virginia, and western Pennsylvania. *Our Country,* which his contemporaries praised as "the Uncle Tom's Cabin of social reform," established his reputation as a major social gospel thinker.[8] By 1916 the volume had sold 176,000 copies.

One of Strong's major theses was that the United States of America—particularly the western part of the country with all of its natural resources—was the place from which to launch a worldwide Protestant missionary enterprise:[9]

> Notwithstanding the great perils which threaten it, I cannot think our civilization will perish; but I believe it is fully in the hands of the Christians of the United States, during the next fifteen or twenty years, to hasten or retard the coming of Christ's kingdom in the world by hundreds, and perhaps thousands, of years. We of this generation and nation occupy the Gibraltar of the ages which commands the world's future.[10]

However, several perils threatened this world mission enterprise: immigration, Roman Catholicism, Mormonism, intemperance, socialism, wealth (depicted as mammonism, materialism, and luxuriousness), and the immorality and congestion of the city.

For Strong, Anglo-Saxonism was more than the classic Darwinian notion of racial distinction; it was a statement of Christianized ethnocentrism. Strong combined the theology of Horace Bushnell, as outlined in his book *Christian Nurture,* and the evolutionary theory of Darwin's *Descent of Man* in order to undergird Anglo-Saxonism.[11] He understood the Anglo-Saxon race to be any European group that spoke the English language and adhered to the Protestant faith. Specifically, the Anglo-Saxon was "representative of two great ideas, which are closely related": civil liberty and spiritual Christianity. Strong argued that the American white Protestant population was the best and most advanced example of Anglo-Saxonism. "Without controversy, these are the forces which, in the past, have contributed most to the elevation of the human race, and they must continue to be, in the future, the most efficient ministers to its progress," he declared. "It follows, then that the Anglo-Saxon, as the great representative of these two ideas, the depository of these two greatest blessings, sustains peculiar relations to the world's future, is divinely commissioned to be, in a peculiar sense, his brother's keeper."[12] Thus Strong advocated assimilation of various ethnic groups into the Anglo-Saxon culture through evangelism, regarding it as the only thing that could save the "inferior races." Quoting Bushnell, he argued, "Any people that is physiologically advanced in culture, though it be only in a degree beyond another which is mingled with it on strictly equal terms, is sure to live down and finally live out its inferior. Nothing can save the inferior race but a ready and pliant assimilation." He stated that the all-conquering Anglo-Saxons had developed an aggressive energy with which they had distinguished themselves as geniuses in colonizing.[13] "Then," he contended, "this race of unequaled energy, with all the majesty of numbers and the might or wealth behind it—the representative, let us hope, of the largest liberty, the purest Christianity, the highest civilization—having developed peculiarly aggressive traits calculated to impress its institutions upon mankind, will spread itself over the earth."

Strong asked rhetorically, "[D]oes it not look as if God were not only preparing in our Anglo-Saxon civilization the die with which to stamp the peoples of the earth, but as if he were also massing behind that die the mighty power with which to press it?"[14]

It is easy to label Strong a racist, but some historians and biographers have been reluctant to do so. As Ralph Luker explains in *The Social Gospel in Black and White,*

> Offensive as Josiah Strong's vision of an Anglo-Saxon eschaton may be, it is not rightly understood as racist. He was not always consistent, but, "Anglo-Saxon" was not really a racial category for Strong. Anglo-Saxons were English-speaking people who were the vehicles of God's redemptive purpose because of their cultural, not racial purity. . . . To convert, to "Anglo-Saxonize," to "Americanize," and to "Christianize" were essentially interchangeable terms for Strong. The church should serve as an "alembic" in which this transformation of other peoples would take place.[15]

Luker places Strong in a broad continuum of racial attitudes in the larger white community of which he was a part. He compares Strong's "radical assimilationism" to Josiah Royce's "conservative assimilationism," Edgar Gardner Murphy's "conservative separatism," and Thomas Dixon Jr.'s "radical separatism."[16] Luker outlines several reactions to Strong by his

nineteenth-century contemporaries in the African American community—John Welsey Edward Bowen, a Methodist Episcopal Church minister; Alexander Crummell, an Episcopal minister;[17] and T. G. Steward—and
suggests that they misinterpreted Strong's motives.[18] But defenders of
social gospel advocates (such as Strong) against the racist label have in
turn misunderstood the critique put forth by Strong's African American
contemporaries.

These men were raising the question of the subtle nature of what
they called, among other things, "caste prejudice." They argued that many
of their white social gospel advocates were at best paternalistic and at
worst racist in their desire to dominate and force their Anglo-Saxon vision
on their perceived wards. This is true in spite of the fact that many social
gospel advocates were former abolitionists and active philanthropists on
behalf of the African American community.

Strong's nomination as president of Atlanta University provides an
example of the African American critique of the motives of their white
benefactors. Just a year before Strong was nominated for the presidency,
Francis Grimké, the prominent black pastor of Fifteenth Street Presbyterian Church in Washington, D.C., wrote a stinging article in the *AME
Church Review* in support of the necessity of placing African American
men in professorial positions in institutions of black higher education.
Grimké was a graduate of Princeton Theological Seminary and the nephew
of the famed white abolitionists and women's rights advocates, Sarah and
Angelina Grimké. Grimké, in the 1885 article titled "Colored Men as Professors in Colored Institutions," argued that higher educational institutions, which were designed for the education of African Americans, were
only partly doing their jobs. He stated that these institutions had two
functions. The first duty was to educate young black men and women and
the second was to afford the opportunity for "colored men to exercise
their gifts as instructors in the higher departments of learning—which has
an important bearing upon the progress of the race." Grimké argued that
role models were crucial to the intellectual and educational development
of blacks, "in that it accustoms the students to see men of their own race
in high and responsible positions, the effect of which is to foster race pride
and to engender a feeling of mutual respect."[19]

Grimké furthered his argument by noting the negative impact of white
role models on blacks: "The intellects of our people are being educated at

the expense of their manhood. In the class-room they see only white professors. Vacancies occur, but they are filled only by white men; the effect of
which is unconsciously to lead them to associate these places and the idea
of fitness for them only with white men."[20] He charged that the opportunity for intellectual development was systematically denied African Americans, and that "our white friends have, in nearly all of these institutions,
reserved [this intellectual role] for themselves." The explanation for this
recalcitrance on the part of whites, Grimké charged, was "to be found in
race prejudice on the one side and selfishness on the other":

> [W]e are excluded because of caste prejudice. I say this in the full
> knowledge of the fact, that in these institutions there are those
> who profess to be our friends; who were, many of them, identi-
> fied with the anti-slavery movement; who bear the name of
> Christ, and are under ordination vows as ministers of the gospel.
> All this is true, and yet this accursed prejudice exists. Abolition
> simply meant freedom for the slave as a man. Christianity, as
> interpreted by the actions of the great majority of white profes-
> sors in this country, means recognition of the Negro, but in his
> place,—as an inferior.[21]

Grimké was describing a subtle form of racism that sought to control the
ability of the African American community to chart its own course.

It was these issues of paternalism and control that Steward identified
as racist in the writings of Strong. Steward took Strong to task in *The End
of the World*, referring to "[t]he frantic floundering of this writer [Strong]
upon this sea of speculation, with not a word from revelation, nor a
principle of sound philosophy by which to guide his course, is strikingly
significant."[22] *The End of the World* was a treatise on eschatology with a primary focus on millennialism. Timothy E. Fulop suggests that Steward's
eschatology fell within the bounds of premillennialist ideology and that
it held exceptionalist views of black Americans and other people of color
with regard to God's judgment of white Christianity.[23] But Steward did
not understand the "end of the world" in conventional premillennialist
terms, nor did his millennialism favor people of color over Anglo-Saxons.
In another article, Steward indicated that he was too impressed with modern notions of science and the influences of newer biblical interpretations
to hold onto traditional ones:

We are bound to define the terms in the light of what may be called the New Learning, unless we choose open warfare with science.

Hence I now contend that in the construction of our theology we are compelled to hear what the Lord our God says in the rocks and in the stars, what He says in the still small voice within us, and what He says in His blessed Word. This increased knowledge compels us to define a new "heaven and earth," "world," "creation," "beginning" and "end."[24]

Steward did critique Anglo-Saxonism for its arrogance and abuse of power, particularly in the way it had violated its Christian responsibility by promoting a racist view of the gospel. Calling Anglo-Saxonism "Clan religion," Steward argued that "[t]he Saxon principle is that of clan, and the grand ideas of liberty so richly expressed in jingling verse and sounding speech are always subordinate to it. . . . Clan, first, last, and always! Only the clan idea has broadened to the extent of a nation in Europe, and to the extent of a color in America. To this idea all others, whether of liberty, justice or religion, are subordinate."[25] Steward did not use the word "clan" loosely. He had been a missionary in the Reconstruction South and had seen the terror and destruction caused by the Ku Klux Klan.

In attempting to undermine the writings of Strong, Steward used his exegetical and scholarly skills to reinterpret the common meaning of the eschatological phrase the "end of the world." After surveying the relevant texts, he argued that the word "world" would be better translated as "age," and "end" as "consummation." Therefore, the "end of the world" would be best translated as the "consummation of the ages":

> While the Kingdom of Heaven is represented as having its obscure beginning, its successive stages of development and its culminating glory, we have seen that this is not the age referred to which is to be brought to its consummation, for the kingdom will reach its happiest condition after the consummation of the age. There is reason to believe further that this phrase, the end of the world, is equivalent to "the consummation of *this* age," i.e., the one now current, in distinction from the ages past, and the ages to come. . . .

> The consummation of the age must, of course, mean the consummation of the things belonging to this age, especially those things which give it character.[26]

Ordinary premillennialism suggested that the world was headed for a destructive end based on its continued ethical deterioration, and that Christ would come to establish his kingdom of a thousand years' reign. Steward, on the other hand, argued that the consummation of the ages refers to the end of the period of domination by the culture and civilization that started with the Roman empire and has continued through its spiritual heirs: Europe and, particularly, America.

Steward admitted that this civilization was as of yet the most advanced. It had the great builders, explorers, and inventors. It felt that it had perfected the great ideas of Western civilization: liberty, fraternity, and equality. In Steward's mind, it also had corrupted these ideas in its effort to spread this civilization. More important, this civilization had used God as its shield in its march toward progress. Steward sarcastically recounts:

> The world is made for the Saxon, who is its lord, and all the other tribes are to clear it up for him. Surely this God is very good to the Saxon, although so very cruel to the Indian, Negro, Chinaman and the rest of mankind. . . .[27]
>
> . . . God is so engaged to give the world to the Saxon that He will use even the vices of their civilization [alcohol and tobacco] to destroy the other inferior peoples of the earth who have before been engaged to prepare it for their habitation. Again, I say, What a very useful God the Saxons have! Oh, that each of the other races had one just as good! As these theological carpenters and sculptors have made this one, perhaps some genius will do as much in the future for the other races. It is an old saying that what has been done may be done.[28]

Although Steward believed that the destruction of Anglo-Saxon culture was inevitable, he did not predict the destruction of the entire world, as did premillennialists. He also severed the connection between the concepts of the "consummation of the age" and the establishment of the kingdom of God that would be established in Christ's triumphal reign. He saw these as two distinct time periods. Because Anglo-Saxon culture had failed to effectively evangelize the world, Christ would delay his return until the gathering in of the Gentiles was completed. Steward defined the Gentiles as "the darker races" who were locked outside of the bounds of the Gospel by the spread of "Saxonism" instead of "Christism": "It is not Saxonism that is to become universal, but Christism. The sin of the age has been in associating Saxonism with Christianity, if not in placing it above Christianity. Saxonism must utterly and signally fail, in order that Christ may be all in all."[29] Steward predicted the violent demise of Anglo-Saxon culture, via a major war between the various white nations of the earth. "We have seen that the prophecies point to a violent end to those nations which are the legitimate successors of Rome," he wrote. "The circumstances of to-day indicate the approach of such a catastrophe." But he was very optimistic that with the downfall of Euro-American domination, a new and more equitable age would arise which would place the various peoples of color on a more equal footing. Steward symbolically represented these nonwhite people as the Egyptians and Ethiopians of Psalm 68:31: "Princes shall come out of Egypt; Ethiopia shall soon stretch out her hands unto God." But ascendancy of the darker races in Steward's view would not duplicate the hegemony of the Europeans; rather, it would be based on a biblical notion of egalitarianism as exemplified in Galatians 3:28–29 and Acts 10:34–35.[30]

Not all of Steward's African American contemporaries agreed with his interpretation. One book reviewer, Benjamin Tanner, questioned Steward's exegetical interpretation of the "end of the world" and differed with him on the question of what he perceived as Steward's dispensational postponement of the conversion of blacks to Christianity. But Tanner wholeheartedly agreed with Steward's assessment of Strong's Anglo-Saxonism and the need for a transfer of power to the "darker races":

> We are free to confess that we have no objection to such a transfer of power; for with Dr. Steward and the thoughtful of all the darker races of the earth, the white man's grinding is simply intolerable; while his emasculated gospel is to be proved; as teaches St. John: "Beloved, believe not every spirit, but prove the spirits, whether they are of God." We know of no higher test than fidelity of Gospel truth. If they respond not to this, be assured they are not of God. And what gospel truth more demanding than that of man's brotherhood—not in empty sentiment, but in deed and truth.[31]

Our Civilization

The End of the World was a precursor to Steward's later, broader view of civilization. Continuing his response to Josiah Strong, he gave a glimpse of the importance he placed on his understanding of civilization in a lecture titled "Our Civilization" given at Wilberforce University after World War I (and later published by the author).[32] For Steward, unlike Strong, civilization was not something that was owned by Anglo-Saxons but a phenomenon which was controlled by no one culture or people. Wilson Jeremiah Moses, in his biography of Alexander Crummell, has argued that Crummell and his counterparts shared with Americans and Europeans an inflated "idea of the triumphs of nineteenth-century civilization." Crummell and other African Americans' understanding of civilization was that it

> implied a historical process, whereby mankind progressively learned the laws of physical, moral, and economic science. The laws were universal—they did not belong to any race or culture. They were discovered, not invented, and hence not the creation of any race or nation. The fact that Europeans were farther along in the process of civilization did not mean that they had been more intelligent, inventive, or creative, merely that they had submitted earlier to the divine and natural law and were now carried along in the current of inevitable progress.[33]

Steward's enthrallment with the civilization of the West was rather more tempered than this. He neither attempted to show what was particularly grand about English or American culture nor peculiar to any nation, or "to the English speaking part of mankind, great as it is."[34] Rather, Steward suggested that the present culture developed before the rise of modern Western civilization and began in the earlier Egyptian and Asian cultures. Europeans had distorted civilization with the issue of race, but people of color could normalize this progressive civilization because they understood the devastation of racism.

Steward's notion of the history of civilization was in some sense cyclical, starting with the rise of the cultures of the East, that is, Egypt and Asia, flowing through the West, and flowing back again to the East, in this case, Africa and African America: "We shall try rather to grasp in view the whole broad current of civilization, that current which taking its rise in the East has now made the circuit of the globe and is dashing its waves of return against the back gates of the orient whence it started."[35] Civilization, Steward believed, consists of all "discovery, science, art, and that belongs to human activity and progress."[36] His understanding of civilization was heavily influenced by the writings of French historian François Guizot and his work *The History of Civilization.*[37] Guizot understood civilization to be comprised of the "progress of society and the progress of individuals; or the melioration of the social system and the expansion of the mind and the faculties of man."[38] The notion of progress based on human freedom was central as well to Steward's understanding of civilization. For him, the other components of civilization, such as law, religion, art, and so forth, could not be successful without the element of freedom. Freedom was humanity's "dearest birthright"; it was the means and ends, the cause and the effect of human progress:

> Freedom is the proper element in which all other parts of civilization move. When at its goal, it includes freedom of the sovereign, freedom of the state, freedom of the arts, of religion, of speech, of the press—in a word, the freedom of MAN [Steward's emphasis]. This is the ideal acme of all progress in the development of the individual and of society. Only the highest possible type of men, can be truly free; men who through the elevation of their nature become a law unto themselves.[39]

It is with this idea of freedom that Steward assessed the ancient civilizations of Egypt, Asia, Greece, and Rome. Each of these groups built upon the successes and discoveries of the other. In Egypt and Asia, "the despots . . . recognized no freedom on the part of their subjects. The ruler alone was free. He was descended from the gods; all others were earth-born." Greece and Rome evolved to have an inkling of the idea of freedom, but they had not expanded the idea to include all within their civilizations. "In Rome," wrote Steward, "we see massive organization, extensive toleration, majestic law, an expanding civilization; but we see no amelioration of the social conditions. Wealth and power were held by the few, while the free paupers, and the hordes of slaves moved and groaned in the depths of misery."[40]

Steward credits the "barbarian cultures" of the Goths, Vandals, and Franks that conquered the Roman Empire with developing the first notion of the "unconquerable passion for personal independence." He argued that these groups were just emerging from cannibalism, but within them "were two principles of the utmost importance, *their love of independence and their respect for their own women.*"[41] He further stated that the path to the present form of civilization of France, Germany, England, and Spain was fraught with convulsion of wars and conquests.

There were certain elements that were common to all the nations which identified with this line of civilization, Steward argued. One element was the desire to develop new skills in philosophical and scientific thinking and religion. The next element was the shift from the development of "theory to things; from fancy to fact." In this phase, humans developed the technology to begin to scientifically understand and evaluate nature. Steward wrote, "We are determined to know this world. . . . We are sounding ocean depths, noting currents and winds, keeping tab on the weather, boring the earth, climbing into the clouds, to know, to know. The heroes of the world today are the vanguard of discovery." Highlighting his continued liberal theological views, Steward argued that to work with nature was to work with God, a mutual cooperation with the laws of nature that was essential to the furtherance of civilization: "Nature with her bounty and benevolence toward men who have now become obedient to her laws, is relieving men, women, and children from drudgery so rapidly that society cannot keep pace in adjustment. To work with nature is to work with God; to read her laws is to listen to the voice of God; to obey them in the building of a house, the launching of a ship, the cultivation of a crop, or the training of a flower is to walk with God."[42]

This benevolence of nature and humanity's cooperation with it contributed to the third characteristic of civilization, namely, "the increased respect of man for man, the augmented and expanded sympathy that binds man to man."[43] It is this third element that expresses Steward's clearest understanding of progress. All of the intellectual, philosophical, and technological developments were evolving for the ultimate promotion of people's concern for other humans without regard to country, race, or other distinctions. Steward saw this evolving humanitarianism move from concerns for materialistic efforts toward more spiritual concerns:

> Man is becoming better fitted to live with man; he is growing away from war; his sympathies are not satisfied now with poems and pictures, he offers food, raiment, and shelter. Materialistic as we may call our age, man was never so spiritual as now. And

although he is but beginning in the field of world-wide knowledge, and has felt only the slightest touches from the world-idea
of a common race with common rights, the approach of the idea
is filling him with a new nobility of soul.[44]

Steward bolstered his contention by calling upon the vision of Saint Paul
and his announcement of the universal brotherhood of humankind.
When Paul announced the "oneness of human blood, and declared that
we are to know no man after the flesh, he proclaimed the dominant chord
of the whole realm of real anthropology, and gave the basis of all social
and political equity. It is by getting into the spiritual man that we find
common ground." Those differences of color, hair, language, customs,
and such, Steward argued, were trivial differences of the flesh. As humans
became more spiritual and reached the realm where they became more
obedient to the truth "that makes men free, we will know as we are known,
and behind every human form and face of whatever hue we will see a
whole man and brother."[45]

It is clear that in *Our Civilization* Steward was not advocating racial
exceptionalism and did not emphasize the potential self-destruction of
Anglo-Saxons as he had earlier. At this point in his life, he argued that this
civilization would evolve into a better form that would rid itself of class
and color distinctions. He suggested that the Anglo-Saxon had the capacity to change and would not necessarily meet the destructive end which
he prophesied in the *End of the World.* Maybe this shift in his thinking
had to do with his sixteen years of experience in military life in which
regimental authority generally superseded the dominance of race.

In his 1904 address "The Army as a Trained Force," he would argue
that the army by the nature of its constitutional aristocracy contributed
to "make effective the doctrines of equality": "The black soldier and the
white soldier carry the same [armament] the same rations, serve under
the same laws, participate in the same experience, wear the same uniform,
are nursed in the same hospitals, and buried in the same cemeteries. . .
[T]he army of our Republic, by its aristocracy of commission, has proved
itself the most effectual barrier against the inundating waves of race discrimination that the country has as yet produced."[46] Even with this optimistic view of the army and race, Steward was less charitable regarding
the larger society and its view of race.

Steward measured the progress of civilization in its shift from the view that "the people belonged to the government" to "the government belongs to the people and its value is measured by its service to them."[47] His optimistic view of human evolution logically led him to a cautiously hopeful view of the abolition of war. This was understandable, given the fact that his lecture "Our Civilization" was given just after World War I. Steward pointed to the development of the Hague Court and the League of Nations as evidence of the potential for peace. Contrasted with his vision in *The End of the World,* Steward here articulated his hope that humanity had the capacity for peace, but his optimism was tempered by the realization that there were continued calls for war as the means to settle international disputes: "The progressive, hopeful spirit is for peace; but the timid and the unbelieving, cry out for fortifications, armies and dreadnoughts." Still, with a type of postmillennial hopefulness, Steward projected his expectant view for peace. "To my mind, the destiny of peace and brotherhood for mankind is near at hand," he wrote. "The expansion of knowledge, the quickening and enlarging of human sympathy, the kindness of heart increasing toward all living things that are beautiful or useful, are both preparatives and harbingers. Our own notion shows what a people practically non-military, can accomplish."[48]

With an eye toward the fallen nature of humanity, Steward suggested that there were three significant obstacles that impeded the development of civilization. Using the imagery of running water as a metaphor for civilization, he indicated that "as water runs it purifies itself in part by the dropping of sediment; but there are some things it cannot drop. I have seen the swollen carcas [*sic*], putrid and stench-giving, float down the Rio Grande intact, to be beaten to pieces only when it has encountered the waves of the Gulf." Noting the tenacity of certain defects, Steward indicated that these "carcasses" must be "beaten to pieces before we shall drop them."[49] He lumped two of these defects of culture together as one: intemperance and prostitution. The other one was racism.

Steward argued that the "rum house and the brothel" were twin evils which worked hand in hand for the downfall of civilization. These evils, as he saw it, were the makings of "young manhood shattered" and "maidens despoiled." They led to the bolstering of the "white slave trade" (which was a misnomer and really included young women of all colors), "herded often by denatured women, for the same vile market—to be sold ofttimes to gray haired, blear eyed, besotted men, who are the shame of their kind."[50]

He proposed a partial antidote for this "disease": the encouragement of "woman suffrage." Here Steward claimed that civilization had moved to open the door for broader participation for women. "The idea is now firmly incorporated in our civilization that woman is deserving of the largest possible freedom," he stated. Steward gave examples of women's contributions as leaders in England and France and argued that American society had opened its doors to women in all fields.[51] Using military language and imagery from the Civil War, he suggested, "Such it may be is the coming of woman suffrage to the aid of the forces for one more charge against rum, vice, and war. No evil can hide, no evil can entrench itself successfully in the presence of the civilization that is almost here."[52]

The next major "carcas" which Steward suggested could not be easily purged from the metaphoric stream was "the fiction, and the night-mare, of race." The founding fathers' broad language, with their use of the phrase "all men," was larger than their hearts, he asserted. White men had grown to abolish slavery, but "the heart of man has not broadened to the extent of seeing only man in man." He argued that the struggle was not just for political and civil rights but rather for "HUMAN" rights. It was an issue of changing the heart rather than merely establishing laws which did not get at the core of the matter: "When the heart is wrong[,] reason is seldom right." Steward connected the issue of race to spiritual and religious concerns, and specifically to his broader vision of the bringing in the postmillennial kingdom and the development of human progress:

> The mere enactment of law will not establish justice. It is only the perfect law of God that converts the soul. The legitimate goal of our civilization is to bring mankind into a loving family. Our world-wide systems of communication and travel, the rising of Esperanto, the world-gatherings for the promotion of common good and the suppression of common evils, show how large the human heart has grown. We increase in size just as we put away hate and fear toward other men and put in their place confidence and love.[53]

As evidence of progress toward racial harmony Steward pointed to the 1911 conference, which he deemed the beginning of "fostering concord

among all races." He and his wife, Susan Steward, attended this conference, and Steward felt that it demonstrated the fact that humanity was
awakening to the reality of racism and was attempting to fight it:[54] "Let
us thank God that the eyes of our understanding are so enlightened that
we can see the evils and that courage is arising within to attack them."[55]

Steward ended his speech with a hopeful prediction regarding this
progressive organism, civilization. It was his belief that civilization would
reach its apogee due to a combination of human effort and the work of
the power of Christ. Affirming his belief in his vision for a Christian post-
millennialism, he declared,

> I have shown you evidences that it already dimly perceives its
> goal and destiny; I have pointed out some of the obstructions that
> lie across the pathway of its progress; it remains but to assure you
> that the goal of this civilization will be reached. I say this not
> because I have deduced the conclusion from premises composed
> of past events; not because I have absolute trust in the law of cause
> and effect; not because I believe in the unity of history and in an
> aggregate humanity with a world-spirit; not alone because I
> believe that humanity is stamped with redemption, and that no
> matter into what depths it has fallen it will rise again; but because
> I believe, that marching in the midst of our civilization is Christ
> the Son of the living God, and that He is to become finally, the
> king of kings and the lord of lords, and that all nations will come
> to serve him. All art, all science, all law all religion, all politics, all
> social movements, will, when man comes into his hour, partake
> of His light and rejoice in His communion.[56]

It is clear that by this time in his life (c. 1918), Steward had somewhat
modified his earlier view of Anglo-Saxonism and become more hopeful
regarding an end to racism. Interestingly, *Our Civilization* also illustrates a
turn to a more orthodox theology on Steward's part, in contrasts to his earlier embrace of the rational philosophical tradition and scientific modernity. This turn was already in evidence nearly twenty years earlier with the
publication of Steward's only work of fiction, *A Charleston Love Story.*

Chapter 5

Rethinking Liberal Religion:
A Charleston Love Story

D avid Wills has suggested that Steward's theological productivity
ended with *The End of the World* in 1888.[1] Steward was, however,
still concerned with the broad question of theological orthodoxy, and he wrote several theological articles after this period. But once
Steward entered the military, his writings turned toward articles on history, military life, and the sociology of the African American community.
He wrote one book during this period, *The Colored Regulars in the United
States Army*,[2] and penned articles concerning the relationship between
the U.S. military and the inhabitants of the United States' new territorial
acquisitions, Cuba, Puerto Rico, and the Philippines. But Steward was
also concerned about some of the larger religious issues of secularization
and liberalism.

Wills has indicated that AME ministers became less productive as
theological writers and increasingly more conservative in their theological outlook during the last part of the century and into the beginning of
the twentieth century.[3] Steward fit this pattern, as his literary productivity on theological topics declined. And though, as we have seen, Steward
was considered one of the church's more liberal theologians, he developed an apologetic for a more conservative rational orthodoxy in his
novel *A Charleston Love Story; or, Hortense Vanross*.[4] Between 1891, when
Steward entered the military, and 1899, when this novel was published,
Steward was an active duty U.S. Army chaplain. While attending to his
various military tasks, he used his creative writing talents to craft this
melancholy, Victorian love story. It is unclear exactly why Steward took

up the cause of what appeared to be a conservative view of Christian orthodoxy in this novel.

William L. Andrews, in the only scholarly analysis of this novel, has suggested that its writing was motivated by Steward's "uncompromising Christian fundamentalism," which did not "deviate from the call that Steward followed throughout his adult life, the call to 'preach Jesus' by whatever means available."[5] Steward continues, "On the most obvious level, therefore, *A Charleston Love Story* is the work of a conservative evangelical mind trying to hold the line against dangerous new trends in religious thinking and ethical practice."[6] Naming Steward's novel as representative of Christian "fundamentalism," as Andrews does, is certainly inaccurate. Not only was the fundamentalist movement a later phenomenon, developing in the first and second decades of the twentieth century,[7] but Steward was hardly a theological conservative. It is true that Steward was concerned with the dangers of certain new trends in religious thinking and ethical practices, but it is also true that Steward saw science and its advances as compatible with Christianity and not at odds with the Gospel. Steward was most clearly representative of the African American wing of the "liberal evangelical" tradition rather than any conservative fundamentalism.

Throughout Steward's early career in the military, he broadened his scholarly and theological interests to include the study of anthropology and psychology. His interest in theology pushed him further into the study of the social sciences; as Steward himself put it, he studied "history and applied science as bearing upon revealed religion."[8] He wrote for several of the leading social gospel and liberal journals and magazines, including the *Independent*. Simultaneously, as a part of his chaplain's duties, Steward organized a temperance society among the soldiers in honor of Blanche K. Bruce (1841–1898), a former teacher and politician and the second African American U.S. senator from Mississippi.[9] Steward was extremely concerned about the piety and moral conduct of his charges. He walked a fine line, preaching a pietistic faith that was firmly committed to an orthodox but rational Christian experience and took into consideration the new scientific results of the time period.

Some of this tension can be seen in his novel. Steward's indebtedness to the common sense philosophical tradition is evident throughout *A Charleston Love Story*. But Steward was attempting to prove to his critics that he was, indeed, evangelical and pietistic, whatever his commitment to a rational orthodoxy. His reaction took on broader significance given the clear shift of many mainline Protestant churches toward liberalism and the further drift of others toward a blending of universalist theology and a more radical communitarian experimentalism in movements such as "free love" and the "water cure." It is interesting to note that Steward staged this discussion outside the context of the African American community; the novel is set in a white, southern community.

Steward constructed his story around the divergent theological beliefs of his two main characters. A conflict regarding Christian orthodoxy was the pivotal point in the relationship between Hortense Vanross, the protagonist, and her antagonist pursuer—and later husband—Leonard Howell.

The novel opens as Leonard Howell, a former northern military officer,[10] woos a southern belle, Hortense Vanross, during the Reconstruction period. Conflict develops when, at some point early in their courtship, they realize they have incongruous understandings of the role and function of religion, particularly the Christian faith. These incompatible approaches cause significant problems. They are both willing to ignore their major theological tensions and marry, primarily because they each feel that they can eventually win the other over to their point of view. Added to this conflict is Howell's developing liberal view toward open marriage and his later infidelity. These theological and matrimonial difficulties send Hortense into a deep depression and ultimately lead to her physical decline and death. Yet her commitment to her faith and her unfailing love for her husband wins him over in the end. Howell, at her deathbed, confesses his faith in her God, gives up his licentious life-style, and commits himself to single-handedly raising their children as Christians.

Clearly, Steward drew from familiar circumstances and experiences within his own life to develop this story line, namely, Charleston and the surrounding area, Steward's station of missionary service with the AME Church, and the American Missionary Association. Charleston was also the hometown of his first wife, Elizabeth Gadsden.[11] Howell's early life is set in southern New Jersey, where Steward was born and spent his early years. Howell is stationed as lieutenant with the famous African American Fifty-fourth Massachusetts Regiment, garrisoning the city of Charleston, a regiment Steward was familiar with through his research for *The Colored Regulars in the United States Army.*[12] After Hortense and Howell marry, they settle in Macon, Georgia. Steward spent three years of missionary ministry in Macon (1868–1871), the longest of his itinerancy during his seven-year ministry in the Reconstruction South. Steward developed two characters in his own image, both serving as moral role models. The Reverend Thomas Gordon is the prototypical northern missionary and represents the best of the social Christianity to which Steward was committed. Like Steward, Gordon is a pastor and teacher who comes south to be a missionary among the freed population. As Steward tells it, Reverend Gordon "was not born to hate. Rich and poor, Northerners and Southerners, black and white, were all very much alike to him. His heart was an overflowing fountain that sent out only sweet waters, and sent them out with such volume and force as to bear down all petty prejudices with their current."[13] The other character in which Steward saw much of himself was Hortense's Macon pastor, the Reverend Dr. Danforth. Like Steward, Dr. Danforth is a seminary-trained orthodox minister and well versed in rational Christian apologetics and liberal religion. Danforth becomes the authoritative defender of Hortense's belief and rational orthodoxy.

As Steward developed the specific theme of theological orthodoxy, he clearly contextualized the novel in the larger arenas of class, race, and hue.[14] To set up the novel, he gave a brief review of the history of slavery in Charleston, including the Denmark Vesey insurrection.[15] He further fleetingly described the class and color distinctions within the antebellum African American community, including the "'free browns,' the center of which was the 'Brown Fellowship Society,' representing persons of mixed blood who were freeborn; and the 'Compact,' a society of Blacks that admitted none to membership saving blacks who had been born in wedlock."[16] The gruesome nature of the slavery system, Steward said, was like an insidious cotton gin which rolled "out its bales of cotton on one side and ooz[ed] out its stream of blood and death on the other."[17]

In turn, Steward described at least three distinct classes of Charleston white society: the old aristocratic families, the middle class, and the poor workers. The aristocrats were the successful merchants, planters "who maintained city residences," lawyers, and politicians. These whites were in the upper class and were the best educated and most cultured. They "enjoyed a distinction founded upon blood, and . . . were generally accorded the first place in everything."[18]

At the other end of the scale was the working class, including the "poor white trash." Steward was sympathetic to the plight of this class. In his unbiased assessment of poor whites, he asserted that many were "upright and respectable." His characterization of poor whites demonstrated that they were not much very economically different from their slave counterparts. Given a different social circumstance and under "freer conditions," Steward felt that poor whites might have "reached the higher ranks of society." In Charleston society they were, however, "permitted no social standing whatever. They existed and looked on; they did not live and partake."[19]

Between these two extremes was the white middle class, which was made up of skilled mechanics, petty merchants, teachers, bookkeepers, and so on. As with the lower class, Steward assessed the middle class as having the "usual proportion of good and bad." He suggested that "among them . . . some of the best people that the city ever produced were to be found." Steward set this social group off from the rest as the most virtuous, asserting that the Victorian domestic virtues which were generated by the southern aristocracy and beyond the reach of the poor "by reason of their social surroundings," "seemed to find congenial homes among many of those who were neither high nor low in the social scale. Here alone the domestic virtues especially received their warmest support and brought forth their best fruit."[20] The Vanross family was this best fruit.

Steward also commented on the general economic situation of the South. His experience as a cashier in the Georgia's Freedman's Savings and Trust Company made him well aware of the complicated economics of the United States, particularly of the Reconstruction South, which had a devastating effect on the poor of the South.[21] Steward portrayed Howell as a shrewd businessman who exploits the opportunity he gains as an employee of a northern banking interest in the South. It is possible that Steward was making his own confession of greed through his character, as Steward was himself a not-so-successful private entrepreneur in the southern cotton industry.[22]

Steward introduced the two main characters to each other in Charleston when, showing that northerners also have "chivalry," Lieutenant Howell intervenes on behalf of Hortense and her mother in the context of a harmless altercation with two black soldiers under Howell's command. While developing his plot, Steward craftily avoids the pitfall of race and the obvious moral issue of the period—slavery—by making the Vanross family one of the nonslaveholding southern families. The Vanrosses consist of a recently widowed mother, three sons, and two daughters. Steward still placed the family in support of the Confederacy, mostly through force of public pressure: "The two older sons knew that if the war came it would be a rich man's war and a poor man's fight; but they also knew the intolerant spirit by which they were surrounded, and for the sake of their mother and sisters they saw that they should be compelled to shoulder muskets." Given their surroundings, the Vanross family is scripted as "closet" abolitionists in the South. Had they been in the North, Steward indicated, they would have been "earnest abolitionists."[23] As it is, they are supportive but paternalistic toward freedpersons and former slaves.

The encounter between the Vanross family and Leonard Howell evolves into a romance between the elder daughter, Hortense, and Leonard. Howell is sent back to the North and mustered out of service when the Fifty-fourth Infantry is disbanded. He returns to Charleston as a civilian carpetbagger, in major part to pursue a relationship with Hortense. In the early stages of this growing love affair, the subject of religion is not discussed, but it comes up as they are close to a marriage proposal and impeded their budding romance.

The Vanross family is Christian "of the old-fashioned, orthodox type." To them the Bible is "the supreme rule of life, and Hortense an earnest defender of its teachings." Leonard, on the other hand, is heavily influenced by the "so-called liberal ideas of New England." Initially, Leonard does not have a precise theological creed but has learned "to doubt orthodoxy . . . and certainly to complain of the restraints of religion." He sees the ardent religionist's claims regarding morality, but he can not obligate himself to their creeds. Once he realizes that he can not dissuade Hortense from her firm Christian beliefs, it becomes clear that continued discussion regarding religion will only push them further apart. He decides that he would rather live in the tension of their theological conflict than lose Hortense's love. Hortense, for her part, is so much in love with Leonard that she is willing to ignore the wide gulf between them. She secretly believes that she can persuade him to her perspective on orthodox Christianity. With covert hope, Hortense presses Leonard to define his beliefs about God. Leonard reluctantly outlines his beliefs. He indicates that he believes in a God of wisdom and love who is not concerned with the individual affairs of human beings. Leonard believes that everything is placed under law and each individual is left to work out his or her own destiny. "I believe the law the best that could be for the whole but not the best for each individual," he says; "I will even grant it to be a law of benevolence, but I think it is fixed; and so I cannot see the value of prayer; nor can I recognize any personal communication with the Divine Being. I lack all that element which is called faith."[24] In short, he does not hold to any orthodox Christian beliefs.

Although Steward did not label Leonard Howell's "so-called liberal ideas of New England," they came closest to transcendentalism.[25] Transcendentalism rejected the belief that the Bible was divinely inspired and it utilized German biblical criticism to debunk what it saw as biblical myth. As a result of this reliance on biblical criticism, the divinity of Jesus was rejected as holding back modern humanity from obtaining true freedom. Revelation and miracles were likewise rejected. Transcendentalism also rejected the revised Lockean version of Scottish common sense philosophy, which helped to set the stage for Unitarian belief and justification of biblical revelation and miracles. God was seen as existent but distant from human affairs, and God's glory and majesty were thought to be best seen in nature. The universe was governed by a set of moral laws that regulated the affairs of humanity. Humanity had the capacity to progress positively and achieve moral good.[26] This was, overall, what Steward attributed to his character Leonard Howell.

It is not clear where Steward initially encountered liberal religious ideas.[27] He was obviously concerned about their influence on middle-class Christianity and saw the liberal movement as a direct threat to Victorian family life. He was very familiar with Frederick Douglass, a frequent attendee and financial supporter of the Metropolitan AME Church in Washington, D.C., when Steward was the pastor there. Douglass was definitely influenced by these liberal ideas of New England. He provided Steward a firsthand account of his ideas regarding religion in a letter responding to Steward's inquiry about his religious beliefs. Because of Douglass's liberal beliefs, it was widely rumored that "he was not a believer in Christianity; and it was further said by some that he had little respect for ministers or religion."[28]

Douglass said in response to Steward's letter that he understood Steward's surprise at his regular attendance and support of the Church, given the accusations of infidelity and atheism directed at him. Douglass's support of the church had nothing to do with the theology espoused from the pulpit, he said, because he greatly differed with Steward regarding

these issues. He questioned Steward's notions of plenary or other inspiration of the Bible, for "if it contains the will of God to man, it is vastly more
important to know what that will is, than to know precisely how that will
has been communicated."[29]

Religion for Douglass was not bound by dogma but by utility. God
and humanity were connected in so far as the men and women reflect the
moral and natural laws of the God of the universe. Regarding Steward's
query concerning Douglass's faith stance, he stated that to him

> God is good! God is light! God is truth! God is love! and to
> glorify God is to lead a life in harmony with these attributes. In
> this respect man is related to his Creator as the watch to its
> maker. A watch glorifies its maker when it answers the end of its
> manufacture, which is to keep good time—always to be true, and
> never to be false in its measurement of time. As God is true, I
> would have man true! As God is holy, I would have man holy! As
> God is pure, I would have man pure. An unclean man in body or
> mind does not glorify his Maker. He may sing praises to the Lord
> and call himself a Christian, but he brings no glory to the Lord,
> no good to his fellow man. Christianity is nothing to me, except
> as it stands as the representative of the sigh of the soul for a
> noble life; for herein is the true glory of God.[30]

It is clear that the relationship between humanity and this universal God
was based on the moral laws which, Douglass believed, were set forth in the
cosmos. Douglass was not an atheist as some thought. He did believe in
God, but his God worked his will through the efforts of people. Christianity was important only so far as it urged people to good works without the
confinement of dogmatic belief. This was clearly within the line of the liberal transcendentalist philosophy Steward imputed to Leonard Howell.

Of course, Steward, as a trained theologian, was acquainted with liberal ideas, and it is highly likely that Steward would have discussed these
ideas with Douglass. Steward counted Douglass as one of his personal
friends.[31] He gave speeches about Douglass's career[32] and shortly after his
death began a biographical sketch on his life. He even ranked Douglass
among the world's great men.[33] Steward believed that Douglass represented
the best of what an American could achieve both in terms of personal
accomplishments and his agitation for human rights. He did not have

qualms about Douglass's political philosophy, and both men believed in a moral law that regulated the universe, a law internalized by human beings.

Yet they differed radically when it came to understanding what part God had in this process. Although Steward's common sense philosophical orientation gave broad latitude to notions of innate goodness, he still believed that goodness emanated from the divine. He felt that liberal theology, disconnected from divine morality, might serve a social-political agenda well but could lead to moral breakdown, especially in family life. He therefore depicted Leonard Howell as a dedicated philanthropist who is particularly concerned for African American advancement but nevertheless illustrates the dangers of liberal religion and its disastrous effects on personal and family life. Transcendentalists searched the limits of freedom and progress, especially in the framework of a humanity unbridled from the constrains of religious dogma and God constructs, and Steward wanted to show the dangers of this unlimited freedom.

Steward wrote his novel during the "Gay Nineties," a time when leisure activities were on the increase. For Steward, the combination of liberal religion, capitalistic pursuits based on selfish instinct, and the developing culture of leisure led to a breakdown of family life and orthodox values. He used secularized movements such as the water cure and free love to represent the dangers of exploring these limits, giving his character, Leonard Howell, an interest in both. Steward used this combination of the flagrant display of wealth tempered by philanthropic ventures and dabbling with secular movements to create what he felt was the sinful nature of Leonard Howell.

Howell's philosophical orientation first comes head to head with the orthodox views of Hortense in her attempt to have their children baptized in the Christian faith. Howell initially refuses to take part in the ceremony but later accepts a compromise to "accompany her to the church and stand with her in the ceremony, but to take no part by word or act that could be construed into a acquiescence in his wife's belief": "Mr. Howell . . . began to talk more of love as the controlling principle of life, and to draw sharp distinctions between the freedom of love and the bondage of society. 'If,' said he, 'mankind could lift their eyes and look upon love and its relations to life as the child of God, instead of seeing only lust, which, with the majority, now crowds love aside, then would they be able to consider this matter in its true light. Love needs no bonds. It will take care of itself.'"[34]

Steward portrayed Howell as having wandered into a philosophy which "he had accepted as religion, and which had driven all love for the church and all regard for the Sabbath, from his breast." Howell constructs a religious, social, and moral creed, which suits his "rapidly deteriorating nature."[35]

Howell regards the relevant difference between Hortense and himself to be the "revealed religion" of orthodoxy and the "natural religion" of transcendentalism. But Steward asserted that the real distinction is that between "revealed religion" and "no religion":[36]

> [Howell] preached purity and love; he advocated freedom of intercourse among friends; he extolled virtue; he condemned the tyranny of custom and conventionalism; he expatiated on a higher form of friendly attraction which should exist between persons of opposite sex, a feeling so far above the corrupt and debased feeling which usually prevailed that impurity could not exist in its presence; he described a possible state of personal purity in which persons might mix in delightful freedom, enjoy-ing and expressing by word and caress the sincerest affection, and yet there would be no evil; he was a dreamer of Eden delights between men, women, and children, surrounded by love, purity, and peace. This he preached to Hortense; this he preached to his household, and this he claimed to practice himself, and urged upon his wife to practice. This was the angel of light into which the filthiest doctrine ever invented by man was transformed, and which came so near deceiving one of God's "elect," the pious and ever faithful Hortense.[37]

In order to vindicate himself from his critics and prove his commit-ment to orthodoxy, Steward, in this novel, crafted a scenario that showed liberal movements and philosophies in their most negative light. Howell's blatant infidelity crushes Hortense's spirit to the point that she loses the will to live and becomes fatality ill. Until she is directly confronted with Howell's infidelity, she sincerely believes that their religious difference has not affected their genuine love for one another. She becomes completely disillusioned with her husband when it becomes clear that his religious and philosophical notions are smoke screens for a much more sinister commitment, namely, his sexual involvement with other women. Yet she maintains her faith in God in the midst of this difficult time.

Indeed, it is Hortense's faithfulness, even unto death, which finally begins to wear on the conscience of Howell. Eventually, Howell begins to feel remorse for his infidelity. In an early morning dream, he has a vision of his deceased mother-in-law who forewarns him of his wife's impending death and his responsibility for her demise. His guilt is further corroborated when he finds that his wife, that same morning, tells him of her independent dream of her mother's visitation to her, beckoning her to the other side. This incident begins Howell's conversion process.

It is interesting to note that given Steward's commitment to rational theology, he has Howell's transformation begin with a mystical experience such as a vision. Was Steward suggesting that some things regarding the Christian faith could not be explained within the rational realm? Howell later confesses and repents to his wife for all of his acts of infidelity: "As soon as Leonard could command words he attempted to make a full confession of his wrongs—painting himself in true colors. He told the story of his duplicity, and of his treachery; of his deceitful philosophy, and of his wicked sinning."[38] Hortense forgives him of his sins toward her, but asks who would continue the task of raising their children in a Christian manner and home. The ultimate test of Howell's repentance and conversion is challenged with this question: "'They are Christian children to some extent, but the work of training is not done yet. I can no longer be with them to carry out the obligations I assumed for them before the Lord in His church. Who, Leonard, will finish my work?' As she said this she fixed on Leonard a look of earnest entreaty, and awaited his answer."[39] His response to this question is the ultimate litmus test to determine the sincerity of his transformation:

> Leonard continued to pace the floor in silence for some time. A deep and fierce struggle was going on within between his pride, his love, and his moral sense. Should he throw overboard all that cargo of theories he had so long been carrying and admit himself to have been deceived by his own subtle reasonings? He had given up his sins; why not jettison the cargo of pestiferous theories which had nourished and defended them in part? His theories never had been sufficient to entirely cover his conduct. Stretch the covering as he would, it was not sufficient to cloak all his misdoings. His theory stopped short at a line drawn between love and lust; but his practice confounded these two passions and

ignored the limitation of his philosophy. Why not discard the theory as being sufficient neither to produce a good life nor to defend a bad one? Somewhat in this line ran Leonard's thoughts as he walked up and down his sick wife's bedroom.[40]

It is with this type of internal debate that Steward has Howell wrestle with his decision to become an active participant in the Christian communion. Christianity finally triumphs over Howell's "cargo of pestiferous theories" with the proclamation, "'My dear wife, I will, God helping me, take hold of the work where you lay it down, and to the best of my ability will carry out the obligations made in the church and which I now assume; I will try to walk before our children in your spirit, that they may be saved from such a life as mine has been. If God will forgive the unchangeable past, I will from this hour, dear Hortense, consecrate myself to the carrying out of your life. You shall live, Hortense.' Then with tears streaming down his cheeks he groaned, 'God be merciful to me a sinner.'"[41] Orthodox Christianity had won the day. Steward had proven that an innate notion of religion without the rational proofs grounded in Christian Scriptures was in fact not religion at all. He ends the book by having Howell move with his children, after Hortense's death, to Brooklyn, where he becomes a faithful member of his brother-in-law's church.

Through *A Charleston Love Story,* Steward could be viewed as enunciating a corrective to his previous discourse in *Divine Attributes,* for which he was severely criticized. Here Steward was admitting what he perceived as the dangers of the common sense philosophical tradition. After Howell's conversion to orthodox Christian faith beside Hortense's deathbed, his "heart was now indeed opening and was giving out real love, and receiving love in return. His love was now taking its place in obedience to reason and conscience, and was enjoying its freedom under law."[42] Steward was to work through other correctives in his life as well. As it is interesting that Steward used a woman protagonist to articulate his corrective in theology, it is his view of women and their role in civil society that will next be addressed.

Chapter 6

Steward, Women,
and Civil Society

W omen spiritually, socially, and intellectually shaped Theophilus Steward and his thinking about civil society. Steward also had specific ideas as to the role women were to play in this civil society. Early in his life, his clerical male mentors within the AME Church also influenced his understanding of women, civil society, and, especially, their restriction from clerical leadership. This view of women's role in civil society would take the shape of limiting women to the spheres of home and, within the church, to working with children and other women. Women's domesticity would be the call of the day early in Steward's life, and he would join other men in championing this sphere for women.

Yet, as in other areas of Steward's life, we shall see that he would vacillate, shift, change, and broaden his views regarding women's roles in civil society, especially within the church and regarding the ordination of women. This evolution of views would be due in part to the direct and indirect challenge of women closest to Steward.

Steward's limited and broadened views of women would not be expressed in his earlier theological works but primarily in his literary work, *Memoirs of Mrs. Rebecca Steward,* published in 1877. Yet Steward gives a glimpse of his vacillating view of women's role in civil society in his series "Distinguished Women of the Bible," which was published in the *Christian Recorder*[1] during his Brooklyn pastorate in 1876. Over several Sundays, Steward preached a series of sermons on distinguished women in the Bible, such as Eve, Ruth, Naomi, Rebecca, and Deborah. In his recounting of the life of Rebecca, the wife of the biblical patriarch Isaac, he highlights her domestic role and demeanor: "She had been fully in sympathy with her parents, working honestly with them in plain simplicity of manners. The best girls are to be found in full subjection to their parents and in full attachment to home."[2] Yet Steward was to highlight the heroic leadership of the biblical prophet Deborah, who broke the gender leadership barrier in ancient Israelite society. He compared the human frailties of Rebecca and Eve to the heroics of Deborah:

> If we saw the depths of unprincipled cunning in Rebekah [*sic*], we saw the heights of unswerving fidelity in Ruth. If in Eve we saw women's weakness, in Rebekah we saw her woman's strength. If in Eve we saw woman passive, in Rebekah was her handling all the weapons of social success with an amazing energy.
>
> And now we come to contemplate a grander scene. We shall see woman today supreme in the nation, at the head of the army, leading a successful revolution and celebrating the uprising of her [Deborah's] nation with brilliant song.[3]

It was clear that Steward wrestled with this issue throughout his life. At times he was the champion of notions of female domesticity and opposed the ordination of women, as will be shown below in the exploration of *Memoirs of Mrs. Rebecca Steward*. This chapter will outline the nexus of these issues in Steward's early thought and show how he used his memorial to his mother to promote domesticity and rebut both the holiness movement and the ordination of women. However, Steward also evolves in his thinking regarding the role of women, especially after leaving his leadership position in the AME Church and expanding his wings in the world of the military and beyond. His growth and change, I shall argue, is influenced by several factors, including his relationship with his second wife, his sister, and others, as well as the changing environment for women within his lifetime.

Memoirs of Mrs. Rebecca Steward

In May 1889, at the Quarto-Centennial Conference of the African Methodist Episcopal Church of South Carolina, Moses Buckingham Salter (a future bishop) spoke these words concerning women and their place in the family, church, and society:

When woman possesses the right character, she exerts a powerful influence on society. Being the leading character of social life, she is in position to do a great good. She can make her influence felt, in words, actions, and general deportment. The community looks to her for a model of excellence in all that is pure and good. A young woman may exert much influence if possessed of the proper character, for on her are the eyes of the world, and when she walks in the path of virtue and rectitude, she is looked upon as the foundation of all good society . . . As a wife, in the true sense of the term, she exerts a powerful influence on her husband. . . .

There is no influence in the home so great as the mother's. Husband, and children alike, look for direction in all its sacred departments. In a well ordered home the wife and mother is the sovereign . . . She shapes the character of the home for time and eternity . . . In the Church and Sunday School she may be a pattern of excellence and good works. The Church looks to her for its best fruits of spiritual labor. Though she is not permitted to hold the reigns of government, yet her very silence has an influence on all the movements of the Church.

When we look at woman filling the position of the minister's wife; when we see that his success often depends upon the wisdom and gentle manners of his wife, we are led to believe that God sometimes calls a man to the ministry because He wants the services of his wife.[4]

This rhetoric of Victorian Christian domesticity was commonly espoused and promoted by the male hierarchy within the AME Church. This vision of the proper role that women should play in home, community, church, and society was part of the larger conception of the development of a civil society that highlighted the dignity of the African American community by AME Church male leadership.

Men were not the only advocates of this view. Some of the most prominent women within the church also embraced and advanced these views. In most cases, these women were the spouses of bishops or upwardly mobile ministers. Mary E. Lee, the wife of Benjamin Lee, a prominent AME clergyman soon to become a bishop, posited in the *AME Church Review* that motherhood and home making were the highest endeavor for women. In praising Sarah Tanner, the wife of Bishop Benjamin Tanner, for choosing marriage and mothering over the profession of teaching, Mary Lee stated, "This is the truest, the grandest view: she entered upon the highest, divinest sphere which is occupied by women; for of all the affairs concerning the civilization of the human family, that of home-making and keeping is the most important. She who enters upon it, enters upon the greatest of responsibilities and the most stupendous of all work."[5]

Such rhetoric did not go unchallenged by other women in the wider church. Some women called on the AME Church to broaden its vision concerning the roles women could and should play beyond the domestic sphere. At the same conference where Salter praised domesticity, Hallie Quinn Brown, principal of women and instructor at Allen University (an AME school in Charleston, South Carolina), boldly spoke on behalf of women's right to develop educationally in the same social and professional spheres as their male counterparts:

> I am an advocate for my sex and myself. [Laughter and applause.] I believe there are as great possibilities in women as there are in men. I believe that the day has long since passed when women are supposed to be able only to be educated to some extent. Women are now launching out into all the industries— familiarizing themselves with the arts and sciences—sustaining themselves on great occasions, and successfully contesting for equality with men in schools and in other departments of life. The time was when women were not allowed to enter certain institutions. The doors are thrown open now in almost every state. We are marching onward grandly. No race can rise any higher than its women. If you keep the women of any race down, you will have a poor set of men.[6]

Mary E. C. Smith, an educator from Edward Water College (an AME School in Jacksonville, Florida) addressed this same gathering on the subject of the "Pioneer Women of East Florida." She praised a number of heroines who co-labored with men in the early development of the Florida Annual Conference within the AME Church.[7]

AME women did informally influence the organizational development and structures within the church, even if they were not included in the ecclesiastical hierarchy. Jualynne Dodson has argued persuasively that women, through the development of female-specific, collective organizations within the AME Church, were able to facilitate "women's participation in decision-making that was the exercise of AME Church power. It was not an official participation and neither women nor their organizations was incorporated in the formal structure of authority."[8] Dodson has argued that bishops regularly consulted with the various women's organizations when making pastoral and other leadership appointments.

Women were able to influence the male leadership because of their ability to raise money or affect the economics of the church. Most of them were connected to the male leadership of the church and tended to be light-skinned and better educated.[9] The best example of this organizational power occurred in 1874, when AME wives of bishops organized the Women's Parent Mite Missionary Society at the urging of Tanner, editor of the _Christian Recorder,_ for the support of the missionary effort in Haiti.[10] These bishops' wives organized the women of the church, starting with the wives of the local pastors. They wrote an open letter in the _Christian Recorder_ as the mechanism of organizing the women church members:

> Dear Sisters—We your sisters and sufferers with you in the common cause of our dear Redeemer, were deeply moved by the letter of our editor, Bro. B. T. Tanner D.D. recently published in the CHRISTIAN RECORDER, asking us to cooperate with the Board of Missions of the A.M.E. Church in its efforts for the evangelization of the world.
>
> We have carefully surveyed the duties named in his letter to us, each of which should move the heart of all good women; and especially those of us who have consecrated our all, jointly with our dear husbands, for the universal spread of the gospel, and the establishment of "that kingdom which shall never be destroyed." But our hearts have been moved, our sympathies and prayers are specially drawn towards Hayti, because of the appeal coming from that feeble church, composed of our dear brethren on that historic island; the memories of which are so fresh in all of our minds. Who does not remember the good and noble Toussaint L'Ouvérture, and others whose blood flowed so freely for the emancipation of our race? The feeble band, residents of that island, lovers of Toussaint's ideas of liberty, and Allen's ideas of our holy religion,

ask us to aid them to a true understanding of the true Christ and his pure religion. In view of this appeal coming to us their sisters, we have agreed to make a special and immediate effort of that inviting field, and ask the cooperation of all of the dear sisters, the lovers of Jesus, in the charges of your husbands.[11]

This debate was of course not a new one in nineteenth-century Protestantism, black or white. It is also a familiar pattern that there were women who promoted the ideology of female virtue and domesticity working within the parameters of male hegemonic control.[12] Carroll Smith-Rosenberg has persuasively argued that the Second Great Awakening opened up the sphere in which white women could actively and publicly participate in revivals: "Male clerics and reformers led this movement, yet women were their most zealous adherents. Through sheer numbers, women dominated the Second Great Awakening's revivals and spiraling church membership. They violated liturgical decorum by praying publicly and by prophesying. Setting Victorian proprieties and family needs to one side, they devoted whole days and nights to revival efforts."[13] On the other hand, Smith-Rosenberg has asserted, once revival religion of the nineteenth century gained ascendancy in American culture and became routinized as the dominant ideology, men backed away from women's active and public leadership in church life and began to promote a new and different role for women:

> Repudiating their prophetesses, such men glorified a novel Victorian figure, the patient and homebound mother and a new institution, the bourgeois family, isolated and nuclear. De-emphasizing the intense piety of revivalistic conversions, clergymen now argued that salvation blossomed within the Christian nursery as a result of loving, maternal discipline. Reinstating the time-honored boundaries encircling woman's sphere, evangelical ministers shepherded their female adherents back towards the contained family and traditional femininity.[14]

Smith-Rosenberg's focus is exclusively on revivalism within white nineteenth-century America. Dodson argues that the Second Great Awakening also provided a similar opening for black women's expressions of preaching and oratory: "Preaching AME women operated in similar, if not the same, spheres of cleric work as did men formally ordained in the Church. In addition, women consistently requested and petitioned the denomination for legitimate authority to carry out preaching activities."[15] Yet there was a similar process developing within the AME Church. From the beginning of the AME Church there had been black women preachers who were not ordained or sanctioned by the church. The most noted ante-bellum example is Jarena Lee.[16] Amanda Berry Smith is the best example of a post–Civil War AME woman who preached without the official sanction of the church.[17] By 1885, Bishop Turner had ordained Sarah Ann Hughes as a deacon only to have her ordination rescinded by the 1888 General Conference.[18] The editor of the *Christian Recorder,* Benjamin F. Lee, expressed his misgivings about the ordination of Hughes, arguing that the church had "not run out of men for pastors. Women have always been great helpers; they have enough work of this kind."[19]

These women preachers were not the only female preachers through-out the late nineteenth century,[20] and the AME Church was not the only black church struggling with this issue. Indeed, women preachers were asserting themselves in the African Methodist Episcopal Zion Church as well.[21] Both Julia A. J. Foote and Mary J. Small were active as preachers in the mid- to late-nineteenth-century AMEZ Church.[22] Foote's ordination as deacon by Bishop James Walker Hood in 1894 also caused a contro-versy, but the AMEZ Church allowed her ordination to stand.[23]

As the AME Church developed institutionally in the latter part of the nineteenth century, its ministers began to maneuver their female followers toward a Victorian notion of feminine domesticity. This was a deliberate process, based in part on certain leaders' desire to move the church toward what they believed was a more acceptable middle-class, rational set of Christian beliefs and practices and a more acceptable form of civil society.

The *Memoirs of Mrs. Rebecca Steward,* a memorial to Steward's recently deceased mother, became one of the primary tools used to pro-mote the ideology of female domesticity within the church. This little volume, published in 1877, was a compilation of diverse materials— including a family history, eulogies by family members and church offi-cials, and letters and essays by Rebecca Steward herself. It served a double purpose. While highlighting and praising the Christian virtues and piety of Rebecca's life, it was also used to lambaste both the growing sanctifi-cation movement and the women preachers who were part of it. Like most of the church's leadership, Steward, during this early stage of his life, defended female domesticity and strongly opposed the sanctification movement and the ordination of women.

Steward's early mentor, Daniel Payne, the most powerful bishop of the AME Church during much of the nineteenth century, has correctly been credited with having significantly influenced the spread of female domesticity and middle-class values. He was also a critic of the sanctification movement, and he opposed women's ordination and preaching.[24] Steward dedicated his mother's memorial volume to Bishop Payne:[25] "In recognition of his learning, talents and piety; and as a testimonial to his high appreciation of female excellence, this little volume is affectionately inscribed."[26]

Why did Steward publish this book? At one level, it provided a way for him and others to process the mourning experience. Steward himself stated that he could never speak publicly about his mother because of the storm of emotions that would break forth. She "was among the most intelligent and most holy of women," he wrote. "Her death brought my second deep sorrow [the first sorrow being the loss of his son, Stephen Hunter], but it came as a cloud with great streams of light breaking through. The departure of our babe had left a tiny trail of light into and through the cloud, the departure of my mother made such rifts that streams of golden glory came through to convert falling tears into the rainbow of hope."[27] Yet this memorial volume was more than a vehicle for Steward's expression of private grief and hope. It also fitted nicely into the larger picture of the version of female domesticity which both Steward and Payne promoted.

Steward indicated that his family and friends urged him to coordinate and write this tribute to his mother. The contributions included an opening poem by William Steward, her eldest son, and a eulogy by Elizabeth Lloyd, her niece. The volume also contained reminiscences and reflections by several prominent AME Church officials. Among others were Bishop Jabez P. Campbell, the eighth bishop of the AME Church; Benjamin Franklin Lee, Rebecca's nephew and later president of Wilberforce University; Benjamin Tanner, editor of the *Christian Recorder;* and Theodore Gould, a nephew and well-known pastor in the AME Church.[28] It also included several essays by Rebecca Steward herself, three of which discussed sanctification and had been published in the *Christian Recorder.* Steward also

contributed a biographical and family history to this collection. In addition, the volume contained correspondence between Rebecca and her
daughter, Alice Felts, though there were no tributes written by Felts or
either of her two sisters for reasons that will be clear later in the chapter.

The volume highlighted Rebecca Steward's role as a mother, wife,
and church and community leader. It accentuated her life as a dedicated
and pious Christian, one who was self-sacrificing, humble, and giving.
Speaking of Rebecca's example of domestic management, Benjamin Lee
indicated that "at the head of the domestic circle, with my uncle, she
appeared to have a clear and high notion of home economy. Her house
was a house of order, pleasure, books, the Bible, religion, and prayer." She
was well read in secular literature and a student and teacher of the Bible,
especially to the young. Steward indicated that his mother "was possessed
of more than ordinary intelligence."[29] Bishop Jabez Campbell gave a
glimpse of Rebecca Steward's education and her influence on her family:
"The early educational advantages of Mrs. Steward were those afforded
by the township School. Here she became a good English scholar, and
supplemented the instruction, thus received, by extensive reading; so that
she became proficient, both as a writer and a conversationalist. . . . Is it
necessary to be said, that we can see the effect of Rebecca Steward's Bible
lessons upon the minds of her children, in giving them an impulse to seek
for things divine?"[30]

She was an extraordinary woman who delighted in reading and writing poetry, short stories, and theological treatises. She enjoyed "good
preaching" and listed as a pleasure the attendance at classic lectures on
Gothic architecture.[31] Theodore Gould observed that Rebecca was such
an informed student of biblical doctrine and the "current or popular
questions of the day" that it caused a "very eminent and learned bishop"
to state after a visit with her, "No one can possibly spend five minutes in
conversation with Sister Steward without being edified." Gould further
indicated that another "intelligent" minister affirmed that she was "one of
the best read women [he] ever had the favor of conversing with." Gould
himself counted his aunt an important mentor. "I looked up to her for
that advice and counsel which had much to do with shaping my early
life," he wrote. "And if I have been worth anything to the church as a minister, her prayers, instructions and counsel have helped to mold me into
what I am."[32]

The volume served to express a model that the leadership of the church and the wider community championed as the model for Christian womanhood. It was highly publicized within the *Christian Recorder,* and one reviewer indicated that *Memoirs* should be one book which "every married man should present to his wife." Another commentator touted, "I wish all the mothers in our land could read this book and be able to say with her, 'I thought the training of my children was part of the work God gave me to do.'" This same commentator further stated, "I especially praise the work for its value as a testimonial to the doctrines I am trying to uphold upon The Influence of Women."[33]

These "doctrines" being upheld upon "The Influence of Women" insinuated that more was at stake with the publication of this volume than the promotion of a certain kind of female homespun life. This particular type of domesticity was dual focused in both home and community. Steward wrote of Rebecca,

> As a wife and a mother, she fulfilled her whole duty in the household. She was intelligent, hospitable, and kind, securing for her children the best company within their reach. By extensive reading and careful study, she prepared herself to entertain the young and the old, the rude, and the refined; and by her executive ability, she could secure the comfort and pleasure of almost any number of guests. Towards the community, she stood as an *unofficious and unostentatious missionary and educator* [emphasis added]. In herself, she suffered the will of God, and gave such an example of patience as is rarely met with.[34]

Of course, in the home, the focus was on the management of the household, cleanliness, thrift, and so on. She also focused on the raising of the children and leading them in their spiritual formation process. Thus both secular and religious pedagogy fell within her purview. Payne indicated, in his 1885 publication *A Treatise on Domestic Education,* that "[i]t is only the mother[,] conscious of the fact that God has made her the special trainer of the infant and youthful mind[,] who will persist in the good work of domestic education, and who will delight in the glorious task." In the community, women and mothers were to be responsible for the Christian education of the youth in particular. Payne divided religious training into two spheres. "[W]hile the father may give to his children an insight into the mysteries of the sublime science of theology," he stated, "the mother may inculcate the simple and practical duties of the Christian religion."[35]

A woman also was supposed to evangelize and spread the gospel in the community, but only, to use Steward's phrase, "as an unofficious and unostentatious missionary and educator."[36] "Unofficious" and "unostentatious" are key words here. They not only referred to the demeanor which women were generally to take in performing their Christian duty but also defined what women must do publicly and officially with no official recognition and no excessive display. The implied rebuke was to "sanctified" women preachers who were pretentious and disruptive of the order and decorum of the church's hierarchy in their zealous organizing and pursuit of women's ordination. Steward, describing his mother's church involvement, was clear about women's appropriate deportment and role in the church:

> In the Sunday-school she became a teacher and was successful
> in that capacity in bringing many souls to Christ. It was her object
> to secure the conversion of every scholar committed to her house
> or the house of one of the neighbors; she managed for some time
> a weekly prayer meeting, composed of the female members of the
> church, and subsequently became an active member of the church
> aid society. Yet, with all this activity, there was no ostentation, no
> public show, no noisy parade, no extravagant shouting. She was an
> uncompromising opponent to woman's preaching, and to all of
> those mutual aid societies bearing high sounding titles.[37]

Steward highlighted several of Rebecca Steward's community activities in order to underline the contrast between his mother's life and works and the holiness women preachers' activities and style as he perceived them. He focused on such endeavors as Sunday school teaching and church-aid-society work to show that she recognized and submitted to the male hierarchy in accepting the appropriate sphere for the involvement of women in church life and evangelical activities. Women were not to be itinerant preachers and evangelists, preaching in different churches. Their evangelistic efforts were to be confined to work with other women and with children in the home. A curious emphasis was given to the fact that Rebecca Steward functioned well in the prayer bands—small groups of women who operated autonomously with in the church for purposes of prayer and mutual support. Dodson has argued that the "[e]arly gender-specific 'prayer-bands' . . . provided African American women with peer companionship for self-measurement and protection as they identified those worm who possessed special gifts to preach the Gospel. Prayer bands also became arenas where preaching gifts were honed, refined through practice."[38]

It was in the prayer bands that the church hierarchy had most difficulty in controlling the activities of women. Although the church's male leadership recognized the spiritual legitimacy of these female-led prayer groups, it worried that these praying bands also encouraged women to exploit their gifts and calling in ways it thought inappropriate. Many women moved from leading a prayer group to preaching at these gatherings. From there they began to preach, at first locally, to other such assemblies, and later to assemblies and in churches far distances from home. In other words, from these praying bands developed the female traveling preachers.

Steward took pains to indicate that Rebecca Steward's exclusively female prayer meetings led her only to more acceptable avenues of service within the church, such as the "church aid societies." These aid societies or "mite" societies were internal church organizations that raised money to support of various mission efforts. As indicated earlier, the Women's Mite Missionary Society of the AME Church were female-led and mostly controlled by the bishops' wives and other upwardly mobile ministerial spouses.[39] Through their fund raising, even these women were able to create a greater degree of autonomy for themselves. This society expanded the role and function of women within the church as well, yet it was contained within the bounds set by the male hierarchy. Steward made it clear that Rebecca Steward functioned without any inappropriate conduct or self-promotion that might challenge the male power structure of the church.

The movement of women preachers for ordination and formal recognition within the AME Church was very active during Rebecca's lifetime. T. G. Steward indicated that around 1869 the "movement for the special promotion of holiness assumed noticeable proportions."[40] Women within the church had unsuccessfully petitioned the general conference in 1844 and in 1852 for ministerial privileges. In 1868, the general conference created the position of stewardess, women who were to assist the male stewards, class leaders, and pastors. Jualynne Dodson has argued that the position of stewardess was created as a "structural alternative to ordination for women who desired to serve the Church."[41] Steward stated that his mother had no sympathy for this movement and "expressed unhesitatingly her disapproval of any religious or political reform, led[,] largely[,] by women."[42] He also referred to his mother's series of articles on sanctification, implying that these articles, which were sharply critical of the sanctification movement, also bore on the issue of women's ordination.[43]

Although Steward indicated that his mother disapproved of women preachers and of any religious or political movement led by women, it was not reflected in her articles. Her articles strictly concentrated on the question of sanctification and her apologetic for the Wesleyan version of this doctrine. The doctrine of sanctification, or second blessing, as espoused by the holiness movement evolved from the Wesleyan doctrine of Christian perfection. This variation stressed the personal religious experience of attainment of perfect love in this life. It argued that after one was first convicted of one's sins, one was saved by justification. At some later point, one had a second and more profound experience of entire sanctification of the soul by God, an experience that washed the soul clean from sin so that one could live a sinless life. Rebecca rejected this idea, contending instead that salvation happened when one accepted Christ as savior. Sanctification was instead a natural part of a Christian's growth process. "If Christ does not mean to save to the *uttermost* why does he invite all the ends of the earth to come and be saved?" she wrote. "He does not say repent and believe *now*, and after a while I will come to wash, cleanse, purify, sanctify you or set you apart; but he says repent and believe *now* and ye shall be saved *now*."[44]

One of Rebecca Steward's articles traced the notion of sanctification from the series of Old Testament covenants through to the covenant of Christ of the New Testament: "It is a mistaken idea that we can be Christians and not be sanctified Christians. . . . Oh! I wish that every Christian would feel that he is a sanctified Christian, and go to work as such. Oh! That every one could feel that to-day I am a pillar in the temple of our God . . . instead of sitting still and dreaming: 'Can I be sanctified, or when can I be sanctified.' Oh! that Christians would awake, and look around, and see what they can do for the Master."[45] Rebecca Steward felt that sanctification was linked to ones action as a Christian. Therefore one should not wait for the sanctification experience, as did those within the holiness movement. Rather, the Christian should "do for the Master," which for her translated into Christian charity or love of neighbor.

In another article, Rebecca made a comparison between adulthood and Christian perfection. She stated that when a baby is born it is perfect but yet not a perfect adult. "His limbs, hands and feet are perfect; of his body there is no part lacking; and under the fostering care, and tender nursing of his mother, the rigid but wholesome discipline of the father, he must grow to perfect *manhood,*—and who can fix the time when the child ceases and when the man begins?" Recasting the Christ figure in a maternal image, she stated, "As soon as we believe we are perfect in Christ; and through the wise and just discipline of God the father, and the loving and tender care of Christ as our mother, being fed with the word, we grow in grace and in the knowledge of the truth daily. We can no more exist in a justified state and not be sanctified, than a child can be born without a *natural mother!*"[46]

Clearly, Rebecca Steward was theologically opposed to the sanctification movement. Her disfavor with this movement did not, however, translate in her writings to an overt rejection of women preachers. In fact, the subject never came up in her writings. It is also clear that it was her son, T. G. Steward, who was significantly opposed to both the sanctification movement and, most especially, women preachers.

We get a glimpse of T. G. Steward's ambivalence toward sanctified women preachers from the account of Amanda Berry Smith, the famous evangelist who was accused of advocating women's ordination. In her autobiography, she recounted an encounter with Steward in 1872. Smith does not call Steward out by full name but simply refers to him by the first letter of his last name, "Brother S.," in order to maintain anonymity. The General Conference of the AME Church was to be held that year in Nashville, Tennessee—the first time such a meeting was held south of the Mason-Dixon line. There was much excitement among the AME Church membership about attending this historic meeting. At an annual conference held in Philadelphia the year before, at which Steward was in attendance, Smith tried to find out the approximate cost of attending this Nashville conference. She indicated that her inquiries about costs were met with hostility when she asked several of the delegates (whom she also did not name). They accused her, Smith said, of desiring to attend the conference to advocate women's ordination, an accusation she denied.

Just as the conference was closing, she ventured to ask "Brother S." about costs. This man, she stated, was elected as a delegate, and she considered him a good friend. Steward's own memory of the election of delegates from the Philadelphia Annual Conference suggests that the only person with a last name that started with S was T. G. Steward:[47]

> Just before the Conference closed I ventured to ask another good brother, who had been elected delegate, and whom I knew very well, and he was so nice, I thought he would tell me. "Brother S.," I said, "how much do you think it will cost?" This was the uppermost thought then—the cost to go to Nashville. "Oh, my sister," he replied, "I don't know; it will take all of a hundred dollars" and with a significant toss of the head shot through the door, and I saw him no more till I met him next year at Nashville; and that was a surprise, but he managed to speak to me, as we both stopped at the Sumner House and sat at the same table.[48]

Steward did not encourage her attendance at a meeting that he felt might bring controversy regarding women in ministry. He tried to avoid her inquiries and was surprised to see her at the Nashville conference. Clearly, from Smith's perspective, she was out of her place.

Besides this incident, it is interesting that Steward's sister, Alice Felts, did not agree with his stance regarding women's ordination. In 1886, nine years after the publication of her mother's memoirs, Felts wrote the *Christian Recorder* in support of Bishop Turner's action of ordaining a woman. Turner had recently ordained Sarah Hughes of the North Carolina conference and Bishop John M. Brown had appointed Margaret Wilson to pastor a local congregation in the New Jersey conference. She pointedly argued that women, who made up two-thirds of the membership and gave three-fourths of the money, shared the financial burden of the church on an equal basis. She also noted that, in order to secure an adequate supply of Sunday school teachers, the church looked the other way on Paul's injunction against women speaking in public. It could therefore also, in all fairness, disregard the law regarding women's ordination:

> Now, if they are equal, or no discrimination is made by the law in taxation or confession of faith, but are required to use the same means of grace, the same attendance on class and prayer meeting, the communion service, the same payment for support of preacher, church and poor—after all this, why the law should then step out and say, so far and no farther shall you go. . . . The

sense of the law seems to me to be, a church member may be so represented in teaching or preaching as deacons, elders, Bishops or General Officers of the Church, and if the should be found able to fill the editor's chair neither the law or the Scripture would object. Indeed, I really think were it so that some of the offices of the Church were filled by women, it would be no more than is due them.[49]

Given Felts's strong sentiments regarding the ordination, one could only speculate how she felt about the way the *Memoirs of Mrs. Rebecca Steward* were used to attack women preachers. One wonders if this explains her conspicuous absence from her mother's memorial.

Sociologist Jualynne Dodson has shown that female preachers, most of whom were of the holiness persuasion, were very active during the mid-nineteenth century. She has also argued that these preaching women, through petitioning for ordination and recognition and by their relentless obedience to the call to preach, forced the church's structures to expand to include women in limited official capacities as stewardesses and deaconesses. Yet by means of this inclusion, the church attempted to limit and control women's preaching activities.[50] Clearly, the *Memoirs of Mrs. Rebecca Steward* were used by her son and others to counter this movement with a different version of Christian piety espoused by a woman.

In "'My Spirit Eye': Some Functions of Spiritual and Visionary Experiences in the Lives of Five Black Women Preachers," Jean M. Humez focused on five nineteenth-century women preachers, including Elizabeth (last name unrecorded), Jarena Lee, Rebecca Cox Jackson, Julia Foote, and Amanda Smith. Humez suggested that one of the reasons for the opposition to women preachers was their strong critique of the increasing sophistication or worldliness of the churches. Humez pointed out that the AME membership, particularly the leadership, was "becoming increasingly well educated, dressed more fashionably, took pleasure in social functions of the churches, approved such things as 'fairs and festivals,' of choral and even instrumental music, and was in general less interested in living a life centered wholly on religious experience and values."[51] This, of course, was the view of the female holiness preachers themselves.

Steward was eager to rebut the view that the church was moving toward a more worldly posture. As well, he also wanted to reject the view that only the holiness preaching women were concerned with issues of piety. It helped that Rebecca Steward did not exemplify this pattern worldliness. It is clear from Rebecca's writings that she was equally concerned about promoting a life of Christian piety and values. She argued that a true sanctified life led to Christian charity: "This is just what God requires of His children, viz.: to be perfect in our love to him, and to have perfect charity, one with another." Steward further indicated that his mother "seemed to have consecrated herself most fully to the Lord, and although she repudiated the theory of the 'second blessing,' yet she doubtless enjoyed all that the strongest advocates of that theory [Holiness] claim[ed]."[52] To counter the claim that the church focused on worldliness and fashion, Steward clearly indicated that his mother was a modest dresser. She wore no earrings, jewelry, or rings.[53] He stated that his mother "repudiated extravagance of all sorts, and sought to avoid everything that might render her noticeable."[54] While proffering the notion that one could be pious and still effectively oppose the tenets of the holiness movement, Steward, through the *Memoirs of Mrs. Rebecca Steward,* reasoned that the notion of female domesticity, especially the focus on education, was not contrary to a deep Christian spirituality. In fact, it supported the idea that Christian piety was enhanced by domestic education.

Steward and the male hierarchy of the AME Church used the *Memoirs of Mrs. Rebecca Steward* to challenge the powerful movement of holiness and its advocates, women preachers, and to set the agenda for female domesticity within the AME Church. As indicated by the subinscription on its title page, Steward published the book to honor his mother: "Her children shall rise up and call her blessed." He also clearly used the volume to perform double duty, to counter women's movements that challenged the religious order of the day.

Susan Maria Smith McKinney Steward

This is not the end of the story of Steward and his understanding of the women's role within the church. In part, Steward's change of attitude toward women may have been due to the influence of his second wife, Susan Maria Smith McKinney, whom he married in 1896.[55] By the end of his life, Steward had gone through a series of changes which helped him move to a more liberal position about the role of women within the church as well as within the larger society. He had truly evolved to a different position from that articulated in his earlier writings, as he had argued for a more limited role for women in society. As his world view expanded, so did his perspective on women. It took a combination of things to push him forward on his thinking regarding women's role in civil society. Besides the strong support for women in the church by Steward's sister Alice, he must have been aware of Frederick Douglass's progressive position on women as Douglass attended his church in Washington, D.C. As has been shown earlier, Steward interacted with Douglass on other matters. It is not inconceivable that he and Douglass interacted on this matter as well.

Steward's departure from the active pastorate within the AME Church and his appointment to the chaplaincy, thereby expanding his geographical horizons, must have had an impact on his views. He was most certainly aware of the developments among women within the black Baptist church with the founding of the National Baptist Convention in 1897[56] and the further development of the National Baptist Women's Convention, Auxiliary movement in 1900.[57] Surely Steward was aware of the continued debate about the ordination of women within the African Methodist Episcopal Zion Church which culminated in the official recognition of women's ordination in 1898. This came on the heels of the founding of the National Association of Colored Women (NACW) in 1896, many of whose leaders, such as Hallie Brown, were influential religious figures. The NACW leadership supported the ordination of women.[58] Still, as late as 1897, Steward recommended against the admission of women to the American Negro Academy, noting that "literary matters and social matters do not mix."[59] At this stage in Steward's evolution, he still made a clear distinction between women's role as literary expositors and educators and men's roles in the more "weightier" social matters of elevating the race.

Susan Steward, a noted medical doctor from New York City, came from a family of professionals, including her sister, Sarah J. S. Garnet, principal of a public school in New York City and the second wife of the famed abolitionist Henry Highland Garnet.[60] Other sisters became professionals as well. Emma Smith Thomas was noted as an "accomplished teacher" and was "successful in the acquisition and investment of money and was a competent advisor in financial affairs." Clara T. Smith Brown was a teacher of piano and organist at Concord Baptist Church of Brooklyn. Mary Smith became a successful owner of a hairdressing business.[61] Both her sister Sarah and she were known to be social activists, concerned with temperance, women's suffrage, education, and missions work.[62] They were also both active in the Woman's Loyal Union (WLU) of New York and Brooklyn. Judith Weisenfeld, in her book *African American Women and Christian Activism: New York's Black YMCA, 1905–1945*, indicated that the organization built a "national reputation for New York's black activist women." They crusaded to "gain access to jobs in sales, an area of employment traditionally restricted to white women, and sought ways to ensure that young African American women received training for such positions."[63] Susan Steward was an active member in the NACW's Wilberforce Club in 1914, before whom she read a paper on "Woman in Medicine."

In this paper, Steward rehearsed the history of women in medicine by starting with the biblical stories of Hebrew midwives, calling them obstetricians. For the historical section of her paper she followed James J. Walsh's book *Old-time Makers of Medicine*.[64] Susan argued that Plato encouraged the education of women in his *Republic*. She highlighted women doctors of the early European Christian and medieval eras, especially the medical writings of twelfth-century Benedictine nun St. Hildegarde of Germany. After acknowledging the decline of women in medicine during the sixteenth century in Europe, she turned to the rise of women doctors in the mid-nineteenth century, focusing on the education of Elizabeth Blackwell, the first American trained female physician, who was admitted to medical school in 1848, and Clemence S. Lozier, the founder and dean of the New York Medical College and Hospital for Women in 1863. Steward augmented this list by including both white and black women doctors of her own time period. She even argued that marriage need not stop women from choosing a medical education. "They are trained in the art of differentiation," she wrote, "and hence, in the delicate matters of the heart, are the better able to make wise selections; so that the medical education of women and marriage need not become a question of discussion with the women who have chosen the profession of medicine as their life-work."[65]

Besides this article, Steward also gave a paper on "Colored American Women"[66] at the First Universal Races Congress held at the University of London, July 26–29, 1911. The purpose of the paper was to lift up as "beacon lights" some notable professional black women in America. "I have tried to hastily tell you of the progress of our women, not yet fifty years away from slavery," she said. "The club spirit prevails among them, as well as among the women of the Caucasian race, and they are working for the intellectual and moral uplifting of the race, having taken as their

motto: 'Lifting as we climb.' What may they not accomplish with the infu-
sion and enthusiasm of such a spirit[?]"[67] In her paper, Steward moved
from eighteenth-century writer Phyllis Wheatley to her nineteenth-century
contemporaries, such as Ida B. Wells-Barnett; Hallie Brown; Mary
Church Terrell; her sister, Sarah Garnet; and Amanda Smith. Considering
T. G. Steward's earlier relationship with Smith, it is significant that Susan
Steward highlighted, in the profession of lecturer, Smith as a woman of
"strong character and intellectual ability."[68]

Steward was a tireless promoter of the rights of women in general and
of African American women in particular. Certainly after her marriage
to T. G. Steward, his attitude changed, as he advocated the active role of
women in all parts of society, especially as participants within the effort
to abolish intemperance[69] and prostitution. Susan Steward died on March 7,
1918, and did not see the arrival of the Nineteenth Amendment of the
Constitution, which gave women the right to vote in 1920, though she
rigorously supported it.

Susan Steward's impact on her husband was certainly profound. It is
not surprising then to find Steward advocating for women's suffrage in his
"Our Civilization" lecture, which was delivered as an address sometime
before the passage of the Nineteenth Amendment. Nor was it strange to see
Steward, in this volume, argue that women's roles were expanding to all
professions from the literary where he had earlier restricted them, to much
broader spheres of influence such as "politics and religion": "She is in literature, music, painting and sculpture; in commerce and manufacture, in
agriculture, stock-raising and dairying, in education from kindergarten to
college; in all the professions, in politics and religion. The freedom which
was regarded as the special patrimony of the man, is now for the whole
household; and the women are destined to give the momentum necessary
to the final victorious charge against the brothel[,] the saloon[,] and war."[70]

Certainly, Steward's marriage to Susan McKinney Steward was a major
factor in his evolution in thinking. As Hallie Brown eulogized Steward's
life, "She could strike, and strike hard, in what she believed to be a righteous cause. With her it was justice on the one side, and injustice on the
other. The line was sharply drawn. There was no middle ground of expe-
diency or compromise."[71]

It is clear that Steward's thinking about roles that women should
play in the development of an African American civil society shifted over
the course of his lifetime. The influence of the strong women in his life

obviously challenged and shaped his thinking on women. Steward's mother was the primary shaper of his early spiritual values, and his second wife helped shape his thinking regarding women and civil society in his later years. Susan Steward was a force Steward certainly could not contain—strong like his mother, opinionated, and devout, but "worldly" in her own right. Being the thinker that he was, Steward, in his older age, came to agree with Susan Steward about women's expanding role in the larger society and far beyond the domestic sphere.

The evolution of Steward's thinking was not limited to the issue of women. He also expanded his ideas regarding racism as a result of his move out of his more provincial church setting. His career as a military chaplain and his travels around the world, which helped reshape his understanding of race as a world phenomenon, will be discussed in the next chapter.

Chapter 7

Race, Imperialism, and the Military: A View from an Army Chaplain

S teward's time as an army chaplain brought him the unpleasant knowledge that race was an international problem with international ramifications. Earlier in his life, Steward believed that "[t]he presence of a so-called *colored man* is the acid test of American culture." He later came to understand that "[w]e are accustomed to think the color question an American question, and to regard the Negro race as the only race affected disadvantageously by it; but a residence of nearly a year in the Orient has taught me that it is a world-wide question, and established the most important cleavage among men."[1]

In a seemingly contradictory move, given Steward's excoriation of Strong and his vision of Anglo-Saxon imperialism in America, Steward accepted a commission as captain in the U.S. Army's Chaplain Corps in 1891. He was assigned to a black regiment, the Twenty-fifth Infantry, was initially stationed in the West, and thereafter increasingly became exposed to the arena of international affairs.

Steward's previous international experience was limited to a short and ill-fated missionary enterprise in Haiti in 1873.[2] While he did have some significant concerns regarding imperialism, he believed the military was important and valuable. Steward was not a pacifist.[3] He also clearly understood the significance of the military in securing the freedom of the former slaves and was acutely aware of the importance of the military presence in the Reconstruction South.[4] War was a "horrible" thing "beyond description or conception,"[5] he believed, but clearly it had its uses.

Steward entered the military chaplaincy with apprehension regarding the treatment that African Americans would receive in the army. He was concerned that he would be restricted in his ability to preach the gospel and assumed that army officers "were not generally kind" to chaplains, especially black chaplains.[6] There seemed to be good reason for this fear, considering that the first black regular army chaplain, Henry V. Plummer, who was attached to the Ninth Cavalry, was court-martialed for intemperance in 1894 just three years after Steward's entrance into the corps. Some believed that his court-martial was precipitated by his advocacy of a colonial expedition to central Africa as part of a larger back-to-Africa scheme.[7]

Given that, Steward's generally optimistic view of black life in the military was significantly influenced by his initial experience in the military. Not knowing what to expect when he arrived at Fort Missoula, Montana, where his regiment was stationed, Steward was pleasantly surprised at the positive reception he received, especially from the commanding officer of the fort and his wife, Col. and Mrs. George L. Andrews. The colonel and his wife extended an invitation to Steward to reside in their home while his quarters were being prepared. Mrs. Andrews was also active in assisting Steward in the religious services for the enlisted men. He called the couple "decidedly Christian." They offered such special attention to Steward and his family in getting them settled that Steward was compelled to highlight their courtesies in a letter to his friend and patron, John Wanamaker, the U.S. postmaster general.[8] Steward, perhaps with the intent of building a political relationship with then-general Benjamin Harrison, described to him in a letter his connection with the army as "pleasant."[9] Steward was also surprised by the friendliness of the other officers at the fort and amazed at the generally positive reception he received from most of the local Montana residents as he preached in many of their churches. He even preached, for an extended time, in the pulpit of the all-white, only Presbyterian church of Missoula.[10] He was especially enthralled with the fact that he had been welcomed to preach in the churches and to eat in the homes of many of the settlers: "Through this region were men who had served in the Confederate Army or their relatives and children, or as some described them, 'The left wing of Price's army who had escaped the surrender.'" He indicated that "they were very cordial to me. . . . Many of them seemed devoutly pious." Even when he was confronted by acts of discrimination, for example, when he was refused dining privileges in a Missoula hotel, Steward was quick to point out the fact that Colonel

Andrews "backed me squarely in my protest and went with me to consult the most prominent lawyer of the place." Steward made such a positive connection to the colonel that he wrote an article praising Andrews at his retirement.[11]

Given this welcome reception, Steward became so enamored of military life that he began a writing campaign, which stretched throughout his military career, designed to accent both the high morals and the heroic performance record of the military in general and the African American soldier in particular. One early example of this effort to highlight black soldiers was an article, titled "The Colored American as a Soldier," in an 1894 issue of *United Service,* a monthly journal of military and naval affairs. Given the specialized nature of this magazine, Steward's initial focus had to be on changing the military's view of African American soldiers. African American soldiers were seen as less honorable and efficient than their white counterparts. Steward felt that the public did not give these men the recognition and respect that they deserved: "These colored regiments have passed all this time, with but little exception, in places far away from popular view, and amid dangers as great and hardships as severe as have been shared by any part of the army. In this dull and trying service they have been carefully weighed in the balances of usefulness, and the general testimony of those whose words are entitled to special weight is, that they have not been found wanting."[12] Steward noted that African American troops won proportionately more medals and certificates for gallantry than their white peers, and that black soldiers were generally healthier than white soldiers based on the surgeon general's report of death rates and admissions in the hospitals for alcoholism. He outlined the history of the Twenty-Fifth Infantry, focusing on its various "remarkable" marches, a history that had never before been published. He supplemented this information with several testimonials from white officers—a captain, colonel, and brigadier general—who had commanded the two black cavalries and two black infantries. Steward ended the article with a hope, one far ahead of his time, for an integrated army: "[T]he writer hereof cannot refrain from saying that he hopes that day will soon come when there will be no more colored soldiers in the army of the United States, but that the special defenders of the flag shall be simply Americans,—all."[13] Steward's defense of the army, specifically black soldiers, led to his decision to write a book on the African American soldier's involvement in the U.S. military. The result was *The Colored Regulars in the United States Army,* published in 1904, just as all four black units—the Ninth and Tenth Cavalry and the Twenty-fourth and Twenty-fifth Infantries—were sent to Cuba.

An introductory letter accompanied the volume by Lt. Gen. Nelson A. Miles, commander of the Army of the United States.[14] Steward reported that Bishop Benjamin W. Arnett had requested that President McKinley have Steward assigned to write a volume on the history of the Colored Regulars, especially dealing with their work in Cuba.[15] In fact, Steward orchestrated the commissioning through his civilian allies in the AME Church.

A brief look at the chain of events gives a clear picture of the way Steward used the military system in his favor. As early as December 9, 1898, while stationed at Fort Logan in Denver, Colorado, Steward had corresponded with the editors of the *Independent* and the *Arena*[16] regarding his partially developed volume on the subject of the recognition of the gallantry of the "colored troops at San Juan."[17] On February 13, 1899, while Steward was away visiting his ill wife in Brooklyn, New York, Colonel Burt made an initial request for Steward's reassignment to Fort Apache, Arizona, to support other black troops, a request that was granted on February 23, 1899.[18] Steward had already had a conflict with Colonel Burt three years earlier when Burt refused to endorse Steward's application to a West Point chaplaincy vacancy.[19] This change of venue was not to Steward's liking, in part because of the potential delay in completing the volume on black soldiers, which was not yet officially sanctioned. Steward solicited the assistance of Bishop Arnett and his old friend, Levi J. Coppin.[20] Arnett wrote President McKinley on February 23, 1899, the same day of Steward's official transfer, requesting that Steward be allowed the necessary time to write the "History of the Colored Regiments." Arnett noted in a follow-up letter to R. A. Alger, secretary of war, that he had personally consulted with President McKinley, who had indicated that "anything that was necessary to accomplish the object he [McKinley] was willing to do." Arnett outlined Steward's needs in order to finish the book, including the rescinding of the transfer orders to Fort Apache:

> The first request is that he be relieved from duty, a reasonable time to collect, arrange and tabulate the information, necessary for the volume. If the necessary time is permitted him, he can arrange the table of contents and submit it to you for your approval. I understand that he has been ordered to move from "camp Logan" to Fort Apache, Arizona. If the order is rescinded,

before the 21st of March, '99, it will save him moving his family
and save expenses. He could make his headquarters at Wilberforce, Ohio, with his children. I hope you will be able to grant this
request in the interest of ten million people.[21]

Writing on behalf of the Minister's Association of Philadelphia, Coppin
wrote to President McKinley, "We the ministers of the A.M.E. Church at
Phil. Pa. have learned with much regret that our ministerial colleague
Chaplain T. G. Steward, of the 25th U.S. Infantry is to be relieved from
duty at Fort Logan and assigned to Fort Apache Arizona. If it would be
agreeable to the Hon. President to have him continued at his present post,
the ministry of the A.M.E. Church with the Bishops, will be placed under
an additional debt of gratitude."[22] Clearly, though in the military full time,
Steward continued to rely on his connections in the AME Church.

In the introduction to *The Colored Regulars,* Steward laid out what he
saw as the role of the military in the development of African Americans'
involvement in civilization: "In the face of slavery and against its teaching
and its power, overcoming the seduction of the master class, and the
coarse and brutal corruption of the baser overseer class, the African slave
persistently strove to clothe himself with the habiliments of civilization,
and so prepared himself for social organization."[23] He traced the development of African Americans from their origin in various parts of Africa to
their conglomeration as "No People," to use the biblical phrase,[24] to the
development of a sense of common identity as a people in America. In
spite of the diverse cultures from which Africans came, he argued, through
the "aid of a common language and a common lot, and cruel yet partially
civilizing control, the whole people were forced into a common outward
form, and to a remarkable extent, into the same ways of thinking"; that is,
they attained peoplehood. Steward was noncommittal regarding a prediction of where the African American community as a whole was headed.
They were "marching from nowhere to somewhere," but without any clear
direction. He mused about four possible scenarios that were prevalent in
his day, but refused to commit to any definite prediction:

> Are we destined to see the African element of America's pop-
> ulation blend with the Euro-American element and be lost in a
> common people? Will the colored American leave this home in
> which as a race he has been born and reared to manhood, and find
> his stage of action somewhere else on God's earth? Will he remain

here as a separate and subordinate people perpetuating the conditions of to-day only that they may become more humiliating and exasperating? Or is there to arise a war of races in which the blacks are to be exterminated? Who knows? Fortunately the historian is not called upon to perform the duties of prophet.[25]

In *The Colored Regulars,* Steward abandoned the role of prophet that he played in *The End of the World,* and assumed that of historical observer. Yet Steward still had an agenda. Among the various options he outlined for African Americans, Steward implied that they should choose to struggle for a sense of self-determination as a distinct group within American society. They should not give up their unique identity but should insist on their acceptance as an equal contributor to the advancement of American civilization. Steward hedged his bets but suggested "this new Afro-American will some how and some where be given an opportunity to express that particular modification of material life that his spiritual nature will demand."[26] Steward argued in favor of military development for African Americans, saying that whether as a "nation among other nations, or as an elementary component of a nation," no people could win and hold a place without winning respect through physical force. "Too often the greatest of all national crimes is to be weak," he postulated. "When the struggle is a quiet one, going on within a nation, and is that of an element seeking a place in the common social life of the country, much the same principles are involved. It is still a question to be settled by force, no matter how highly the claim of the weaker may be favored by reason and justice."[27] Justifying his advocacy of military or disciplined physical power, Steward argued that physical strength, along with intellectual and material strength, was a necessary component of a triadic power relationship for the emergence of a "special people" from "an unhappy condition." He contended that African Americans had, through the trials of slavery and emancipation, proven and continued to prove their abilities in the realm of intellect, material, and physical abilities. *The Colored Regulars* was an attempt to highlight how African Americans had evolved from slavery during the American Revolution, with limited knowledge of "the spirit or the training of the soldier," through the Civil War, in which he "secured his standing as a soldier," to the present period just after the Spanish American War in which he emerged as a "new soldier," taking "his rank with America's best, and in appearance, skill, physique, manners conduct and courage prov[ing] himself worthy of the position he holds."[28]

Steward used a slave spiritual, "Do You Think I'll Make a Soldier?" to highlight the importance of the book. The song accented the dilemma which African Americans found themselves in regarding the army and the general perception of their lack of fitness to serve in the military. From the nation's earliest days, Steward argued, African Americans had proven themselves gallant soldiers, yet it was continually asked if they were fit for service: "It is not: Will I make a soldier? but: Do you think I will make a soldier? It is one thing to 'make a soldier,' another thing to have men think so. The question of fact was settled a century ago; the question of opinion is still unsettled."[29]

Pointing to black soldiers' participation in such martial campaigns as the American Revolution, the War of 1812, and the Civil War, Steward asserted that "the martial spirit is not foreign to the Negro character, as has been abundantly proved in both ancient and modern times."[30] He pointed also to the pre-Christian exploits of the Egyptian civilization and to the martial spirit of the Maroons of Trinidad, British Guiana, St. Domingo, and Florida. He gave special note to the spirit of Toussaint L'Ouvérture, the leader of the Haitian Revolution, as the best modern example of states-manship and military leadership within the African context, equal to that of Europeans. He even pointed to the military organizations of Zulu and other South African tribes as examples of Africans' familiarity with mili-tarism. Drawing upon the work of a contemporary historian, George Washington Williams,[31] Steward claimed that "[i]f the Afro-American should fail in this particular it will not be because of any lack of the military element in the African side of his character, or for any lack of 'remorseless military audacity' in the original Negro."[32]

Steward inserted his article, "How the Black St. Domingo Legion Saved the Patriot Army in the Siege of Savannah, 1779,"[33] into the *Colored Regu-lars* to demonstrate how people of African descent had distinguished themselves during the American Revolution. It also highlighted the con-nection between the Haitian Revolution and the American Revolution, chronicling the fact that a regiment of volunteer free mulatto and black Haitian troops were instrumental in saving the city of Savannah from British occupation when the combined forces of Americans and their French allies were unable to do so. Some of these volunteers later became major leaders and officers in the Haitian Revolution, including several of its generals and its first president, Henry Christophe. The inclusion of this article built a case for the contribution of people of color to the broader notions of democracy and independence:[34] "The Black men of the Antilles who fought in the siege of Savannah, enjoy unquestionably the proud historical distinction of being the physical conductors that bore away from our altars the sacred fire of liberty to rekindle it in their own land; and also of becoming the humble but important link that served to unite the Two Americas in the bond of enlightened independence."[35]

On the American side after the Revolutionary War, Steward was quick to point out the valor and expertise of African American soldiers and officers. He also summarized the history of discrimination by the U.S. military toward its black officers and enlisted men, from the Civil War to the Spanish-American War, giving special mention to the harsh treatment received by young, black West Point cadets. They "endured hardships disgraceful to their country, and when entering the army were not given that cordial welcome by their brother officers, becoming an 'officer and gentleman,' both to give and receive." Steward included in this section of *The Colored Regulars* a chapter on colored officers written by his son, Capt. Frank R. Steward, who held bachelor of arts and bachelor of laws degrees from Harvard and was an officer of the Forty-ninth U.S. Volunteer Infantry. Frank Steward argued even more forcefully that "the commissioned ranks of the army and navy [had been] the stubbornest to yield to the newly enfranchised." He further argued that the prevailing sentiment of the times was that "Negroes cannot command" nor would black troops "follow and obey officers of their own race."[36] Frank Steward offered several examples of the sterling leadership of African American officers to debunk this widespread view. His defense of black officers was clearly supported by the larger African American community. The slogan "No Officers, No Fight!" coined by a black newspaper, the *Richmond Planet,* summed up opposition to the policy of recruiting black volunteers without the training and promotion of black officers.[37]

The Spanish-American War and American Imperialism in the Caribbean

T. G. Steward was well aware of tensions surrounding African American leadership, or the lack thereof, in the military, particularly as he was assigned to recruit for the enlistment of black troops in the volunteer army. In one sense, his job was easy: many African Americans initially felt that the Spanish-American War was a war for the liberation of fellow blacks in Cuba from European control. But many blacks formed volunteer companies under the command of African American officers only to be rejected in most states, especially in the South, making Steward's job of recruitment ever more difficult.[38]

Steward was clear that he supported the United States' intervention in the war with Spain concerning Cuba. He was careful to indicate that the bombing of the warship *Maine* was not enough to bring the country into war. He felt that the motive of revenge and the hatred felt by the American populous was un-Christian to say the least. He argued that a more noble cause was that of aiding Cuban nationals in their struggle for freedom from Spain: "On behalf of the starving reconcentrados, and in aid of the noble Cuban patriot, we might justly arm and equip ourselves for the purpose of driving Spanish rule from the Western Hemisphere." He added, "This view appealed to all lovers of freedom, to all true patriots, and to the Christian and philanthropist." Steward even noted with irony the inconsistency of southern leaders supporting the war effort on behalf of "the aspirations of the colored Cuban patriots and soldiers" while at the same time being "utterly opposed to Negroes or colored men having any share in ruling at home."[39]

Still, Steward was clear about his belief that the war was a just war. He felt that the United States was led to war "simply to liberate Cuba from the iniquitous and cruel yoke of Spain, and to save thousands of impoverished Cubans from death by starvation." It is clear that Steward's view carried with it a paternalistic attitude toward the oppressed. He stressed the fact that "great care" was given not to recognize the Cuban government "in any form" and that "it seemed to be understood that we were to do the fighting both with our navy and our army, the Cubans being invited to co-operate with us, rather than that we should co-operate with them. We were to be the liberators and saviors of a people crushed to the very gates of death."[40]

Even in the midst of this call for patriotism, Steward was aware of the continued racism that African Americans faced in the United States, and he was concerned for other people of color in these newly captured territories. As imperialist efforts of the United States rose during the end of the nineteenth century, exemplified by the Spanish-American War and other exploits, so did racism and terrorism against African Americans in the form of lynching. The *Chicago Tribune* estimated that between 1882 and 1899, 2,533 black men and women had been lynched without legal proceedings.[41] Many in the African American community articulated what they saw as the contradiction between America's interceding on behalf of people of color in Cuba's struggle with Spain and the continued hostile treatment of African Americans at home and in the military. Steward was concerned and spoke out in a variety of ways. He was more than willing to discuss the negative treatment of black soldiers in the South. He commented freely on the treatment he and his family received during their trip to the South, stating that they "could not eat with the other officers of the regiment under a Southern sky." The troops were also segregated from white soldiers once they reached Chattanooga en route to the staging point for Cuba in Key West, Florida. In light of these experiences, Steward wrote to the *Independent*, "United States commission could not make clean what the South pronounces unclean; and these men whose brawny arms are expected to uphold the flag of the great nation had a 'realizing sense' of the weakness of their flag as they saw the Government blue spit upon by a custom as mean as it is silly and degrading. A glorious dilemma that will be for the Cuban Negro, to usher him into the condition of the American Negro."[42] Steward spoke, in outrage, about the brutal and savage murder of Sam Hose in Georgia by a white mob after Hose had been accused of the murder and rape of a white woman. He described in his essay, in gory detail, the way the white crowd made a spectacle of Hose's lynching, torturing him by cutting off his ears and other body parts prior to burning him, and then tearing his body to pieces to sell as souvenirs. "The people temporarily threw aside law, order and civilization and indulged themselves in a delirium of diabolism," he wrote. He described the subsequent hanging of Rev. Elijah Strickland, whose crime was that of trying to protect Hose from the mob. These "anarchists," Stewart claimed, had but contempt for civilization and governmental authority, and the nation was obliged to do one of three things:

1. Either to stand by and see its black citizens successfully disrobed of all their rights and left at the mercy of their white neighbors, and bear its full share of the odium of all these horrid outrages.

2. Or cut loose from the South and let that section bear its own iniquities.

3. Or assert itself as a nation, and establish the reign of justice and humanity over every foot of land beneath the sway of its flag.[43]

Steward, however, had a very difficult time recognizing the racial inconsistencies within the Army itself. His captivation with the military sometimes caused him to lose objectivity in his interpretation of issues and events. While others were pointing to the discriminatory policies of the army, Steward was on the defense. In particular, in 1898, as the United States was preparing for their war with Spain, there was much discussion regarding the resignation of six black officers of the black Sixth Virginia Infantry, a volunteer regiment, who were in conflict with their white commander. The group resignations were precipitated by orders for each of the six officers to come before a board of examiners after the all white First Georgia had fired on the Sixth Virginia Infantry.[44] The black officers were replaced with white officers, rather than from among the rank-and-file as many of the black volunteers had hoped. In response, the enlisted black volunteer soldiers staged a work stoppage. This crisis brought the question of discrimination in the army before the public eye. Shortly after this incident, Steward came to the defense of the army and its treatment of regular army officers. In an article in the *Colored American,* Steward wrote that he had read many articles that did the army a great injustice. He made a clear distinction between the newly formed volunteer army and the regular army: "I shall speak in this paper only of the regular army, which is in my estimation an ideal military organization, unequaled in many respects by any other body of men of like number anywhere in the world." He strongly refuted the idea that there was prejudice in the regular army and affirmed that he had not seen anywhere else "black men and white men mingle so freely and so fraternally as in the army of the United States."[45] He went on to deny any prejudice among the white officers in these black units. "The Negro soldier has a friend in almost every officer that has ever served with black troops," he declared. "The Negro is a friend winner." He indicated that there were four black captains in the regular army and that they were treated fairly. Ultimately, he skirted the issue of promotions to officers from the rank-and-file by indicating that he had only known one "to make the trial, and more favors were shown him than I have ever known above to a white candidate."[46] He ended by suggesting that the army in fact treated African Americans more fairly than other institutions:

> The army today instead of being the worst, is really the best place. It is in advance of Howard University; of Lincoln University; of many of the schools, and of the churches. No white Methodist

minister of this country ever treated me one fifth as well as I have
been treated by three fourths of the army officers with whom I
have had to do. A Negro Methodist minister among his white
brethren even in Philadelphia never received a tithe of the cour-
tesy that the black army chaplain often receives from the officers
with whom he serves.[47]

Steward did not mention the Sixth Virginia Volunteer Infantry incident in *The Colored Regulars,* reinforcing his stance as apologist for the
army. He did, however, admit to the level of discrimination experienced
by the volunteer army, whose units were mustered out of service at the
end of the war efforts in 1899. The public outcry against black officers
and their troops was so loud that Steward noted that "[t]he three hundred
colored officers became an object at which both prejudice and jealousy
could strike; but to reach them the reputation of the entire colored con-
tingent must be assailed." Not only did the civilian population in Colorado
mistreat them when white troops were far more disruptive, but the mustering out of the volunteers meant the removal from service of black officers.[48] Steward admitted that the discharge of the black volunteers and
their officers had a depressing effect on the larger African American
community and thus spawned a wave of protest from the African American press. "With a few exceptions, these protests were encouched [*sic*] in
respectful language toward the President and his advisers, but the grounds
upon which they were based were so fair and just, that right-thinking
men could not avoid their force," Steward lamented.[49]

On the whole, though, Steward maintained that the army was the best
place for the African American masses to gain the social skills they needed
to enter into civil society. Yet even with this apologetic for the military,
Steward was greatly concerned for the broader role that race played in
American social and political life and its effects on foreign countries. Given
the American proclivity toward segregation, discrimination, and racism,
especially in the South, he challenged the United States toward a peaceful
benevolence in the way it ruled the occupied islands of Cuba and Puerto
Rico after the Spanish-American War. His concern was that the Cuban
people, who had experienced domination by Spain would not stand for
racial mistreatment by whites, would act as radicals, and would plan revolution. To Steward's credit, he argued that the United States was obligated
to hand over Cuba to the Cubans as a sovereign island. As for Puerto Rico,

he felt that the U.S. government could not "rightfully retain it, except with the consent of the Porto Ricans themselves." His hope was that these countries coming under U.S. control as the spoils of the war, would choose American citizenship or close alignment based on the benevolent action of the military:

> It is important for the people of the United States and for the people of these islands that the garrisons sent there should be of the best type of our people, physically and morally, that they might command the respect of the West Indians, and so win their esteem that they should ultimately willingly vote themselves under our flag.
>
> Whether this shall be the result, or whether they shall dwell with us as malcontents, ever plotting revolution and breeding assassins, depends very much upon how we begin with them. They are few in numbers and contemptible in power, but to attempt to crush them would be as costly as it would be infamous, and would demand of the civilized nations of the earth a "humanitarian war" against our misrule."[50]

Steward therefore recommended that in order to "bring about harmony and to obviate disagreeable conflicts," black southern soldiers, who were used to the climate and were morally upright, be placed in these garrisons in the territories along with white liberal soldiers from the North and West. White southerners should be avoided at all cost "because the strife that would follow would be irrepressible. In brief, a word to the wise is sufficient." Steward felt that the residents of these islands could be either "citizens or wards." He argued that as wards, "West Indians" would be more costly to manage than "our Indians" because [they, the West Indians are] more intelligent and better situated."[51] He reminded his readers of the tactical mistake that Napoleon had made by not recognizing the desire of the Haitians to be recognized and treated as French citizens. The attempt to subdue St. Domingo had cost "sixty thousand European lives and failed," he noted. "Had Napoleon been wise and governed the island through the great Toussaint, it would have remained the Empire's proudest ornament." He ended his challenge with the statement that "[w]ith care and generosity on our part, Cuba and Porto Rico may become not only our ever faithful allies, but active and valuable parts of our Great

Republic. With harsh and ungenerous treatment they may become the abodes of our bitterest and most active foes."[52]

Steward was also mildly critical of imperialistic colonialism, but here we see the tension with which Steward lived. On the one hand he desired to see Cuba and Puerto Rico exercise self-determination about their future. Yet he was so caught up in the spirit of Americanism that the best option he could see for these groups was alignment with the United States—and this in spite of his awareness of the ills of racism within the American context. As much as he criticized Josiah Strong for his brand of religious ethnocentrism, Steward was supporting the same expansionist views. Further, he defended the use of black troops as the enforcers of U.S. imperialism. Steward did, however, recover some of his earlier opposition to imperialism and racism during and after his tour of duty in the Philippines.

Steward in the Philippines

The Spanish-American War was carried out not only in Cuba but also in the Philippine Islands. From 1899 to 1902 Steward developed a firsthand appreciation of the role the U.S. Army was playing in the Philippines when he was stationed there. His attitude toward the Philippine conflict was encumbered by the same source of tensions that accompanied his evaluation of the conflict over Cuba.

Because of the Treaty of Paris (December 10, 1898) between Spain and the United States, the United States acquired control of Puerto Rico, Guam, and the Philippines. Led by Emilio Aguinaldo, Filipinos began a rebellion against Spain before the American occupation of the Philippines. As soon as the rebelling nationalists became aware that the United States had no intention of granting independence to the Philippines as they had done with Cuba, they mounted an eventually unsuccessful campaign against the American armed forces, which included the African American Twenty-fifth Infantry. At home in the United States there was a rising tide of anti-imperialist sentiment, especially in the African American community. Although African Americans generally supported the Cuba campaign, the same was not true with the campaign in the Philippines. According to military historian Bernard Nalty, this was due in part to the fact that African Americans did not feel the same affinity with Filipinos that they did with the Cubans, who they "considered brothers and fellow victims of oppression." Bishop Turner and others who opposed the Cuban campaign stepped up their opposition and condemned those who waged an "unholy war of conquest" against Aguinaldo and his "feeble band of sable patriots." Even Booker T. Washington, who had supported black soldiers' involvement in the Spanish-American War, now questioned the viability of the expansion into the Philippines, indicating that "[u]ntil our nation has settled the Indian and Negro problems, I do not think we have a right to assume more social problems."[53]

The rebelling Filipinos waged a fierce guerrilla campaign, and it soon became clear that the pacification effort would have little effect. Steward saw the limits of this strategy, noting that military governments were rarely accepted, except "as a defense against anarchy"—not the situation in the Philippines. Steward stated that the military had intended to be "fair and just," but the rebels continued to be active, and it was unclear how much support "the peaceful natives of the towns" gave to the "hostilities" of the "insurgents": "Those who were 'amigos' in the day might be 'enemigos' at night; so that it was necessary for the military to use considerable vigilance even over those who were quietly pursuing their daily occupations. The pacification of the country went on slowly, accompanied with much difficulty and some loss of life."[54]

While Steward saw the "insurgents" as a problem for the American army, he became increasingly aware of the impact that American-styled racism was having on the Philippines. He also began to appreciate the affinity between other peoples of color and the African American. During his stay in the Philippines, in addition to his regular chaplain's duties, Steward was responsible for educational development in the Zambales province, and it was there that he became an astute observer of the cultural, social, and political life of the Filipino people.

It was in this context that Steward began to make an international connection between racism and imperialism. The effects of the racist attitudes of some Americans, both civilians and military, were far-reaching.[55] One black soldier stationed in the Philippines observed that "already there is nowhere in Manila you can hardly get accommodated and you are welcomed nowhere." The reality prompted him to further state that it was "enough to make a colored man hate the flag of the United States." Another soldier wrote, "The whites have begun to establish their diabolical race hatred in all its home rancor . . . even endeavoring to propagate the phobia among the Spaniards and Filipinos so as to be sure of the foundation of their supremacy when the civil rule . . . is established."[56] Evidence suggests that most of the white soldiers referred to the natives as "niggers."[57] Patrick Mason, a sergeant in the Twenty-fourth Infantry, wrote the *Cleveland Gazette* with his observations on the connection between racism and imperialism:

> I have not had any fighting to do since I have been here and don't care to do any. I feel sorry for these people and all that have come under the control of the United States. I don't believe they will be justly dealt by. The first thing in the morning is the "Nigger" and the last thing at night is the "Nigger." You have no idea the way these people are treated by the Americans here. I know their feeling toward them [Filipinos], as they speak their opinion in my presence thinking I am white. . . . The poor whites don't believe that anyone has any right to live but the white American, or to enjoy any rights or privileges that the white man enjoys. . . . I must not say much as I am a soldier. The natives are a patient, burden-bearing people.[58]

Like Mason, Steward's experience in the Philippines began to shift his sentiments toward a more critical view of the American occupation. He watched as Americans attempted to create divisions within the Filipino people and justify the presence of the occupational forces, suggesting that the islands' various ethnic groups could not peaceably coexist. Steward even stated that the head of the Civil Commission, William H. Taft, following this thinking, saw these ethnic groups as "factional." In a fragment of a manuscript written about the Filipinos, Steward claimed, "Three years' close observation has convinced me that the tribal differences are unimportant, and that no active tribal animosities exist. In their army, in their journals, in their social gatherings, in their churches no mention is made of the different so-called tribes." If there were any factional differences, Steward felt they were a result of the intrusion of the American occupation. He reported that a Zambal woman who had not participated in the insurrection told him that about "one tenth of the educated people are willing to accept American rule, but that the nine tenth wish independence."[59] Steward indicated that in spite of the fact that the Filipino people were not in the slightest way in danger of rising up against the American occupation, it was not right to interpret their passivity as widespread. The people did not see in

American domination[,] the realization of their ideals and there is likely to be discontent. They regard the rule of the Americans only as an inevitable means to an end, the benevolent intentions of good Americans may win them over in time. The treatment accorded them under the civil government is most liberal and the commission in all its ways has been an honor to the country. Governor Taft's methods and policy are worthy of the American name, still the people wish for independence. Should our government pilot them to the goal they desire it will accomplish the greatest marvel of history. Why cannot we do it? We can if we are great enough.[60]

Steward also described a conversation with an educated East Indian merchant who reported "expressions of discontent" and a determination among the people to "break their chains." He told Steward that "England would have to say her prayer within three years" and used terms such as "the white man" and "the colored man" to speak of the desire to drive the English merchants out of the Indian trade, especially out of the cotton industry. Steward could not verify the veracity of this man's story concerning a nascent movement for Indian independence, but he used the conversation as a way to show "the effect of England's Colorphobia."[61] The last paragraph of the manuscript fragment about the Filipinos focused on the notion of unity between the "East Indian, Chinese, Filipinos, and the Afro-American." Steward noted that they readily mingled and that color appeared to be "growing into a bond of union among them." From this he inferred that it was each of these groups' commitment to religion that solidified this unity. "It is among these people that you find deep and all controlling *religion*, he wrote. "Fear and devotion with respect to things divine and reverence for parents among East Indians, Chinese, Japanese, and Filipinos so far as I have observed exceed anything I had ever imagined before."[62]

These Filipino experiences pushed Steward back to connecting his concern for race with his earlier discussion regarding Christianity. In his 1900 diary, which he published in his autobiography, Steward indicated that nothing was clearer than "the fact that the color question is dividing the world." Harkening back to his discussion in *The End of the World*, Steward feared that just as it was "wicked to be *black* in America," the day would come when it would "be wicked to be *white*." But now Steward extended this to the international scene: "It is not Christianity that is dividing the world but COLOR. The color line is an awful fact; and on it the world's great battle is to come, either economically or with the sword. It is a most happy thing for the American Negro that he has been kicked, cuffed and shot out of the white race. This excludes him from the destiny of that race and allots him a portion with the age to come."[63] Steward's experience in Asia rekindled his concern for the consummation of this age and the arrival of the new age to come. The age of the Anglo-Saxon, even with the rise of imperialism, seemed to Steward to be at the beginning of the end. As noted earlier, Steward vacillated once again toward an exceptionalist position regarding race while expanding his ideas on race to encompass an international perspective. He was never entirely stable in his view on this matter.

After his experience in the Philippines, Steward was now concerned for the development of a new leadership for the rising age he anticipated for the African and Asian. Writing to the *Christian Recorder* about his experience in the Philippines, he gave his readers a glimpse of his future goals. Looking toward his retirement from the army in five years, he indicated that he wanted to spend the remainder of his life "helping to train young colored men from the United States, from the West Indies, from the Philippines and from India, as well as Africa, for the great work of preaching the gospel to the New World that is now struggling for birth." This struggle, "painted as the death struggle is, in my belief, the birth struggle. Light is again to come from the East, and a new wave will break forth to take its westward march. The pigmented races are to arise and shine creating a language and a literature entirely free from the fallacies, sophistries and contempt of race prejudice."[64] This proved to be an accurate prediction of his future endeavors. After mustering out of the military in 1906, Steward joined the faculty of Wilberforce University, where he continued his lifelong efforts at "race improvement" through liberal arts education.

Steward at Wilberforce University

As late as 1920, Steward, then seventy-seven years old, wrote two other articles regarding race and imperialism. These articles reiterated Steward's internal conflict over issues of race, civilization, and religion. He was hopeful but not certain that Western civilization could raise itself above the question of color and be inclusive of people of color. If it could not, then it would pass away and, possibly in a violent manner, give rise to a new age of people of color.

In "The Race Issue, So-Called, a Social Matter Only," Steward argued that to be forced outside of the civil and political structures is to "be almost dehumanized." Yet he felt so strongly about these structures, he argued that "if one should come in possession of civil and political rights all else would regulate itself. Men are therefore sometimes content to urge their claims for these rights as special, and leave the social matter out of sight."[65] Sympathetic and "enlightened white friends" demand equal rights in the area of politics and voting boxes, and call for full citizenship participation for African Americans in the "name of our common Americanism," he argued, but at the same time "they stand firmly on the ground that he should continue to be a social outlaw." Steward contended that the objection to civil and political rights for blacks stemmed for the most part from "the unwillingness of whites to admit him into the body social, as an actual partaker of and partner in, all that is meant when the terms Americanism, and American people are used."[66] Whites in America had conspired with whites of other countries in "forming a social compact into which no man marked by them as 'colored' can enter," he asserted. According to this compact, "colored" people must not be allowed in "business prominence, political place, military rank, [or] literary eminence" because once admitted, they might "overcome the social barriers which now exist." Steward argued that "[t]he fiction of race is often invoked to excuse not only the absurdity of this claim of superiority, but also the many horrid outrages which arise from this essentially immoral base."[67]

All of what Steward called the anthropological sciences (physiology, philology, and sociology), as well as chemistry and medical science, he asserted, demonstrated the fact that the notion of race was a fiction and that "the human race was one." As the study of comparative religion pointed to the oneness of God, it also pointed to the oneness of humanity. Steward felt that this was especially true for Christianity as he understood it. Reaching straight back to his AME heritage, he wrote, "One humanity and one God and Father of us all, are the two summaries of its anthropology and its theology."[68]

Entering further into religious language, Steward warned that error and falsehood would soon fade and that either Christ's kingdom would stand or "the gates of hell will have prevailed over the Church which He

Himself built upon the Rock." Reaffirming his faith, Steward declared that the "enormous falsehood of inferior races must disappear and the enormous fraud practiced upon so large a body of mankind must cease," or it will be possible to maintain that man had "set at nought the reign of truth and God": "I arraign not merely the outrages, the lynchings, the seductions, the rapes, the robberies and murders, the vile subjection of unprotected females, but the whole false and wicked system which makes a large body of civilized and Christian people social outlaws. The evil is fundamental, and in this land universal, although varying somewhat in degree in different localities."[69]

As for a prediction concerning the future, Steward, characteristically, offered two different options. The first prospect was optimistic, an echo of his conclusion in *Our Civilization* that civilization could, as flowing water, purify itself of the dross by stirring the human conscience. Humanity had the capacity for self-critique and change. In the age of the new science of psychology, people were well aware of the concept of conscience. Steward argued that if the conscience could be awakened "as God's witness to truth," it would draw humans to be obedient to its claims, and victory over racism would be won without the threat of strife. "Men will see the truth and see the God of truth, and will arise to the glory of His kingdom," he proclaimed.

The second option, decidedly more pessimistic, was the way of violent revolution. If humanity would not listen to reason, it would listen to violence, blood, and burnings that Steward suggested might shake the world "more than Calvary's tragedy." To suggest that this potential revolution would agitate the world more than Christ's death on the cross revealed the weight Steward gave his concern for racism and its effects on all humanity. He ended this article with a benediction: "Let us pray that such a lot may not befall the present day civilization. But we know, unless all nature is a lie, that when God shall arise and the order for action is given, the bugles of the Almighty will never sound retreat."[70]

We get some hint that Steward at least partially believed his own millennial predictions of the consummation of the Anglo-Saxon age in an article he wrote in July 1920, "The White World Peril Fore=cast [*sic*] and Facts, Lothrop Stoddard's Book." The article was a short review of Lothrop Stoddard's book, *Rising Tide of Color against White World Supremacy.*[71] Born in New England, Stoddard received a law degree and doctorate from

Harvard University and was one of the more significant racial theorists of the interwar period.[72] Steward compared his own prophesy—the demise of the Anglo-Saxon age through war and the ascendancy of the darker races—with Stoddard's view of the world. Stoddard felt that the white world was destroying itself, particularly through the Great War, which had just ended. With the energy of whites spent fighting among themselves, he felt they were leaving themselves too weak to ward off what he called "the rising tide of people of color." His fear was that African and Asian people would take over as whites dissipated their energies fighting among themselves. Steward felt that this book, though based on a racist premise, vindicated his predictions in *The End of the World* more than thirty years earlier:[73] "Having reached the end of its journey geographically, it is rapidly reaching its limit intellectually and physically, . . . the nations which now dominate the earth and the race which now would regard itself as the power behind the throne in the Divine administration, will have fulfilled their day and their mission, and new nations born, as it were, in a day, will come out of darkness and walk in the light of the one great God, with whom there are no superior races and no inferior races."[74]

Steward vacillated between the exceptionalist and the universalist positions much of his life. Clearly he was not a full-fledged black nationalist of the Bishop Turner or Marcus Garvey varieties. His military experiences with whites, his long view of Western civilization as expressed in *Our Civilization,* and his general optimism toward human moral agency had influenced his thought far too much for him to feel comfortable in this camp. Yet his experiences in the Reconstruction South, his intellectual musing in *The End of the World* on race, imperialism, and the Protestant experience, and his later encounters in the Philippines helped to temper Steward's optimism toward humanity's capacity for good. Specifically, he questioned the ability of the white race to rid itself of racism, and he continued to see the potential for people of color to model a new age of Christian equality.

Conclusion

Theophilus G. Steward lived a long, full, and active life. He was a complex man who immersed himself in the life of a rapidly changing America. It was an America that shifted in technology, philosophy, and theology; an America that held out a dream of freedom and equality for African Americans and then dashed it cruelly. Born in 1843, Steward lived through the end of chattel slavery, he lived through the tumultuous Reconstruction period, and he lived to see legal second-class citizenship institutionalized in the form of Jim Crow laws and segregation laws throughout the United States, especially in the South. During his lifetime, white benevolence molded into white paternalism. Steward watched—and participated—as America extended its imperial control over peoples of color in the Americas, Africa, and Asia.

Steward was first and foremost a thinker. He did not follow the traditional path and of thinkers who consciously sit down and develop a theological or philosophical road map by which to live or teach. Rather, his theology evolved with his changing circumstances and opportunities. It is clear that throughout his life he was constantly in a process of shifting and reassessing his philosophy and theology. He worked toward a vision of an integrated society that was grounded in a strong commitment to blacks determining their own destiny. In nearly every thing he did and wrote, Steward's first avenue of engagement was theological. He deeply believed that African Americans could only develop as a people if they developed a theological framework and approach that could address the evolving scientific and modern trends of the day.

One of the facets and dimensions of Steward that made him stand out in his time was understanding the importance of developing a theological underpinning for the African American church, which would provide a guide to understanding the changing intellectual world of his day. He felt that his theology had to be rational yet still retain the basic beliefs of the Christian faith. This combination, he believed, would be able to respond to the challenges of science and modernity. At the same time, he had to relate to a church that was largely theologically conservative and predominantly composed of poorly educated ministers. Attempting to maneuver between these various forces was difficult at best. Eventually, Steward and his theology were branded too controversial by conservative forces in the AME church. Part of the controversy over his theology came as a result of his commitment to education as a tool to develop self-determination.

Throughout Steward's life, education remained a central theme. He was both a teacher and advocate for education at almost every major period of his life. Steward believed that if African Americans were going to exercise self-determination and create a civil society, education was essential. The major purpose of education was to develop two spheres within the individual: the intellect, which responded to a classical liberal arts education, and moral character. Striking a balance between these two spheres was not easy. Steward's views on precisely how the educational process was to be carried out changed over the course of his life. Over time, he lessened his earlier focus on the importance of classical education and the development of the mind, instead placing emphasis on the importance of moral force. He never gave up his concern for the cultivation of the mind, yet his change of venue from the church as the primary institution of civil society to the military provided him with a different set of lenses through which to view African Americans' struggles for educational attainment. His involvement with poor black soldiers helped him see the limitations of classical training in this population. Steward was not opposed to technical education; on the contrary, he felt that African Americans must develop at all levels if they were to become self-determining and self-sufficient. This shift in focus from classical education to moral training could be interpreted as a move toward a more conservative perspective, although Steward saw this as merely playing two sides of the same coin.

There are parallels between Steward's changing attitudes toward theology and his developing educational philosophy. During his military experience, Steward revised his more liberal theological beliefs, those that helped to ostracize him from the church he had served for so long. He maintained his view of the compatibility of science and Christianity. He was clearly representative of the African American wing of the liberal evangelical tradition, and he continued his study of rapidly developing scientific and evolutionary theories. But through the genre of fiction, Steward showed the dangerous outer limits of theological liberalism beyond which he felt one could not maintain a proper moral perspective.

Steward lived in tensions that in some ways were irreconcilable. On the one hand, he was committed to a notion of American democracy that he felt was the most highly evolved type of civilization on Earth. In fact, as Martin Luther King Jr. would seventy years later, Steward regarded the idea of democracy as the pinnacle of modern civilization. Democracy had its flaws, such as racism, but these defects could be cleaned up. On the other hand, because of his vision for African American self-determination and civil society, Steward was driven to critique American racism and imperialism. He wanted to prove that African Americans could also build a cultured society.

At times these two visions converged, and at other times they con- flicted. Steward could critique Josiah Strong because Strong privileged Anglo-Saxons as guardians of Christian civilization and its development. But Steward's involvement with the U.S. military at points seemed con- tradictory to his strong stance against the racist ideologies of the period. Yet he saw the military as a way for African Americans to access a broader society and to grow in discipline and moral virtue. He felt these moral virtues were important to prepare African Americans for participation in democracy in general and institutions of black civil society in particular. He also saw blacks' military participation as a way of earning good will in white American society by proving that African Americans were as capable and loyal as whites.

Through his military experience, especially in the Philippines, Steward broadened his notion of racism. He made an international connection between racism and imperialism, challenging the United States to change its foreign policies regarding Haiti, Puerto Rico, Cuba, and the Philippines during a time when they were coming under attack by American and other powers. Steward asked the United States to recognize these nations' rights to self-determination as well.

Throughout his life, Steward was a man driven to find ways, through the church, theology, education, and the military, to build strategies of self-determination for the African American community which would allow them to participate in the larger American society.

Steward died at Wilberforce University doing what he loved: training young African American men and women to be leaders in a rapidly changing world, one which was still hostile to this group of talented students. He died somewhat alienated from the AME Church, the very institution which nurtured him as a child and young adult, providing him with adventure and opportunities to serve the African American community during one of the most critical periods in American history. It was in the AME Church that he learned the nature of politics and the value of education, and it was here that he was encouraged to excel academically. He placed much hope in the church as the institution which would elevate African Americans to new heights. For Steward this vision was only partially fulfilled. This does not mean that his life should be seen in some tragic sense; rather, we should see him as one of many African American leaders who dedicated their lives to the task of uplifting their people, the church, and the world with a hopeful and triumphant vision for humankind. This triumphant and hopeful vision for humankind still raises challenges for contemporary black theologians and religious thinkers in their quest for the creation of a late-twentieth-century version of "civil society."

As Steward understood that the world around him was changing, he broadened himself to explore other institutions which might aid the pursuit of African American self-determination. As Steward's situation changed, so did his strategies. What sometimes appeared to be contradiction may in fact have been an expression of his creativity, a creativity that was critical during the nadir period, when new options, ones in addition to the black church, needed to be found. He did not have the luxury of overlooking any possible option or arena which could be used as an instrument of change. Though very much a man of his time, Steward left a legacy that remains useful today for any who seek to follow him.

Notes

Introduction

1. James H. Cone, *Black Power and Black Theology,* Twentieth Anniversary Edition (New York: HarperSanFrancisco, 1989).
2. Gayraud S. Wilmore, *Black Religion and Black Radicalism: An Interpretation of the Religious History of African Americans,* 3d ed. (Maryknoll, N.Y.: Orbis Books, 1998).
3. For a critique of this movement and its limited impact on the majority of African American churches, see the chapter titled "The New Black Revolution: The Black Consciousness Movement and the Black Church," in *The Black Church in the African American Experience,* by C. Eric Lincoln and Lawrence H. Mamiya (Durham, N.C.: Duke Univ. Press, 1990), 164–95.
4. In the African American historical context Cornel West has used Gramsci's term "organic intellectual" to categorize a particular type of black leadership in the nineteenth and twentieth centuries. See his book *Prophetic Fragments* (Grand Rapids, Mich., and Trenton, N.J.: William B. Eerdmans Publishing and African World Press, 1988), 3. See also Antonio Gramsci, *Selections from the Prison Notebooks of Antonio Gramsci,* ed. and trans. Quintin Hoare and Geoffrey Nowell Smith (New York: International Publishers, 1983), 3–23.
5. Reverdy C. Ransom, *The Pilgrimage of Harriet Ransom's Son* (Nashville: AME Sunday School Union, n.d.), 66.
6. For a chronological look at the life of Theophilus Gould Steward, see William Seraile, *Voice of Dissent: Theophilus Gould Steward (1843–1924) and Black America* (Brooklyn, N.Y.: Carlson Publishing, 1992).
7. See Rayford W. Logan, *The Betrayal of the Negro: From Rutherford B. Hayes to Woodrow Wilson* (London: Collier Books, 1965) (originally published as *The Negro in American Life and Thought: The Nadir, 1877–1901* [New York: Dial, 1954]). Historians have debated as the length of time this nadir experience lasted. Logan's first edition of this work limited the time frame from 1877 to 1901. But as a result of the broad discussion Logan extended the

period to the end of Woodrow Wilson's presidency in 1921. This broadened time period coincides with Steward's ministry and life, as he was active as both a minister and thinker during this time.

8. W. E. B. Du Bois, *The Souls of Black Folk* (1903; New York: A Signet Classic, 1969), 45.

9. Evelyn Brooks Higginbotham, *Righteous Discontent: The Women's Movement in the Black Baptist Church 1880–1920* (Cambridge: Harvard Univ. Press, 1993), 10. Jürgen Habermas popularized the notion of the "public sphere," the term Higginbotham uses for what I am calling "civil society." Habermas indicated that the public sphere was the "realm of our social life in which something approaching public opinion can be formed." See Jürgen Habermas, "The Public Sphere: An Encyclopedia Article (1964)," *New German Critique* 1 (Fall 1974): 49–55.

10. Peter L. Berger and Richard John Neuhaus, *To Empower People: The Role of Mediating Structures in Public Policy* (Washington, D.C.: American Enterprise Institute for Public Policy Research, 1977), 2. G. W. F. Hegel understood civil society to be that sphere or those institutions in society that stood between the family and the state or the governing institution which controlled the lives of individuals. See G. W. F. Hegel, *Elements of the Philosophy of Right*, ed. Allen W. Wood and trans. H. B. Nisbet (Cambridge: Cambridge Univ. Press, 1991). Hegel further indicated that civil society was "an association of members as self-sufficient individuals in what is therefore a formal universality, occasioned by their needs and by the legal constitution as a means of security for persons and property, and by an external order for their particular and common interests." Hegel, *Elements*, 198.

11. Berger and Neuhaus, *To Empower People*, 3.

12. Higginbotham, *Righteous Discontent*, 10.

13. See Cornel West, *Prophesy Deliverance! An Afro-American Revolutionary Christianity* (Philadelphia: Westminster Press, 1982), 71–72. West theorizes that the African American exceptionalist tradition praises the uniqueness and superiority of African American culture and personality. The assimilationist tradition sees African American culture and personality as pathological. The marginalist tradition postulates that African American culture is restrictive, constraining, and confining.

14. Ibid., 71.

15. Theophilus Gould Steward, *Fifty Years in the Gospel Ministry: From 1864 to 1914*, with an introduction by Rev. Reverdy C. Ransom (Philadelphia: AME Book Concern, n.d.), 287.

16. William Steward to Edwin P. Smith, 21 May 1869, American Missionary Association Archives, Fisk Univ..

17. Barbara J. Fields, "Ideology and Race in American History," in *Region, Race, and Reconstruction: Essays in Honor of C. Vann Woodward*, ed. J. Morgan Kousser and James M. McPherson (New York: Oxford Univ. Press, 1982), 144. Much has been written about the social construction of the idea of race. For

a discussion of the distinction of racial social construction, see Lucius Outlaw, "Toward a Critical Theory of 'Race,'" in *Anatomy of Racism,* ed. David Theo Goldberg (Minneapolis: Univ. of Minnesota Press, 1990), 58–82. For a discussion of the origin of modern racism, see West, *Prophesy Deliverance!* especially chapter 2. For a discussion of the intersection of race, class, and gender as social construction, see Evelyn Brooks Higginbotham, "African-American Women's History and the Metalanguage of Race," *Signs* 17, no. 2 (Winter 1992): 251–74.

18. Steward, *Fifty Years,* 287, 288, 70.
19. Although Gouldtown was a rural community, it may have fit the pattern of larger communities in terms of its notions of skin color and social stratification and class makeup in northern cities. Lighter-skinned blacks were more likely to be emancipated and tended to have greater access to opportunities than their darker counterparts. For a discussion of this phenomenon, see Theodore Hershberg and Henry Williams, "Mulattos and Blacks: Intra-group Color Differences and Social Stratification in Nineteenth-Century Philadelphia," in *Philadelphia: Work, Space, Family, and Group Experience in the Nineteenth/ Century: Essays toward an Interdisciplinary History of the City,* ed. Theodore Hershberg (New York: Oxford Univ. Press, 1981), 392–434.
20. From studies of mulattos in three northern antebellum cities it is clear that mulattos tended to be financially better off and to have greater access to literacy and education than their black counterparts. They also tended to follow self-conscious marriage patterns of marrying other mulattos, thus establishing a clear caste and class arrangement. For a discussion of this recurring arrangement, see James Oliver Horton, "Shades of Color: The Mulatto in Three Antebellum Northern Communities," *Afro-Americans in N. Y. Life and History* 8, no. 2 (July 1984): 37–59.
21. This self-determination among Gouldtowners was misleadingly termed "black nationalism" by Clement Alexander Price in *Freedom Not Far Distant.* Price attempted to describe the formation and continuation of Gouldtown as a racially separate community. He argued that these communities separated themselves from other black communities based on their mulatto distinctions. However, Price overstated his claim that these communities were expressions of black nationalism. Clement Alexander Price, ed., *Freedom Not Far Distant: A Documentary History of Afro-Americans in New Jersey* (Newark: New Jersey Historical Society, 1980), 134–35.
22. Du Bois, *Souls of Black Folk,* with introductions by Nathan Hare and Alvin F. Poussaint (New York: New American Library, 1982), 54.
23. Examples of this historiography are Sterling Stuckey, *The Ideological Origins of Black Nationalism* (Boston: Beacon Press, 1972), 1–29, and John H. Bracey Jr., August Meier, and Elliot Rudwick, eds., *Black Nationalism in America* (New York: Bobbs-Merrill, 1970). See their introduction on pages xxv to lx. Even in this volume Meier and Rudwick differ with Bracey on the way they saw black nationalist ideology develop in America. Meier and Rudwick saw an

inconsistent "ebb and flow" while Bracey argued for a clear pattern which was "slow and winding, but persistent and intensifying." See Bracey, Meier, and Rudwick, *Black Nationalism,* lii–lx.

24. It has been debated as to which of these two ideologies have dominated the lives and history of Afro-America. I think that Robert L. Allen in *Black Awakening in Capitalist America* correctly asserts, "A glance at history suggests that it would be more correct to say that nationalism, and overt separatism, are ever-present undercurrents in the collective black psyche which constantly interact with the assimilationist tendency and, in times of crisis, rise to the surface to become major themes."

25. As there is a self-determinationist strategy which could serve the end of either a separatist or an assimilationist philosophy, there is also an inclusivist strategy which could serve the ends of either of these philosophies. Henry H. Garnet, who became a black emigrationist in the 1850s, called upon whites to financially support his efforts in the African Colonization Society. See Joel Schor, *Henry Highland Garnet: A Voice of Black Radicalism in the Nineteenth Century* (Westport, Conn.: Greenwood Press, 1977), 156. Also see Floyd J. Miller, *The Search for a Black Nationality* (Urbana: Univ. of Illinois Press, 1975).

26. Leonard I. Sweet, *Black Images of America, 1784–1870* (New York: W. W. Norton, 1976), 5.

27. See Donald G. Mathews, "The Second Great Awakening as an Organizing Process," in *Religion in American History: Interpretive Essays,* ed. John M. Mulder and John F. Wilson (Englewood Cliffs, N.J.: Prentice-Hall, 1978) 199–217.

28. The issue of America's rapid industrialization and its impact on African Americans is not directly confronted in Steward's writing. Obviously his work on education relates to this theme. Other African American clerical contemporaries were taking up the issue of industrialization and its impact on the black community. For instance, see a Thanksgiving Day sermon given by the Reverend Reverdy C. Ransom titled "The Industrial and Social Condition of the Negro." It was delivered on 26 November 1896 at Bethel AME Church in Chicago and printed in the *A.M.E. Church Review* (Jan.–Mar. 1988): 9–17.

29. See Paul Griffin, "The Theology of Black Rational Orthodoxy, 1863 to 1935" (paper presented at the annual meeting of the American Academy of Religion, Atlanta, Ga., 22–25 Nov. 1986), 8–9. See also Griffin's *Black Theology as the Foundation of Three Methodist Colleges* (Washington, D.C.: Univ. of America Press, 1984).

30. Griffin, "Theology of Black Rational Orthodoxy," 8.

31. Theophilus Gould Steward, *The End of the World; or, Clearing the Way for the Fullness of the Gentiles,* with an Exposition of Psalm 68:31 by James A. Handy, D.D. (Philadelphia: AME Church Book Rooms, 1888); Josiah Strong, *Our Country,* 2d ed. (New York: Baker and Taylor, 1891; reprint, Cambridge: Belknap Press, Harvard Univ. Press, 1963).

Chapter 1

1. Theophilus Gould Steward, *Memoirs of Mrs. Rebecca Steward, Containing a Full Sketch of Her Life, with Various Selections from Her Writings and Letters; Also Contributions from Bishop Campbell, D.D., Prof. B. F. Lee of Wilberforce University, B. T. Tanner, D.D., Editor of the Christian Recorder, Rev. T. Gould, Mrs. Elizabeth Lloyd, and Wm. Steward* (Philadelphia: Publications Department of the AME Church, 1877), 18, and *My First Four Years in the Itinerary of the African Methodist Episcopal Church* (Brooklyn: n.p., 1876), 3; Theophilus Steward, with William Steward, *Gouldtown: A Very Remarkable Settlement of Ancient Date* (Philadelphia: J. B. Lippincott, 1913), 95.

2. It is not clear if Gould's legal status was free, indentured, or slave.

3. See Steward, *Gouldtown*, 9–56, especially 50, and see also Steward, *Memoirs*, 11–15.

4. For a comparison with other "mulatto" communities who saw themselves as Afro-Americans see Barry Brewton, *Almost White* (Toronto: Collier, 1969), 165–70. See also Joel Williamson, *New People: Miscegenation and Mulattoes in the United States* (New York: Free Press, 1980).

5. Steward, *Gouldtown*, 12.

6. Ibid., 19.

7. Steward, *Fifty Years*, ix.

8. Steward, letter, Theophilus Gould Steward Papers, Archive Collection, Schomburg Center for Research in Black Culture, New York Public Library (hereafter cited as Steward Papers).

9. Bishop Payne was seen as the mentor for several generations of young clergy. For an example of his mentoring role in the development of church leadership, see William B. Gravely, "James Lynch and the Black Christian Mission During Reconstruction," in *Black Apostles at Home and Abroad: Afro-Americans and the Christian Mission from the Revolution to Reconstruction*, ed. David W. Wills and Richard Newman (Boston: G. K. Hall, 1982), 161–88. For a look at the life of Daniel A. Payne, see Josephus Roosevelt Coan, *The Life of Daniel Alexander Payne LL.D.* (Philadelphia: AME Book Concern 1935) and see Payne's autobiography, *Recollections of Seventy Years* with an introduction by Rev. F. J. Grimké (Nashville: Publishing House of the AME Sunday School Union, 1888).

10. Steward, *Fifty Years*, 91.

11. Ibid., 65. See also M. A. Broadstone, "Rev. Theophilus Gould Steward and S. Maria Steward, M.D.," in *History of Greene County, Ohio* (Indianapolis: B. F. Bowen, 1918), 2:971.

12. All but three of the sons survived Steward in death. Stephen died in infancy in 1876 of tuberculosis. James, the eldest son, died in Washington in June 1893. Before his death, he graduated from the Institute for Colored Children,

the well-known school in Philadelphia run by Fannie Jackson Coppin. James was trained as a carriage maker and was certified "at the highest grade" to teach school in Washington. Walter also preceded his father in death in 1904 at eighteen years old. The remaining sons obtained higher education and became professionals in their respective fields. Charles and Frank, after completing high school in Washington and one year at Philips Exeter Academy in New Hampshire, attended Harvard University. Charles became a successful dentist after graduation from Tufts University medical school in Boston. He married Maude Trotter, the daughter of Boston activist William Monroe Trotter. Together, Charles and Maude Steward became socialites and civil rights activists in black Boston. Frank attended law school at Harvard University and became a captain in the Forty-Ninth volunteer regiment during the Spanish-American War. He later became a practicing lawyer in Pittsburgh and an elector for the Electoral College in Pennsylvania. Benjamin, trained as a physician at the University of Minnesota Medical School, established a medical practice in Boston. Theophilus Bolden graduated from Wilberforce University and became a high school teacher in Kansas City, Missouri. Gustavus Adolphus also graduated from Wilberforce University. He later completed a theology degree from Oberlin School of Theology and eventually became part owner of a black-owned, Columbus–based insurance company, the Supreme Life and Casualty Company.

13. For a discussion of the role of Henry McNeal Turner in Georgia politics, see Stephen Ward Angell, *Bishop Henry McNeal Turner and the African-American Religion in the South* (Knoxville: Univ. of Tennessee Press, 1992), 91.

14. Scarborough's father was a member of the Macon A. M. E. Church. Steward mentions the tutorial relationship with Scarborough in his Journal 1868–1871, Steward Papers (hereafter cited as Steward, Journal 1868–1871).

15. Coppin was to later follow Steward in his graduation from the Divinity School of the Protestant Episcopal Church in West Philadelphia in 1887. Levi J. Coppin, *Unwritten History* (1919; reprint, New York: Negro Univ. Press, 1968), 199. Steward, *Fifty Years,* 144–45; Steward, *Fifty Years,* 148.

16. Theophilus Gould Steward, *My First Four Years in the Itinerary of the African Methodist Episcopal Church* (Brooklyn: By the Author, 1876), and Steward, *Memoirs.*

17. Steward, *Fifty Years,* 157–66, 166. Steward indicated that his Hebrew teacher was William L. Roy, author of *A New Catechetical Hebrew and English Grammar* (New York: Stanford & Swords, 1854).

18. See Rufus L. Perry, *The Cushite; or, The Descendants of Ham as Found in the Sacred Scriptures and in the Writings of Ancient Historians and Poets from Noah to the Christian Era* (Springfield, Mass.: Willey, 1893). For description on the life of Perry, see the sketch in William J. Simmons, *Men of Mark: Eminent, Progressive and Rising* (Cleveland: Geo M. Rewell, 1887; New York: Arno Press and the New York Times, 1968).

19. Steward, *Fifty Years,* 181–82.

20. Ibid., 225.

21. Theophilus Gould Steward, *Death, Hades, and the Resurrection* (Philadel-
    phia, 1883); *The Divine Attributes: Being an Examination of What Is Said of
    God, with Relation to Nature and Sentiment, and Rational Creatures, with
    Special Treatment of Omnipresence, with Analysis and Notes,* Tawawa Series
    in Systematic Divinity, No. 1 (Philadelphia: Christian Recorder Print, 1884);
    Theophilus Gould Steward, *Genesis Re-Read; or The Latest Conclusions of
    Physical Science, Viewed in Their Relation to the Mosaic Record, To Which Is
    Annexed an Important Chapter on the Direct Evidence of Christianity, by
    Bishop J. P. Campbell, D.D., LL. D.* (Philadelphia: AME Book Rooms, 1885).

22. Steward, *Fifty Years,* 238.

23. Steward, *End of the World.* See also Strong, *Our Country.*

24. The African Methodist Episcopal Church system has historically been organ-
    ized in a hierarchy with bishops presiding over Episcopal districts, a large
    geographical area which is further broken down into smaller districts. Dis-
    trict elders preside over the ministers in the local district under the supervi-
    sion of the bishop. Each local district meets with its clergy on a quarterly
    basis. Each of the local districts under the bishop's jurisdiction meet together
    on an annual basis, thus the annual conference. They elect delegates to the
    general conference who vote on the various laws and policies for the church.

25. See Wesley J. Gaines, *African Methodism in the South; or, Twenty-Five Years of
    Freedom,* with an introduction by W. S. Scarborough (Atlanta: Franklin, 1890).

26. Steward, *Fifty Years,* 240–41, 240.

27. See Charles Killian, "Daniel Payne and the AME General Conference of 1888:
    A Display of Contrasts," *A.M.E. Church Review* 102, no. 330 (Apr.–June
    1988): 10; *Indianapolis News,* 22 May 1888.

28. *Indianapolis News,* 25 May 1888.

29. Steward, *Fifty Years,* 256.

30. Ibid., 266–67.

31. See Steward's comments on Dr. Steward in "Brooklyn News," *Christian
    Recorder,* 31 May 1877, p. 1: "As an event worthy of note, I mention the fact
    that during the afternoon service much to my surprise, Dr Susan S. McKinney
    who has for many years been the acceptable organist of the church and one of
    the most capable and earnest workers in the community came forward and
    united with the church. She was previously a member of St. Paul's Episcopal
    Church, but has at length decided for Methodism. I trust the change will be
    advantages to herself and Bridge St. church however it may affect St. [Paul's]
    church. The cordial welcome she received was decidedly pleasing."

32. McKinney Steward was the physician in residence at Wilberforce University
    in the latter years of her life. For a look at her life, see Broadstone, "Rev.
    Theophilus Gould Steward and S. Maria Steward." See also Maritcha R. Lyons,
    "Susan S. (McKinney) Steward," in *Homespun Heroines and Other Women of*

Distinction, ed. Hallie Q. Brown (Xenia, Ohio: Aldine Publishing, 1926; reprint, Freeport, N.Y.: Books for Libraries Press, 1971). Also see William Seraile, "Susan McKinney Steward: New York States First African-American Woman Physician," *Afro-Americans in New York Life and History,* 9 July 1985, 27–44.

33. See Steward, *Fifty Years,* 365, 274.

34. Theophilus G. Steward, "The Army as a Trained Force," in *Masterpieces of Negro Eloquence,* ed. Alice Moore Dunbar Nelson (New York: Bookery Publishing, 1914; Johnson Reprint Corporation, 1970), 289. This address was delivered to the Chicago AME General Conference in 1904.

35. Steward, *Fifty Years,* 359–63. This military equality was elusive at best as is borne out in American military history. The Brownsville incident was a case in point Steward's own regiment (after his retirement) was dishonorably discharged from the Army on less than convincing evidence. Steward placed most of the blame on the racist environment in Texas rather than on the army and the president of the United States, who discharged the three companies.

36. Steward, "Army as a Trained Force," 290.

37. Theophilus Gould Steward, "Garrisoning Cuba and Porto Rico [*sic*]," *Independent,* 29 Dec. 1898, p. 1927.

38. He was a founding member in the American Negro Academy, an organization of distinguished African American men dedicated to analyzing the condition of the African American community. He wrote two articles for the Academy: "How the Black St. Domingo Legion Saved the Patriot Army in the Siege of Savannah, 1799," *American Negro Academy* 5 (1899), and "Message of San Domingo to the African Race," *Papers of the American Negro Academy,* 28, 29, Dec. 1915, 25–37.

39. Theophilus Gould Steward, *A Charleston Love Story; or, Hortense Vanross* (New York: F. Tennyson Neely, 1899) and Theophilus Gould Steward, *The Colored Regulars in the United States Army: With a Sketch of the History of the Colored American, and an Account of His Services in the Wars of the Country, from the Period of the Revolutionary War to 1899,* Introductory Letter from Lieutenant-General Nelson A. Miles (Philadelphia: AME Book Concern, 1904; reprint, New York: Arno Press and the New York Times, 1969).

40. Theophilus Gould Steward, ed., *Active Service; or, Religious Work Among U.S. Soldiers,* with an introduction by John B. Ketchum, Corresponding Secretary, Etc. (New York: United States Army Aid Association, n.d.).

41. Steward, *Gouldtown,* and Theophilus Gould Steward, *The Haitian Revolution: 1791 to 1804 or Side Lights on the French Revolution* (1971; New York: Russell and Russell, 1914).

Chapter 2

1. This model of Christian egalitarianism was captured in the AME Church's motto, "God our Father; Christ our Redeemer; Man our Brother."

2. Steward, *Fifty Years,* 216–17.

3. Ibid., xvii. At the time of the writing of the introduction to Steward's auto-biography, Ransom was the editor of the *A.M.E. Church Review*. He later became a bishop in the AME Church.

4. Steward, *Memoirs*, 19, 27, 36, 72–73. Gould credited his aunt, Rebecca, as being a mentor for him. "I looked up to her for that advice and counsel which had much to do with shaping my early life," he wrote. "And if I have been worth anything to the church as a minister, her prayers, instructions and counsel have helped to mould me into what I am."

5. Ibid., 47. Steward was not baptized until after he was twenty-one years of age, seven months after he was ordained; see Steward, *My First Four Years*, 7.

6. Steward, *Memoirs*, 19.

7. See Steward, *My First Four Years*, 5–6. It is clear that Gouldtown had a school, the Lummis School, which was moved to Gouldtown in 1834 and dedicated as Ebenezer AME Church and served both as a church and a school until 1860. The present school in Gouldtown was built around this structure (see *Trinity A.M.E. Church Gouldtown, NJ, 200th Year Anniversary 1792–1992*).

8. Steward, *Fifty Years*, 181.

9. See ibid., 148, where Steward indicated that he studied French while in his first pastorate in Delaware, under a "professor from Paris" in preparation for his short and unsuccessful missionary trip to Haiti. He continued his study of French when he was transferred to pastor in Brooklyn, New York. "Before reaching the age of sixteen," Isaiah C. Wears noted, "Steward mastered the studies of surveying and navigation, and made considerable progress in the study of the German language." For an estimation of Steward's facility in the German language, see Isaiah C. Wears, "Rev. Theophilus Gould Steward, D.D., Chaplain U.S. Army," *A.M.E. Church Review* 10 (July 1894): 140. Steward recounted an encounter in South Carolina with a white woman of German ancestry: "The little learning I possessed, being able at that time to converse quite easily in German, seemed to them—the poor whites—almost marvelous" (*Fifty Years*, 69). Steward indicated that he had been tutored in both Hebrew (holding a certificate of proficiency in Hebrew) and Greek prior to his admission to the seminary (*Fifty Years*, 181); T. G. Steward's individual report under G.O. 41, A.G.O. 16 Dec. 1894.

10. Steward, *Fifty Years*, 183; T. G. Steward's individual report under G.O. 41, A.G.O. 16 Dec. 1894.

11. Daniel A. Payne to George Whipple, 6 July 1865, and T. G. Steward to George Whipple, July 1865, American Missionary Association Collection, Amistad Research Center, Tulane Univ. (hereafter cited as AMA Collection). See also Steward, *Fifty Years*, 31–34, 65–66, and 73.

12. For a discussion of the conflict over financial support, particularly the discrepancy in the amount proposed by Bishop Payne and the actual amount received, see Clara Merritt De Boer, "The Role of Afro-Americans in the Origin and Work of the American Missionary Association: 1839–1877" (Ph.D. diss., Rutgers Univ., State Univ. of New Jersey, 1973), 417–18, especially notes 12 and 13.

13. T. G. Steward to George Whipple, July 1865 and 10 Nov. 1865, AMA Collection.
14. Steward, *Fifty Years*, 73. NEFAS in 1865 joined with several other smaller freedmen's associations and created the American Freedmen's Aid Commission (AFAC). It was a loose coalition of freedmen's associations from the Northeast and Midwest. As shall be seen later, the issue of religion created an ideological breach in the AFAC. The Northeast organizations, of which NEFAS was one, based in Boston, New York, and Philadelphia, adhered to a secular educational philosophy. The Midwest groups, primarily in Cincinnati and Chicago, were much more evangelical in their educational philosophy. The AFAC disbanded in 1869. For a discussion of the various freedmen's aid societies, see Robert C. Morris, *Reading, 'Riting, and Reconstruction: The Education of Freedmen in the South, 1861–1870* (Chicago: Univ. of Chicago Press, 1981), 1–53.
15. "The Union Commission," *American Missionary,* Nov. 1866, 246, 249.
16. Joe M. Richardson, *Christian Reconstruction: The American Missionary Association and Southern Blacks, 1861–1890* (Athens: Univ. of Georgia Press, 1986), 73. See also Richard B. Drake, "Freedman's Aid Societies and Sectional Compromise," *Journal of Southern History* 29, no. 2 (May 1963): 176–77.
17. See O. B. Frothingham, "Education and Religion," *Independent* 18 (12 July 1866): 1. For a discussion of this debate, see also Ronald E. Butchart, *Northern Schools, Southern Blacks, and Reconstruction: Freedmen's Education, 1862– 1875* (Westport, Conn.: Greenwood Press, 1980), 33–52.
18. Frothingham, "Education and Religion," 1. See also "The Union Commission," *American Missionary,* Nov. 1866, 248.
19. See the *Boston Recorder,* 10 Aug. 1866; "Union Commission," 248–49.
20. Butchart, *Northern Schools,* 49.
21. By 1873, the AMA had softened its aggressive policy of freedperson's education in the South. The economic crisis brought on by the depression of that same year contributed to this change. Reconstruction historian Richard B. Drake has argued that the AMA departed from its insistence upon immediate racial equality and compromised with the developing white southern power structure. By 1878, the AMA denied that it had ever claimed that the races were equal but rather that "all men shall be regarded as equal before God and the law." Drake, "Freedman's Aid Societies," 182–83.
22. T. G. Steward to Strieby and Whipple, 28 June 1865, AMA Collection.
23. Steward, *Fifty Years,* 100.
24. Ibid.
25. Ibid., 101.
26. Ibid., 101, 102.
27. Ibid. 102–3.
28. Prov. 8:14: "Counsel is mine, and sound wisdom: I am understanding; I have strength"; Francis Bacon, "Meditationes Sacrae," in *The Works of Francis Bacon, Baron of Verulam, Viscount St. Albans, and Lord High Chancellor of England,* collected and edited by James Spedding, Robert Leslie Ellis, and

Douglas Denon Heath (Boston: Brown and Taggard, 1860), 14:95. The actual quote reads, "[F]or knowledge itself is power."

29. Steward, *Fifty Years,* 104.
30. The sermon, preached on 1 November 1868 during his pastorate in Macon, Georgia, was later published in a book of six sermons, five of which were preached in South Carolina and Georgia; see Theophilus Gould Steward, *Pioneer Echoes* (Baltimore: Hoffman, 1889).
31. Steward, *Pioneer Echoes,* 31–34.
32. Ibid., 36–37.
33. Ibid., 37.
34. Ibid., 37–38.
35. Ibid., 38.
36. Ibid., 39. In developing his later theological work, *The End of the World,* Steward drew upon the works of English geologist Hugh Miller, especially *The Testimony of the Rocks; or, Geology in Its Bearings on the Two Theologies, Natural and Revealed* (Boston: Gould and Lincoln, 1857). See also Miller's autobiography, *An Autobiography. My Schools and Schoolmasters; or, The Story of My Education* (Boston: Gould and Lincoln, 1857).
37. William H. Becker, "The Black Church: Manhood and Mission," *Journal of the American Academy of Religion* 40, no. 3 (Sept. 1972): 317. He contended that the term had four distinguishable but interrelated aspects, as they were evidenced in the black church tradition: (1) leadership, self-assertion, (2) independence, (3) black identity, and (4) vocation.
38. Steward, *Pioneer Echoes,* 39–40.
39. Albert J. Raboteau, "'Ethiopia Shall Soon Stretch Forth Her Hands': Black Destiny in Nineteenth-Century America" (University Lecture in Religion at Arizona State Univ., 27 Jan. 1983), 5.
40. Steward, *Pioneer Echoes,* 40.
41. For a good discussion of Steward's involvement in the Delaware educational struggle, see Ronald L. Lewis, "Reverend T. G. Steward and the Education of Blacks in Reconstruction Delaware," *Delaware History* 19 (Spring–Summer 1981).
42. See Harold B. Hancock, "The Status of the Negro in Delaware after the Civil War, 1865–75," *Delaware History* 13 (Apr. 1968): 61; and Harold C. Livesay, "Delaware Blacks, 1865–1915," in *Readings in Delaware History,* ed. Carol E. Hoffecker (Newark: Univ. of Delaware Press, 1973), 126.
43. For a glimpse of the condition of Afro-American life in Delaware see Hancock, "Status of the Negro," 57–63.
44. Laws of Delaware, XIII, C. 81; quoted from Hancock, "Status of the Negro," 60.
45. Carol E. Hoffecker, "The Politics of Exclusion: Blacks in Late Nineteenth-Century Wilmington, Delaware," *Delaware History* 16, no. 1 (Apr. 1974): 65. See also Amy M. Hiller, "The Disfranchisement of Delaware Negroes in the Late Nineteenth Century," *Delaware History* 8 (1966): 124–53.

46. "Colored Men in Council," *Delaware State Journal,* 28 Sept. 1872; see also "Colored Convention," *Delaware State Journal,* 21 Dec. 1872.
47. Hancock, "Status of the Negro," 64; Theophilus Gould Steward, "Religious and Social Condition of the Colored People of Delaware" *Christian Recorder,* 3 Apr. 1873, p. 8.
48. Lewis, "Reverend T. G. Steward and the Education of Blacks," 160.
49. The association was initially called the Delaware Association for the Moral Improvement and Education of the Colored People. See Henry C. Conrad, *A Glimpse of the Colored Schools of Delaware: A Paper Read before the Annual Meeting of the State Teachers' Association, Held at Rehoboth Beach, Delaware, August 21, 1883* (Wilmington, Del.: James and Webb, 1883), 6.
50. "Colored Education." *Daily Commercial,* 12 Mar. 1870.
51. Conrad, *Glimpse of the Colored Schools,* 9; "Colored Education." *Daily Commercial,* 12 Mar. 1870.
52. Conrad, *Glimpse of the Colored Schools,* 7.
53. Linda Perkins, in "Fanny Jackson Coppin and the Institute for Colored Youth: A Model of Nineteenth Century Black Female Educational and Community Leadership, 1837–1902" (Ph.D. diss., Univ. of Illinois at Urbana-Champaign, 1978), 109, suggested that in the early 1870s, in spite of the fact that the Philadelphia Quakers aided blacks in developing and funding segregated educational institution such as the Institute for Colored Youth, "most were unusually silent on issues that would elevate and aid blacks politically or economically." It was not clear whether this attitude was the same in Delaware as in Philadelphia, but what was clear was the Quaker-dominated Delaware Association for the Education of Colored People's reluctance to advocate for public funding of black education in the public arena.
54. Steward, *Fifty Years,* 146.
55. Ibid., 148.
56. Day (1825–1900), born free in New York City, was an abolitionist, editor of several periodicals, an educator, and an AMEZ minister. During his stay in the mid-Atlantic states, he was assigned to the Freedman's Aid Association and became the inspector general of schools for the refugees and freedmen in Maryland and Delaware. In 1869, at great risk to his life, he organized blacks as voters. For more on Day, see Rayford W. Logan and Michael R. Winston, eds., *Dictionary of American Negro Biography* (New York: W. W. Norton, 1982), 163–65; and Simmons, *Men of Mark,* 978–84.
57. "Colored Men in Council."
58. Livesay, "Delaware Blacks," 128. Livesay suggested that the limited victory of the Republican Party was aided by a split in the state Democratic Party ranks with some animosity toward Greeley, who headed both the Liberal Republican Party and the Democratic Party tickets. As a result of this animus some attempted to organize a "White Man's Party" but were unsuccessful (see "The White Men," *Delaware State Journal,* 17 Aug. 1872).
59. Hiller, "Disfranchisement of Delaware Negroes," 138.

60. Steward, *Fifty Years,* 147–48; Lewis, "Reverend T. G. Steward and the Education of Blacks," 163.
61. "Colored Convention"; the article was also printed in *Every Evening,* 17 Dec. 1872.
62. The white newspapers named Day's paper *Our Mutual Progress,* but Steward and others listed the periodical as *Our National Progress.*
63. "Colored Convention"; Ronald L. Lewis, in his "Reverend T. G. Steward and the Education of Blacks," incorrectly stated that the opposition came from "white Republicans" (163).
64. "Colored Convention."
65. Ibid.
66. "A Letter from Rev. T. G. Steward," *Every Evening,* 18 Dec. 1872. His response was covered in several periodicals as well. See also *Delaware State Journal,* 21 Dec. 1872.
67. "Letter from Rev. T. G. Steward."
68. Ibid.
69. For a discussion of the conflict between the AMEZ and the AME Churches, see Clarence E. Walker, *A Rock in a Weary Land: The African Methodist Episcopal Church During the Civil War and Reconstruction* (Baton Rouge: Louisiana State Univ. Press, 1982), 94–103; See also Katharine L. Dvorak, *An African-American Exodus: The Segregation of the Southern Churches* (Brooklyn, N.Y.: Carlson Publishing, 1991), 129–32, 138–42.
70. Logan and Winston, *Dictionary of American Negro Biography,* 165.
71. Lewis, "Reverend T. G. Steward and the Education of Blacks," 164. Daniel P. Hamilton, Steward's loyal churchman, was also active on the credentials committee with Steward, and served on the Publications Committee with Levi J. Coppin. Steward wrote and gave the crucial resolution in the convention and he wrote the address which was published to the public. Steward, *Fifty Years,* 193.
72. *Proceedings of the Convention of Colored People,* Dover, Del., 9 Jan. 1873, 4–5.
73. Ibid., 5; "Letter from Rev. T. G. Steward."
74. *Proceedings of the Convention of Colored People,* Dover, Del., 9 Jan. 1873, 6–7; Steward, *Fifty Years,* 147–48; Lewis, "Reverend T. G. Steward and the Education of Blacks," 165–66.
75. "Religious and Social Condition of the Colored People of Delaware," *Christian Recorder,* 3 Apr. 1873, p. 8. He indicated that there were only 25 black pastors in Delaware for a black population of 23,000 with only 5,551 church members.
76. Ibid.
77. Ibid.
78. Ibid.
79. "Colored Schools in Delaware," *Daily Commercial,* 3 Feb. 1875; see also the article which outlined the progress of black education in Delaware in the same issue, "Colored Education in Delaware," *Daily Commercial,* 3 Feb. 1875.

80. Lewis, "Reverend T. G. Steward and the Education of Blacks," 170.

81. Conrad, *Glimpse of the Colored Schools*, 7.

82. Hoffecker, "Politics of Exclusion," 67.

83. Conrad, *Glimpse of the Colored Schools*, 8, 12.

84. Steward, *Fifty Years*, 194.

85. Lewis, "Reverend T. G. Steward and the Education of Blacks," 172, 174.

86. Alice Weld, "Public Education in Delaware," *Christian Recorder*, 7 Dec. 1882. See also Ronald L. Lewis, ed., "Reverend T. G. Stewart and 'Mixed' Schools in Delaware, 1882," *Delaware History* 19 (Spring–Summer 1980): 53–58. This edited article has several inaccuracies, including the misspelling of his name. Lewis corrects these mistakes in his later article which is footnoted above, "Reverend T. G. Steward and the Education." This edited article was based on Alice Weld's recording of Steward's speech and later published in the *Christian Recorder*, 7 Dec. 1882, titled "Public Education in Delaware." She was a member of his congregation.

87. Lewis, "Reverend T. G. Stewart and 'Mixed' Schools," 55–58.

88. Ibid., 58.

89. Conrad, *Glimpse at the Colored Schools*, 13.

90. Steward, *Fifty Years*, 187, 194–95.

91. See "Trouble at Bethel Church," *Morning News*, 30 Apr. 1883; and Steward, *Fifty Years*, 195.

92. Steward, *Fifty Years*, 195–96.

93. Steward's appointment as chaplain of the Twenty-fifth Infantry by President Benjamin Harrison was orchestrated by John Roy Lynch, representative of Mississippi in Congress from 1873 to 1883 and at the time of Steward's appointment auditor of the treasury for the Navy Department (see John Roy Lynch, *Reminiscences of an Active Life: The Autobiography of John Roy Lynch*, ed. and with an introduction by John Hope Franklin [Chicago: Univ. of Chicago Press, 1970], 329–30). Also supporting Steward's nomination was Blanche K. Bruce, the second black senator from Mississippi, who at the time of Steward's nomination was the Washington, D.C., recorder of deeds. Lynch was also partly responsible for the appointment of Bruce as recorder of deeds (from 1889 to 1893). See Lynch, *Reminiscences*, 331–32; Steward, *Fifty Years*, 266–67; Willard B. Gatewood, *Aristocrats of Color: The Black Elite, 1880–1920* (Indianapolis: Indiana Univ. Press, 1990), 35. The third person to support Steward was the Philadelphia businessman and postmaster general of the United States, John Wanamaker. See Steward, *Fifty Years*, 267; John Wanamaker, "Letter to the Secretary of War," 26 May 1891, Selected ACP, T. G. Steward, RG 94, NA; Steward, *Fifty Years*, 267.

94. Monthly Report, T. G. Steward, 18 Nov. 1891, Revised Statutes section, Selected ACP, T. G. Steward, RG 94, NA. See also Act of Congress, 28 July 1866, Chap. 299, Sec. 30. While stationed in the Philippines with his unit, Steward was also given the responsibility of organizing an American-style

school system in Zambales Province for Filipinos; see Theophilus Gould Steward, "Two Years in Luzon. II. Examining Schools, Etc.," *Colored American Magazine,* Jan.–Feb. 1902, 164–70; Steward, *Fifty Years,* 318–35.

95. Earl F. Stover, *Up from Handymen: The United States Army Chaplaincy, 1865–1920* (Washington, D.C.: Office of the Chief of Chaplains, Department of the Army, 1977), 3:88.

96. Stover, *Up from Handymen,* 49. In some ways the post–Civil War army chaplaincy role as educator was an extension of the earlier collaboration of the northern churchmen and the army chaplaincy during the Civil War and southern Reconstruction period. It was not uncommon for chaplains, both active and retired, to serve the new freedpersons. Many of the active chaplains gave instructions to the black Civil War units.

97. In Steward's case he also found the time to supply local Presbyterian and Methodist pulpits when they were without a local pastor. He also delivered eight lectures to the women and spouses of the officers of Fort Missoula: three lectures on Queen Elizabeth, one on Empress Catherine II of Russia, and three concerning distinguished French women during the French Revolution. He also lectured to the officers of the fort on "The Historical Importance of Queen Elizabeth's Reign" and "The Siege of Savannah," the latter published as "How the Black St. Domingo Legion Saved the Patriot Army in the Siege of Savannah, 1799." See Steward, *Fifty Years,* 279; Individual Service Report 1, May 1895, 1 May 1897, Selected ACP, T. G. Steward, RG 94, NA; Steward, "How the Black St. Domingo Legion Saved the Patriot Army."

98. See Cephas C. Bateman, "The Army Chaplain Among U.S. Soldiers," in Steward, *Active Service,* 30–33.

99. Steward, *Fifty Years,* 268–74; Theophilus Gould Steward, "Colonel George L. Andrews," *Harper's Weekly,* 7 May 1892, 437; T. G. Steward to John Wanamaker, 8 Oct. 1891, Selected ACP, T. G. Steward, RG 94, NA.

100. Colonel A. Burt to the Adjutant General U.S. Army, 13 Feb. 1899, Selected ACP, T. G. Steward, RG 94, NA. Colonel Burt placed a request to transfer Steward. Part of the reason given was that "Chaplain Steward is of no value whatever beyond his Chaplain's functions and there are many posts in Arizona and New Mexico garrisoned by colored soldiers who have no opportunities of receiving religious attention, particularly from a Chaplain of their own color."

101. Theophilus Gould Steward, "The Morals of the Army," *Independent,* 11 Feb. 1892, p. 7. Steward was also adamantly in favor of abstinence and a supporter of prohibition in and out of the military. He made his views clear in an article titled "The Canteen in the Army," *Harper's Weekly* 36, no. 1842 (9 Apr. 1892): 350–51.

102. Steward, "Morals of the Army," 7.

103. Theophilus Gould Steward, "Washington and Crummell," *Colored American,* 19 Nov. 1898, p. 6. Crummell died on 10 September 1898.

104. See Alexander Crummell, *Civilization: The Primal Need of the Race,* Occasional Papers No. 3 (Washington, D.C.: American Negro Academy). For a look at the American Negro Academy, see Alfred A. Moss Jr., *The American Negro Academy: Voice of the Talented Tenth* (Baton Rouge: Louisiana State Univ. Press, 1981). For a discussion of Alexander Crummell's view of civilization, see Wilson Jeremiah Moses, *Alexander Crummell: A Study of Civilization and Discontent* (New York: Oxford Univ. Press, 1989).

105. Steward, "Washington and Crummell," 6.

106. Ibid. In general, Steward was more attuned to Crummell than Washington. In fact, Steward took a critical stance against Washington in a review of his book, *Up from Slavery.* The occasion was a review, found in his personal papers, of African American literature. He compared three autobiographies: Richard Allen, Frederick Douglass, and Booker T. Washington. In essence he gave a critique of Washington's philosophy as pernicious: "Viewed from a moral and political standpoint [this book] . . . is in no sense a contribution toward the enfranchisement of the race but rather must its weight go to the other side. To follow Washington to the abandonment of all our higher aspirations would be folly in the extreme."

107. Steward, "Washington and Crummell."

108. Ibid.

109. Ibid.

110. See Steward, *Fifty Years,* 261–62.

111. Steward, "Washington and Crummell."

112. Ibid.

113. Ibid.

114. Ibid.

115. Theophilus Gould Steward, *The Army as a Trained Force and the Birth of the Republic: Addresses* (Cincinnati: By the Author, c. 1904), 18.

116. For a history of Wilberforce University, see William A. Joiner, *A Half Century of Freedom of the Negro in Ohio,* comp. and arr. W. A. Joiner (Xenia, Ohio: Smith Adv. [1915]); Frederick Alphonso McGinnis, *A History and an Interpretation of Wilberforce University* (Wilberforce, Ohio: Brown Publishing, 1941).

117. Steward noted in his early Georgia diary that he tutored William S. Scarborough. See diary entry dated 6 Nov. 1868, Steward Papers. For a look at Scarborough's life, see the two articles by Francis P. Weisneburger, "William Sanders Scarborough: Early Life and Years at Wilberforce," *Ohio History* 71, no. 3 (Oct. 1962): 203–26, and "William Sanders Scarborough: Scholarship, the Negro, Religion, and Politics," *Ohio History* 72, no. 1 (Jan. 1963): 25–50.

118. For a brief discussion of this heated election, see McGinnis, *History and an Interpretation,* 55.

119. See Efficiency Report in the case of T. G. Steward, 1 July 1899, and T. G. Steward to Adjutant General, 14 Sept. 1899, Selected ACP, T. G. Steward, RG 94, NA.

120. See Dwight Oliver Wendell Holmes, *The Evolution of the Negro College* (New York: Bureau of Publications, Teacher's College, Columbia Univ., 1934), 74, 186–204; McGinnis, *History and an Interpretation*, 11–12.

121. See *Wilberforce Bulletin*, ser. 4, 3 (June 1918: 16–19).

122. See Theophilus Gould Steward's *Our Civilization; A Popular Lecture* (By the author, c. 1919), 5–6, where he identified ancient civilizations as "Egypt" and "all parts of Asia"; Joiner, *Half Century of Freedom*, 97–101.

123. Perry, *Cushites*. See Joiner, *Half Century of Freedom*, 97 and 100.

124. George Washington Williams, *History of the Negro Race in America from 1619 to 1880, Negroes as Slaves, as Soldiers, and as Citizens; Together with a Preliminary Consideration of the Unity of the Human Family, an Historical Sketch of Africa, and an Account of the Negro Governments of Sierra Leone and Liberia*, vols. 1 and 2 (New York: G. P. Putnam's Sons, 1883). John Hope Franklin in his biography of Williams, *George Washington Williams: A Biography* (Chicago: Univ. of Chicago Press, 1985), 109, indicated that the book was "comprehensive, extending in the first volume from a discussion of biblical ethnology and African civilizations through the colonial and revolutionary periods. The second volume dealt with the antebellum years, the Civil War, and Reconstruction."

125. Steward, *Haitian Revolution*.

126. See Anthony M. Platt, *E. Franklin Frazier Reconsidered* (New Brunswick, N.J.: Rutgers Univ. Press, 1991), 21.

127. Steward, *Fifty Years*, 367–68.

128. T. G. Steward to Frank Steward, 3 Mar. 1923, Steward Papers.

Chapter 3

1. Richard Allen, *The Life Experience and Gospel Labors of the Rt. Rev. Richard Allen*, with an introduction by George A. Singleton (Nashville: Abingdon Press, 1960), 29–30.

2. See Griffin, "Theology of Black Rational Orthodoxy," 8–9. See also Griffin's *Black Theology*.

3. Nathan O. Hatch, *The Democratization of American Christianity* (New Haven: Yale Univ. Press, 1989), 112.

4. For another view of the development of education within the AME clergy, see the two-part article, Larry Murphy, "Education and Preparation for the Ministry in the African Methodist Episcopal Church, 1787–1900," *A.M.E. Church Review* 101, no. 322 (Apr.–June 1986): 19–33, and Larry Murphy, "Education and Preparation for the Ministry in the African Methodist Episcopal Church, 1787–1900," *A.M.E. Church Review* 101, no. 323 (July–Sept. 1986).

5. Payne, *Recollections*, 220.

6. During the time period of 1840s, Payne says that only Gettysburg Seminary, Oberlin College, and Oneida Institute were accessible to African Americans. See ibid., 222.

7. Daniel A. Payne, *History of the African Methodist Episcopal Church*, ed. by Rev. C. S. Smith, two parts in 1 vol. (Nashville: Publishing House of the AME Sunday School Union, 1891; New York: Arno Press and the New York Times, 1969), 53–54.

8. George A. Singleton, *The Romance of African Methodism: A Study of the African Methodist Episcopal Church* (New York: Exposition Press, 1952), 90.

9. Quoted from the opening speech of the conference chairman, Samuel Davis, in the *Minutes of the National Convention of Colored Citizens: Held at Buffalo on the 15th, 16th, 17th, 18th, and 19th of August 1843 for the Purpose of Considering Their Moral and Political Condition as American Citizens* (New York: Piercy and Reed, 1843), 3. Also found in Howard H. Bell, ed., *Minutes of the Proceedings of the National Negro Conventions 1830–1864* (New York: Arno Press and the New York Times, 1969). The minutes will be noted hereafter as *1843 National Convention*. For a look at the issues of the northern free African American community, see the standard works Benjamin Quarles, *Black Abolitionists* (New York: Oxford Univ. Press, 1975); Leon F. Litwack, *North of Slavery: The Negro in the Free States, 1790–1860* (Chicago: Univ. of Chicago Press, 1961); and Sweet, *Black Images of America.*

10. Payne, *Recollections,* 21, 79.

11. This was especially true for Daniel A. Payne. See chapter 6 in ibid., 56–71.

12. Payne, *History,* 141. It is unclear as to the specific books which were recommended for the study of ecclesiastical history and natural and revealed theology. It is possible that Paley's *Natural Theology* was one of the books. It was a common text of the day.

13. Payne, *History,* 141.

14. Daniel A. Payne to George Whipple, 6 July 1865, AMA Collection. See also Steward, *Fifty Years,* 31–34.

15. Steward, *Memoirs,* 19; Steward, *My First Four Years,* 5–6; Steward, *Fifty Years,* 181.

16. The urgent need for ministers and their use at a young and premature stage is highlighted by the fact that Steward was a pastor prior to his own baptism. Steward recounts the significance of his youthfulness during this time: "On joining the conference I expressed a desire to go South, but it was not thought best at that time, and I was appointed to a little church in South Camden, called Macedonia. Many years afterward I meet a man who had been a class leader in middle age at the time of my pastorate there, and remarked to him that I had at one time been his pastor. He could not recollect me at all. After much explanation he finally called up my ministry by remarking, 'O, I do remember; [the annual] conference sent us a boy one year; are you that boy?' It was not unpleasant for me to acknowledge the fact" (*Fifty Years,* 22–23).

17. It could be Edward Garbett, *God's Word Written: The Doctrine of the Inspiration of Holy Scripture Explained and Enforced* (London: Religious Tract Society, 1866.)

18. Steward, Journal 1868–1871.
19. Coppin, *Unwritten History,* 199. Coppin stated, "The minister who impressed me most at this really formative period of my life was Dr. Theophilus Gould Steward. I cannot say that I listened very critically to sermons previous to the time that he became my pastor. . . . But the advent of Dr. Steward marked the turning point of my idea of preaching. . . . If any one became very demonstrative under the preaching of Dr. Steward, it was more on account of what he said than his manner of saying it. He had none of the 'rousnum' that a 'Methodist Preacher' was supposed to have, and to bring in at least, toward the close of his sermon if not before. . . . Many adverse criticisms could be heard upon the style of the new preacher. Some characterized him as a Presbyterian, and others as a lecturer. Dr. Steward knew perfectly well what was going on, but he also knew what the people needed, and paid no attention to the criticisms of those who were no more capable of sitting in judgment upon a theological discourse, or denominational tenets, than they were upon geology, or political economy. As for me, I found myself so absorbed in what I heard from the pulpit Sunday after Sunday, . . . that there was no place so attractive to me as Bethel Church, and no service so helpful as the Sunday morning services, where sermons, fresh, well prepared, and delivered more and more forcefully as the response from the pew was more cordial, became the very bread of life to the soul and a means of enlightenment to the mind" (197–200).
20. Steward, Journal 1868–1871.
21. Philadelphia Conference of the African Methodist Episcopal Church, *Annual Minutes of the Philadelphia Conference of the African Methodist Episcopal Church Held in Smyrna, Delaware, May 11–17, A.D. 1881* (Philadelphia: Christian Recorder Print, 1881), 35–36.
22. Turner called the text "Systematic Theology," but the title was most likely *Elements of Divinity,* by Thomas Neely Ralston (Cincinnati: Poe & Hitchcock, 1863).
23. Henry McNeal Turner, "The Bishops on Theology," *Christian Recorder,* 18 Sept. 1884, p. 1.
24. Ibid. Turner disavows what he calls rumors regarding the rejection of Wakefield's work in the ME Church. He argues that, to the contrary, the ME Church had listed the book on its list of studies for its ministry.
25. Ibid.
26. B. W. Arnett and S. T. Mitchell, comps., *The Wilberforce Alumnal: A Comprehensive Review of the Origin, Development and Present Status of Wilberforce University* (Xenia, Ohio: Printed at the Gazette Office, 1885), 45.
27. It is not clear if this was an extension of the former or whether it was the same organization with a modified name. The Rev. Benjamin W. Arnett was listed as manager of both. According to *The Wilberforce Alumnal,* Steward was also credited with being elected to the chair of theology of Wilberforce University in 1884, but he declined. It is not clear if the chair was synonymous with the

deanship of TTSLA. Another curious attribution to Steward is found in the *Interdenominational Theological Center 1988–1991 Catalog,* which listed him as the first dean of theology at Morris Brown College: "Turner Theological Seminary began as a department of Morris Brown College in 1894, nine years after the Board of Trustees first gave approval on September 23, 1885. The Reverend T. G. Steward, D.D., a former United States Army chaplain, was later elected to the deanship. In the interim, the Reverend E. L. Chew was also elected to the deanship, but the Reverend E. W. Lee, a former principal who was later elected President of Morris Brown College, was the first to serve" (11).

28. "The Tawawa Theological Class," *Christian Recorder,* 29 Nov. 1883, p. 3.
29. *Death, Hades and Resurrection* has not been located; "Tawawa Theological Class," 3.
30. Daniel R. Goodwin to T. G. Steward, 17 Dec. 1883, Steward Papers.
31. Letter fragment, Steward Papers. See also B. F. Lee, "Death, Hades, and the Resurrection," *Christian Recorder,* 21 Feb. 1884. Lee writes, "The book is really an addition to Eschatology. The author makes no pretension to proving, with out biblical statements, that "death does not end all," but in Scripture light so presents his case that the opposite side is certainly unable to prove that the "grave is the end of man."
32. It is not clear if the first two books were ever published. David Wood Wills, in his "Aspects of Social Thought in the African Methodist Episcopal Church 1884–1910" (Ph.D. diss., Harvard Univ., 1975), 114 n. 52, also suggests that the first two books were never published. Although *Incarnation and Atonement* was evidently never published, an article of Steward's was published in the *A.M.E. Church Review* 9, no. 3 (1893) titled "The Doctrine of the Incarnation Stated."
33. Steward, *Divine Attributes.*
34. See Sydney E. Ahlstrom, "The Scottish Philosophy and American Theology," *Church History* 24 (1955): 257–72; Mark A. Noll, "Common Sense Traditions and American Evangelical Thought," *American Quarterly* 37 (Summer 1985): 216–38; James H. Moorhead, "James Addison Alexander: Common Sense, Romanticism and Biblical Criticism at Princeton," *Journal of Presbyterian History* 53 (1975): 51–65; and A. Grave, *The Scottish Philosophy of Common Sense* (Oxford: Oxford Univ. Press, 1960). For a view of the influence of common sense philosophy on Unitarianism, see Paul F. Boller Jr., *American Transcendentalism, 1830–1860: An Intellectual Inquiry* (New York: G. P. Putnam's Sons, 1974), esp. 42–44; Conrad Wright, *The Beginnings of Unitarianism in America* (Boston: Starr King Press, 1955), 135–60; Daniel Walker Howe, *The Unitarian Conscience* (Cambridge: Harvard Univ. Press, 1970), 27–44, 69–92.
35. Steward, *Divine Attributes,* 110–111.
36. Turner, "Bishops on Theology," 1.
37. Theophilus Gould Steward, "'Dr. Steward's Book' Protested by the Florida Conference," *Christian Recorder,* 15 Jan. 1885.

38. *Minutes of the Nineteenth Florida Annual Conference of the African Methodists Episcopal Church,* Nov. 1884, 31.
39. Payne, *Recollections,* 239.
40. Steward, *Divine Attributes,* 3.
41. Ibid., 4, 5.
42. See Rudolf Otto, *The Idea of the Holy; An Inquiry into the Non-Rational Factor in the Idea of the Divine and Its Relation to the Rational,* trans. John W. Harvey (London: Oxford Univ. Press, 1923).
43. Steward, *Divine Attributes,* 5–6.
44. Ibid., 4–5.
45. Benjamin Tucker Tanner, "Divine Attributes," *Christian Recorder,* 31 Jan. 1884, 3.
46. Tanner, "Divine Attributes," 3.
47. Steward, *Divine Attributes,* 59–60. Steward here quoted Joseph Butler, *Ethical Discourses and Essay on Virtue,* arranged as a Treatise on Moral Philosophy; and edited, with an analysis, by J. T. Champlin, D.D. (Boston: John P. Jewett, 1859), 121–22.
48. Steward, *Divine Attributes,* 60.
49. David Wills describes Steward's *Divine Attributes* as "thoroughly" traditional in its views, but many of Steward's peers, including Payne and Tanner, disagreed. See Wills, "Aspects of Social Thought," 114. Steward's earlier published sermon, *The Incarnation of the Son of God* was more theological orthodoxy, but already Steward was giving a nod to rationality. See Theophilus Gould Steward, *The Incarnation of the Son of God: Annual Sermon Preached at Wilberforce University June 13th, 1881* (Philadelphia: AME Book Rooms, 1881), 13.
50. Here I borrow and modify Kenneth Cauthen's definition of the various theological traditions in *The Impact of American Religious Liberalism* (Washington, D.C.: Univ. Press of America, 1983). He defines a continuum of theological traditions, including modernistic liberalism, evangelical liberalism, conservatism, and fundamentalism. I use liberal evangelicalism as a variant of conservatism which gives more weight to the concerns of modernity while at the same time affirming Christian orthodoxy.
51. See, for example, William R. Hutchison, *The Modernist Impulse in American Protestantism* (New York: Oxford Univ. Press, 1976).
52. Steward, *Genesis Re-Read;* see *New York Times,* Sept. 23, 1876.
53. See Paul A. Carter, *The Spiritual Crisis of the Gilded Age* (DeKalb: Northern Illinois Univ. Press, 1971), esp. chap. 2.
54. See William Lloyd Van Deburg, "Rejected of Men: The changing Religious Views of William Lloyd Garrison and Frederick Douglass" (Ph.D. diss., Michigan State Univ., 1973), 311. See also Douglass to William Whipper, 9 June 1870, American Negro Historical Society Papers, Leon Gardiner Collection, Historical Society of Pennsylvania.

55. Douglass to William Whipper, 9 June 1870. See also Van Deburg, "Rejected of Men," 311–12.

56. See Frederick May Holland, *Frederick Douglass: The Colored Orator* (New York: Funk and Wagnals, 1891), 335–36. See also Van Deburg, "Rejected of Men," 312.

57. *Christian Recorder,* 27 Aug. 1874, p. 6.

58. See *Christian Recorder,* 2 Nov. 1876, p. 4.

59. James A. Handy, "The Mystery of Man," *A.M.E. Church Review* 2 (July 1885): 20. For a similar reaction to evolution, see also D. B. Williams, "The Harmony between the Bible and Science Concerning Primitive Man," *A.M.E. Church Review,* 9 (July 1892), 19–20.

60. Rufus Perry was a significant presence in Steward's life. Steward indicated in his autobiography that Perry, who graduated from Kalamazoo Seminary in 1861, taught him Greek. See Steward, *Fifty Years,* 166. Steward was a regular contributor in Perry's *National Monitor.* According to Oscar Fay Adams's *Dictionary of American Authors* (Boston: Houghton, Mifflin & Co., 1897), Perry was widely known as a linguist. He was also the author of a significant volume titled *The Cushite, or, the Descendants of Ham.*

61. The discrepancies between the two copies can be explained by the fact that the autobiographic version was a reproduction from memory or a later edited rendering. Steward himself indicated that he did not preach from a manuscript but from notes. "I did not then, and do not now preach from manuscript; nor do I memorize my discourses. Thus it is not at all probable that I used the exact words as written. My custom has been during my half century of preaching, to work out all of my ideas, writing them out in the order in which I intend to present them, and trust to the occasion for the language" (*Fifty Years,* 41). One would assume that excerpts of the shorter one published just after the lecture would be the more accurate of the two. Conversely, it could also be that the *Christian Recorder* copy was a significantly edited version of the original lecture. See *Christian Recorder,* 2 Nov. 1876, p. 8; and Steward, *Fifty Years,* 157–66.

62. *Christian Recorder,* 2 Nov. 1876, p. 8.

63. *New York Times,* 19 Sept. 1876, p. 8.

64. Ibid.

65. Steward, *Fifty Years,* 158, 159, 160.

66. *New York Times,* 19 Sept. 1876, p. 8.

67. Ibid.

68. Steward, *Fifty Years,* 162–63.

69. Ibid., 165. Here, Steward was following the work of O. M. Mitchel's *Astronomy of the Bible* (New York: Oakley and Mason, 1868), a well-known nineteenth-century astronomer, whose writings attempted to harmonize the Mosaic account with scientific discoveries of the time period. As we shall see later, Steward drew heavily upon Mitchel's work in his writing of *Genesis Re-Read.* Steward's quote was a more of a paraphrase than an actual quote. The actual

quote read, "The most [that] can be derived from the explorations of geology, is the conclusion that the introduction of animal and vegetable life was contemporaneous. This is but negative testimony, and only demonstrates the fact, that no vegetable remains have been preserved which grew prior to the introduction of animal life on earth."

70. Steward, *Fifty Years,* 165.
71. "A Few Notes on 'Genesis Re-Read,'" *Christian Recorder,* 28 Jan. 1886, p. 1.
72. Ibid.
73. Ibid.
74. Steward, *Genesis Re-Read,* 88.
75. Ibid., 96.
76. Benjamin T. Tanner, "Genesis Re-Read," *A.M.E. Church Review* 2 (Jan. 1886): 235.
77. Steward, *Genesis Re-Read,* 53, 171.
78. Ibid., 56.
79. Ibid., 89, 90.
80. Ibid., 91, 93.
81. Tanner, "Genesis Re-Read," 236.
82. Ibid., 237.
83. Wills, "Aspects of Social Thought," 130. Benjamin Tucker Tanner was a prolific writer in his own right. Several of the volumes which he published focused on the place of Africans within the Bible. They include *The Negro's Origin* (Philadelphia: African Methodist Episcopal Depository, 1869); *The Color of Solomon—What?* (Philadelphia: A. M. E. Book Concern, 1895); *The Descent of the Negro* (n.p.: n.p., 1898); and *The Negro in Holy Writ* (Philadelphia: n. p., 1902).

Chapter 4

1. The plan was ill-fated from the beginning, according to Edwin S. Redkey, because of "inexperienced planning and incompetent operation by the ship's white captain, the company lost the ship 'Azor' in debtor's court." See Edwin S. Redkey, *Black Exodus: Black Nationalist and Back-to-Africa Movements, 1890–1910* (New Haven: Yale Univ. Press, 1969), 22.
2. See the Committee on African Migration report, which was written by T. G. Steward, Theodore Gould, Benjamin Tanner, and Leonard Patterson and published in the *Christian Recorder,* 16 May 1878.
3. See Redkey, *Black Exodus,* 30; and George Brown Tindall, *South Carolina Negroes, 1877–1890* (Columbia: Univ. of South Carolina Press, 1952), 153–68; also Nell Irvin Painter, *Exodusters: Black Migration to Kansas after Reconstruction* (New York: Alfred A. Knopf, 1977), esp. 84–95.
4. See Steward Papers. Further, Steward excoriated Washington's critique of African American clergy: "The man who would arise either to oppress or slander the class of men [the black clergy], sinks himself below Christian

respect." See Theophilus Gould Steward, "Washington Slander," *Christian Recorder*, 15 Jan. 1891.

5. Strong, *Our Country*.

6. Steward, *End of the World*.

7. Strong, *Our Country*. Other works by Strong which furthered his views are *The New Era; or, The Coming Kingdom* (New York: Baker and Taylor, 1893) and *The Next Great Awakening* (New York: Baker and Taylor, 1902).

8. Quoted in Dorothea R. Muller, "Josiah Strong and American Nationalism: A Reevaluation," *Journal of American History* 53, no. 3 (Dec. 1966): 487. See also Henry F. May, *Protestant Churches and Industrial America* (New York: Octagon Books, 1963), 114–15.

9. For a look at Strong's view of social and global mission, see Wendy Jane Deichmann, "Josiah Strong: Practical Theologian and Social Crusader for a Global Kingdom" (Ph.D. diss., Drew Univ., 1991).

10. See Strong, *Our Country*, 180.

11. See ibid., 175–80. See also Horace Bushnell, *Christian Nurture* (New York: Scribner's, Armstrong, 1876), 195–223. Strong's quote of Darwin is cited as "Descent of Man, Part I, page 142." It is clear that Strong drew upon Darwinian and social Darwinist theories of natural selection in order to bolster his idea of Anglo-Saxonism: "Mr. Darwin is not only disposed to see, in the superior vigor of our people, an illustration of his favorite theory of natural selection, but even intimates that the world's history thus far has been simply preparatory for our future, and tributary to it." Strong, *Our Country*, 170.

12. Strong, *Our Country*, 161.

13. Ibid., 175, 173. See also Muller, "Josiah Strong," 489.

14. Strong, *Our Country*, 175, 165.

15. Ralph E. Luker, *The Social Gospel in Black and White: American Racial Reform, 1885–1912* (Chapel Hill: Univ. of North Carolina Press, 1991), 270–71. For other views of Strong's apologists, see Muller, "Josiah Strong," 487; Ronald C. White Jr., *Liberty and Justice for All: Racial Reform and The Social Gospel* (San Francisco: Harper and Row, Publishers, 1990), 18–22. For examples of the view of imperial and racial expansionism, see Richard Hofstadter, *Social Darwinism in American Thought* (New York: George Braziller, 1959), 170–200; Thomas F. Gossett, *Race: The History of an Idea in America* (New York: Schocken Books, 1965), 176–97.

16. Luker, *Social Gospel*, 268. Dixon was the author of *The Leopard's Spot* and *The Clansman*.

17. Bowen was a highly educated man who was also acquainted with Steward (see Theophilus Gould Steward, "The Bishops of the Methodist Episcopal Church," *Christian Recorder*, 13 Nov. 1890). He received his bachelor of sacred theology degree from Boston School of Theology in 1885 and two years later was granted the degree of doctor of philosophy by the same institution. This was only the second Ph.D. granted to an African American in America. For a

sketch of J. W. E. Bowen, see Logan and Winston, *Dictionary of American Negro Biography.* Steward was also an acquaintance of Crummell's as they both pastored prominent churches in the Washington, D.C., African American community. A look at Alexander Crummell's life can be found in the biography by Moses, *Alexander Crummell.* Steward also wrote an article comparing the philosophies of Crummell and Booker T. Washington, See Steward, "Washington and Crummell," 6.

18. Luker, *Social Gospel,* 272. Luker pointed to several facts to build his case for Strong's nonracist attitude. He noted that Strong as a youth was impressed by John Brown, the radical abolitionist, and argued that just after the publication of Strong's book he was nominated to the presidency of Atlanta University, which was organized by Strong's own denomination, the Congregationalist, on behalf of the newly freed slaves. Luker stated, "It may have been an error to nominate so radical an assimilationist as president of Atlanta University; it was a shocking error if he is rightly regarded as a racist. . . . If his nomination as president of Atlanta University was an error, it went unnoticed. His sister, Mary, joined the faculty of the AMA's Talladega College in 1893; later, he served on its board of trustees."

19. Francis Grimké, "Colored Men as Professors in Colored Institutions," *A.M.E. Church Review* 2, no. 2 (Oct. 1885): 142. Francis Grimké was reacting to recent events in Washington in which the board of trustees of Howard University, of which he was a member, voted to hire a white professor over a qualified African American. Grimké and the two other black men on the board were supporting the black candidate and were outvoted by their white counterparts. Grimké, "Colored Men," 142.

20. Ibid., 142–43.

21. Ibid., 145.

22. Steward, *End of the World,* 77.

23. Timothy E. Fulop, "'The Future Golden Day of the Race': Millennialism and Black Americans in the Nadir, 1877–1901," *Harvard Theological Review* 84, no. 1 (1991): 91. Fulop develops three ideal types of African American millennial thought. Cultural millennialism focused on the ideology of the United States as the redeemer nation if the world. Emphasis was placed on Western civilization, education, Anglo-Saxon culture, American democracy, and republicanism. This was closest to the Anglo-Saxonism of Josiah Strong. Many of its proponents argued for assimilation or amalgamation. Millennial Ethiopianism centered on a pan-African millennialism in which a future golden age led by people of color would emerge. This new age would also bring God's judgment of white society and Western civilization. Fulop placed Steward's thought in this category. Progressive millennialism focused on more traditional postmillennial thought. It highlighted the optimistic role of the church, missions, and reform that would give birth to the millennium on earth. It focused on racial equality and harmony but was also held a prophetic stance toward the notion of Anglo-Saxonism.

24. Theophilus G. Steward, "A New Reading of an Old Phrase: The End of the World ('Η συνιελεια του αιωνοσ)" *A.M.E. Church Review* 5 (Jan. 1889): 205.

25. Steward, *End of the World*, 72–73.

26. Ibid., 112. Steward generally followed the interpretation of Henry Alford, at the time Dean of Canterbury, in his *The New Testament for English Readers: Containing the Authorized Version, with Marginal Corrections of Readings and Renderings; and a Critical and Explanatory*, vols. 1 and 2 (London: Rivingtons, 1868, 1872).

27. Steward, *End of the World*, 74–75.

28. Ibid., 76.

29. Ibid., 135.

30. Ibid., 114, 135, 117. Galatians states, "There is neither Jew nor Greek, there is neither bond nor free, there is neither male nor female: for ye are all one in Christ Jesus. And if ye be Christ's, then are ye Abraham's seed and heirs according to the promise." And Acts states, "Of a truth I perceive that God is no respecter of persons: But in every nation he that feareth him and worketh righteousness is accepted with him."

31. See Benjamin Tanner's review of Steward's book in "Book and Pamphlet Table," *A.M.E. Church Review* 4 (May 1887): 461–67. See also the review by Benjamin F. Lee in the AME Churches weekly organ, *Christian Recorder*, 12 Apr. 1888: "This work is not a dissertation on Milleriteism. It is not an attempt to show that the popular idea of the millennium is about to be realized, but an effort to set forth the idea that prophesies, promises and preaching point to a millennium in which the narrow lines stretched by Anglo-Saxon expositors shall have no place in Christian development.... The scientific character of the work rest upon somewhat extraordinary Scripture construction and expositions."

32. Steward, *Our Civilization*.

33. Moses, *Alexander Crummell*, 7.

34. Steward, *Our Civilization*, 13.

35. Ibid., 13.

36. Steward, *Our Civilization*, 5.

37. See François Guizot, *The History of Civilization from the Fall of the Roman Empire the French Revolution*, trans. William Hazlitt (London: Bell and Daldy, 1873). For a discussion of Guizot's life and the influence of his writings on American thought, see Charles A. and Mary R. Beard, *The American Spirit: A Study of the Idea of Civilization in the United States* (New York: Macmillan, 1942), 4:88–94.

38. Beard, *American Spirit*, 91.

39. Steward, *Our Civilization*, 10.

40. Ibid., 5–6, 7.

41. Ibid., 11. Steward interjected the subject of women into his discussion of civilization for the first time. What is important here about this interjection

is the fact that he included women in this broader discussion of freedom. Steward stops just short of romanticizing the nature of the relationship between the sexes in early German history by indicating that "their respect for their women was so great that the civilized Romans were struck with astonishment by it. Yet these rugged barbarians like all savages believed that women should do the work, while the lords fought, drank and gambled." Steward is still following the work of Guizot, who indicated that the nature of the relationship between the sexes was not based on a romanticizing of ancient Germans, but rather, "it was in the effects of a strongly marked social position, in the progress and preponderance of domestic manners, that the importance of women in Europe originated; and the preponderance of domestic manners became, very early, an essential characteristic of the feudal system." See Guizot, *History of Civilization,* 70–73. In essence, Guizot suggested that under feudalism, women became more valuable in the family arrangement.

42. Steward, *Our Civilization,* 15, 17.
43. Ibid.
44. Ibid., 18.
45. Ibid.
46. Steward, *Army as a Trained Force,* 24.
47. Steward, *Our Civilization,* 18–19.
48. Ibid., 21.
49. Ibid., 22.
50. Ibid., 23.
51. Ibid., 24, 25.
52. Ibid., 26.
53. Ibid., 27–28.
54. See the conference papers, G. Spiller, ed., *Papers on Inter-Racial Problems Communicated to the First Universal Races Congress Held at the University of London, July 26–29, 1911* (London: P. S. King and Son, 1911).
55. Steward, *Our Civilization,* 28.
56. Ibid., 28–29.

Chapter 5

1. Wills, "Aspects of Social Thought," 135.
2. Steward, *Colored Regulars.*
3. Wills, "Aspects of Social Thought," 136.
4. Steward, *Charleston Love Story,* 52.
5. William L. Andrews, "Liberal Religion and Free Love: An Undiscovered Afro-American Novel of the 1890's," *MELUS: The Journal of the Society for the Study of the Multi-Ethnic Literature of the United States* 9, no. 1 (Spring 1982): 28.
6. Andrews, "Liberal Religion and Free Love," 33.

7. Most of American Protestantism saw itself as Evangelical throughout the nineteenth century. As George M. Marsden argued concerning the twentieth-century phenomenon of fundamentalism and evangelicalism, it was also true of the nineteenth-century that "almost all nineteenth-century American Protestants had been evangelical, that is, part of a coalition reflecting a merger of pietist and Reformed heritages and growing out of the eighteenth- and nineteenth-century awakenings in America. Typically, all sorts of subtraditions within this evangelical movement emphasized revivalism and the accompanying doctrines of Christ's atonement, the necessity of regeneration, the sole authority of the Bible, and the separated life of holiness marked by avoidance of notorious bar-room vices. All fundamentalists wanted to preserve this nineteenth-century heritage, and so all fundamentalists were evangelicals. But in the early twentieth century, by no means all evangelicals were fundamentalists. Not all traditional evangelicals were militant. Moreover many who still called themselves evangelicals were liberals or modernists who had abandoned most of the distinctive emphasis of the awakenings; so the term evangelical had lost its usefulness" (George M. Marsden, "Fundamentalism and American Evangelicalism," in *The Variety of American Evangelicalism,* ed. Donald W. Dayton and Robert K. Johnston [Univ. of Tennessee Press, 1991], 23–24).

8. T. G. Steward's individual report under G.O. 41, A.G.O. Dec. 16, 1894.

9. See biographical sketch of Bruce in Logan and Winston, *Dictionary of American Negro Biography,* 74–76.

10. The "Howell" character was clearly fictional, as there was no record of a Lieutenant Howell enlisted with the Fifty-fourth Infantry. According to the infantry's roster, found in Luis F. Emilio's *Brave Black Regiment,* 327–92, there was no Lt. Leonard Howell listed among the volunteers (Emilio, *A Brave Black Regiment: History of the Fifty-Fourth Regiment of Massachusetts Volunteer Infantry, 1863–1865,* 2d ed., Revised and Corrected, with Appendix upon Treatment of Colored Prisoners of War [Boston: Boston Book, 1894; New York: Arno Press and the New York Times, 1969]). There were several lieutenants who fit the general profile, but none were born in south Jersey. Steward built the character, Howell, on some general features that might have fit several actual lieutenants. He was a northern-born, white, single, ambitious male with limited or basic education and of an artisan or farming background, whose only way to advance into the rank of commissioned officer was to accept command over an African American regiment. See Emilio, *Brave Black Regiment,* 7 and Steward, *Charleston Love Story,* 50–51.

11. Steward, *Fifty Years,* 64–65.

12. All of the commissioned officers in the various African American regiments were white men. This was true up until the end of the war, when the Fifty-fourth was mustered out of service. A few African Americans were commissioned and mustered to other reorganized "colored troops." See also Emilio, *Brave Black Regiment,* 315.

13. Steward, *Charleston Love Story*, 121. Steward regarded his own ministry in a similar fashion. As with Steward, in part due to the zeal with which he pursued the ministry and his adjustment to the climate, Gordon contracted malaria and typhoid fever and was forced to return North to recuperate. Like Steward, Gordon had desired to return to his ministry in the South but, unlike Steward, due to health reasons, is persuaded to take a pastorate in Brooklyn. Gordon eventually marries Lavinia Vanross, the younger sister of Hortense in Charleston on January 1, in the same city and on the same day that Steward married Elizabeth Gadsden. See Steward, *My First Four Years*, 27 and 132.

14. I use "hue" to designate the phenomena within the African American community in which class distinctions are based on gradations of skin color, with the lighter-skinned blacks in a more privileged position. The closer a person of mixed ancestry of black and white comes to mirroring Caucasians in skin color and hair texture, the more privileged they feel themselves to be. Even though Steward's skin was lighter, there was no indication that he carried such attitudes.

15. For a discussion of the Denmark Vesey rebellion, see Robert Starobin, "Denmark Vesey's Slave Conspiracy of 1822: A Study in Rebellion and Resistance," in *American Slavery: The Question of Resistance*, ed. John Bracey et al. (Belmont, Calif.: Wadsworth, 1970), 142–57.

16. Steward, *Charleston Love Story*, 39–40. The free Charleston African American community had several differing class and caste societies, including the Brown Fellowship Society, the most elite of these groups; the Humane Brotherhood, a limited number (thirty-five) of "respectable Free Dark Men"; and the Friendly Moralist Society, which required certified mulatto status. See especially Michael P. Johnson and James L. Roark, *Black Masters: A Free Family of Color in the Old South* (New York: W. W. Norton, 1984), 212–15. Also see E. Horace Fitchett, "The Free Negro in Charleston, South Carolina" (Ph.D. diss., Univ. of Chicago, 1950).

17. Steward, *Charleston Love Story*, 42.

18. Ibid., 36–37.

19. Ibid. Steward's sympathy for the poor went contrary to the popular literature of the times, which tended to disparage poor whites as well as blacks. Andrews compared Steward's novel to that of novelists such as Thomas Nelson Page's *Red Rock*, published in 1898, in which poor whites were portrayed as the whipping boy of the white upper classes and former slaves were seen as dangerous. See Andrews, "Liberal Religion and Free Love," 29, 31. It is interesting to discern Steward's motivation for such a "fair" assessment of white Charlestonians. How much had to do with his commitment to integration is unclear. Surely there were many who sympathized with the southern racist spirit of the times. Steward seems to minimize this in his assessment.

20. Steward, *Charleston Love Story*, 38–39.

21. Steward, *Fifty Years*, 125–27. It is also interesting to note that Steward was a co-owner of a merchant commission business, Sneed and Steward, as a cotton broker, just as his character Leonard Howell was. Steward indicated that his co-owner, N. D. Sneed, was a former U.S. soldier. Sneed is not listed among either the officers or enlisted men of the Fifty-fourth Regiment. But it is still clear that Steward drew much of the background from his own life experiences.

22. Of this failed business venture in cotton, Steward wrote, "Had I followed the advice of the experienced and conservative men with whom I came in contact I would have saved myself from the embarrassment which followed my venture. Mr. Hollingsworth told me not to buy any cotton, but to content myself with selling on commission. Others cautioned me about advancing money upon the growing crops. These were all southern men, and I fully believed in their honor; but my youth and the golden visions which it painted, bewitched me, and I bought cotton, and advanced my last dollar and all my credit upon the cotton crop of 1870. When the fall came, the political excitement and other causes, completely upset the social fabric that had up to that time gained so little in the way of stability, and my money that had gone into the cotton fields did not come back. I found myself bankrupt, and was convinced anew that business was not my calling" (Steward, *Fifty Years*, 125–27).

23. Steward, *Charleston Love Story*, 43, 44.

24. Ibid., 65, 66, 88–89.

25. The term "transcendentalist" was initially used by Immanual Kant in *Critique of Pure Reason*, which was studied by many members of the "New School," the term they would have preferred to use. Kant's philosophy was a major focus of their thinking. For a look at the influence of Kant on the transcendentalists, see William R. Hutchison, *The Transcendentalist Ministers: Church Reform in the New England Renaissance* (New Haven: Yale Univ. Press, 1959), 22–28; and René Wellek, "Emerson and German Philosophy," *New England Quarterly* 16 (1942): 41–62. Even the designation "transcendental" was a label assigned to the movement by its critics. The movement reluctantly accepted the name. Steward must have known the concern for nomenclature, thus declaring the movement the "so-called liberal ideas of New England." As evasive as he was regarding its name, it was as illusive in definition. Transcendentalism, theologically, was a very broad movement and a precise meaning of the term is difficult to establish. In fact, most persons within the movement refused to give it a precise definition for fear that it, the definition, would breed dogmatism. It was dogma that they felt enslaved the individual, keeping him or her from breaking free from the evils of Christianity, which relied on nonrational faith claims. Donald N. Koster has aptly indicated that "[f]riend and foe alike have tried [to define Transcendentalism] but none seems to have succeeded to the complete satisfaction of anyone." See Lawrence C. Porter, "Transcendentalism: A Self-Portrait," *New England Quarterly* (Mar. 1962): 33, and Donald N. Koster, *Transcendentalism in America* (Boston: G. K. Hall, 1975), 1.

26. Anne C. Rose, *Transcendentalism as a Social Movement, 1830–1850* (New Haven: Yale Univ. Press, 1981), 38–69. Alexander Kern, "The Rise of Transcendentism," in Harry Hayden Clark, ed., *Transitions in American Literary History* (Durham, N.C.: Duke Univ. Press, 1953) has identified twenty such common themes with in the transcendentalist movement, which includes the above-mentioned ones; see 250–51. For a view of Unitarianism and common sense, see Wright, *Beginnings of Unitarianism,* 135–60; Howe, *Unitarian Conscience,* 27–44, 69–92.
27. He may have encountered this movement through his theological studies at the Episcopal Divinity School at Philadelphia. One of his character alter-egos, the Reverend Dr. Danforth, indicated that he had encountered this movement: "Mr. Howell had flattered himself that these were new ideas to the minister, when, as a matter of fact, Mr. Danforth had studied them in all possible forms, and given due consideration to every vestige of their importance in his seminary days, while studying his 'Hooker,' and following his 'syllabus'" (201).
28. Steward, *Fifty Years,* 231.
29. Ibid., 234.
30. Ibid., 233. See also Frederick Douglass to Theophilus G. Steward, 27 July 1886, Douglass Papers, Library of Congress; see also Van Deburg, "Rejected of Men," 316–17.
31. Steward, *Fifty Years,* 236. Metropolitan was a popular church, attended by many of Washington's upwardly mobile and elite families. After Steward's tenure at Metropolitan, Douglass's funeral rites were also performed there. In a letter to John R. Lynch, Steward indicated that he regarded Frederick Douglass as a personal friend. See AGO Steward Letter June 2 1891.
32. See Presbyterian Church of Missoula resolution, dated 13 Mar. 1895, in Selected ACP, T. G. Steward, RG 94, NA.
33. Note fragment, Steward Papers.
34. Steward, *Charleston Love Story,* 177–78.
35. Ibid., 212, 193.
36. Ibid., 201.
37. Ibid., 205–6.
38. Ibid., 225–26.
39. Ibid., 230.
40. Ibid., 230–31.
41. Ibid., 232.
42. Ibid., 239.

Chapter 6

1. Only two of these articles survived in the extant copies of the *Christian Recorder* newspaper.
2. T. G. Steward, "Distinguished Women of the Bible—Rebecca," *Christian Recorder,* 30 Mar. 1876, p. 8.

3. T. G. Steward, "Distinguished Women of the Bible—Deborah," *Christian Recorder,* 27 Apr. 1876, p. 8.

4. Rev. Moses B. Saulter [Salter], "Woman, Her Influence," *Proceedings of the Quarto-Centennial Conference of the African M.E. Church of South Carolina at Charleston, S.C., May 15, 16, and 17, 1889,* ed. Benjamin W. Arnett (1890), 82–83. It is interesting to note that Salter was a former assistant of Theophilus Gould Steward, the focus of this paper, while Steward was a missionary in the Reconstruction South Carolina. See T. G. Steward, *Fifty Years of Gospel Ministry* (Philadelphia: AME Book Concern, n.d.), 86–87. Also see Steward, *My First Four Years,* 33. Here Steward indicated that he "had an open door to the hearts of several young men and gave Wm. Thomas, M. B. Salters [*sic*] and others, were by me first brought before the public as preachers, and I opened my pulpit freely to them."

5. M. E. Lee, "The Home-Maker," *A.M.E. Church Review* 18 no. 1 (July 1891): 64. Benjamin Lee would elected bishop within one year of this article's publication. Sarah and Benjamin Tanner were the parents of Henry Ossawa Tanner, the famous late-nineteenth-century expatriate African American painter.

6. See the address by Hallie Quinn Brown in Arnett, *Proceedings of the Quarto-Centennial Conference,* 100–102. For another AME woman that argues for the education of black women, see Hannah Jones, "Women as Educators," *A.M.E. Church Review* 9, no. 3 (Jan. 1882): 321–26.

7. M. E. C. Smith, "Pioneer Women of East Florida," in Arnett, *Proceedings of the Quarto-Centennial Conference,* 181–86.

8. Jualynne Dodson, "Power and Surrogate Leadership: Black Women and Organized Religion," *Sage* 5, no. 2 (Fall 1988): 39.

9. Jualynne Dodson, "Women's Ministries and the African Methodist Episcopal Tradition," in *Religious Institutions and Women's Leadership: New Roles Inside the Mainstream,* ed. Catherine Wessinger (Columbia: Univ. of South Carolina Press, 1996), 133. Dodson highlighted the caste and class nature of the AME Church by mentioning the skin color and education status of these women.

10. See Richard R. Wright Jr., comp., *Encyclopaedia of African Methodism,* 2d ed. (Philadelphia: Book Concern of the AME Church, 1947), 423–25.

11. "An Open Letter," *Christian Recorder,* 14 May 1874, p. 1.

12. See, for example, Kathryn K. Sklar, *Catharine Beecher: A Study in American Domesticity* (New York: Norton, 1976).

13. Carroll Smith-Rosenberg, "Women and Religious Revivals: Anti-Ritualism, Liminality, and the Emergence of the American Bourgeoisie," in *The Evangelical Tradition in America,* ed. Leonard I. Sweet (Macon: Ga.: Mercer Univ. Press, 1984), 200.

14. Smith-Rosenberg, "Women and Religious Revivals," 202–3.

15. Dodson, "Power and Surrogate Leadership," 40.

16. See Jarena Lee, *The Life and Religious Experience of Jarena Lee, a Coloured Lady, Giving an Account of Her Call to Preach the Gospel,* in William L.

Andrews, *Sisters of the Spirit: Three Black Women's Autobiographies of the Nineteenth Century* (Bloomington: Indiana Univ. Press, 1986). Jualynne Dodson argues that Richard Allen did not officially ordain Jarena Lee, as this would have delegitimized "the young Church among the larger, more powerful white community of Methodists, not to mention within the Protestant community in general. But Richard Allen could see that within situations of scarcity, all available and successful resources should be used." See Dodson, "Women's Ministries," 125–26.

17. Amanda Smith, *An Autobiography: The Story of the Lord's Dealing with Mrs. Amanda Smith, the Colored Evangelist* (1893; reprint, New York: Oxford Univ. Press, 1988).

18. See Stephen Ward Angell, "The Controversy over Women's Ministry in the African Methodist Episcopal Church during The 1800's: The Case of Sarah Ann Hughes," in *This Far by Faith: Readings in African-American Women's Religious Biography,* ed. Judith Weisenfeld and Richard Newman (New York: Routledge, 1996).

19. See the *Christian Recorder,* 10 Dec. 1885. Also found in Angell, "Controversy over Women's Ministry," 104.

20. For a look at a sampling of black women preachers and their extant sermons, see Bettye Collier-Thomas, ed., *Daughters of Thunder: Black Women Preachers and Their Sermons, 1850–1979* (San Francisco: Jossey-Bass Publishers, 1998).

21. Less is known of the preaching and lay women's development in the nineteenth-century black Baptist tradition in part because of the independent nature of the Baptist polity. More historical information begins to emerge in the early twentieth century on black Baptist women after the organization of the National Baptist Convention in 1896. For a discussion of the women's organizational development within the black Baptist movement, see Higginbotham, *Righteous Discontent.*

22. For sketches of their lives, see Collier-Thomas, *Daughters of Thunder,* chaps. 2 and 4.

23. For more information on this controversy, see Sandy Dwayne Martin, *For God and Race: The Religious and Political Leadership of AMEZ Bishop James Walker Hood* (Columbia: Univ. of South Carolina Press, 1999).

24. See David W. Wills, "Womanhood and Domesticity in the A.M.E. Tradition: The Influence of Daniel Alexander Payne," in *Black Apostles at Home and Abroad: Afro-Americans and the Christian Mission from the Revolution to Reconstruction,* ed. David W. Wills and Richard Newman (Boston: G. K. Hall, 1982), 133–46.

25. Bishop Payne was seen as the mentor for several generations of young clergy. Steward was numbered among them. For an example of his mentoring role in the development of church leadership, see Gravely, "James Lynch."

26. Steward, *Memoirs,* 1.

27. Steward, *Fifty Years,* 172.

28. Benjamin Lee and Benjamin Tanner would both become bishops in the AME Church.
29. Steward, *Memoirs*, 62; Steward, *My First Four Years*, 5.
30. Steward, *Memoirs*, 53.
31. Ibid., 27, 36.
32. Ibid., 72–73.
33. "A New Book," *Christian Recorder*, 17 Jan. 1878, p. 3.
34. Steward, *Memoirs*, 20–21.
35. Daniel A. Payne, *A Treatise on Domestic Education* (1885; reprint, Freeport, N.Y.: Books for Libraries Press, 1971), 136–37.
36. Steward, *Memoirs*, 20–21.
37. Ibid., 45.
38. Dodson, "Power and Surrogate Leadership," 40.
39. See "An Open Letter" by the bishops' wives as a response to the request for the development of a missions' support society, *Christian Recorder*, 21 May 1874, p. 1.
40. Steward, *Memoirs*, 22.
41. Jualynne Dodson, "Nineteenth-Century AME Preaching Women," in *Women in New Worlds*, ed. Hilah F. Thomas and Rosemary Skinner Keller (Nashville: Abingdon, 1981), 281. See also Charles Spencer Smith, *A History of the African Methodist Episcopal Church* (Philadelphia: Book Concern of the AME Church, 1922), 81.
42. Steward, *Memoirs*, 22.
43. There were at least four articles published in the *Christian Recorder* between December 1872 and January 1873. Steward reprinted three of them in the *Memoirs*. Steward's understanding of sanctification was significantly influenced by his mother.
44. Steward, *Memoirs*, 23.
45. Ibid., 110.
46. Ibid., 116.
47. Steward wrote that the delegates chosen from the Philadelphia Annual Conference to attend the 1872 General Conference in Nashville were "Joshua Woodlin, James Morris Williams, Robert F. Wayman, George E. Boyer, Joseph H. Smith, Thomas A. Cuff, James Hollon and Theophilus G. Steward. James Hollon and Joseph H. Smith later declined and H. H. Lewis and Jeremiah Young were elected to fill the vacancies." See Steward, *Fifty Years*, 142.
48. Smith, *Autobiography*, 198–200.
49. Alice S. Felts, "Women in the Church," *Christian Recorder*, 18 Feb. 1886, p. 1.
50. By 1900, the AME Church officially brought into the structure the title deaconess. These women, who were "consecrated" but not ordained by the bishop, were to function as social work and social service providers within the church and not as official clergy. See Dodson, "Nineteenth-Century AME Preaching Women," 288–89.

51. See also the discussion of holiness women and their confrontation with the AME Church hierarchy in Jean McMahon Humez, "'My Spirit Eye': Some Functions of Spiritual and Visionary Experience in the Lives of Five Black Women Preachers, 1810–1880," in *Women and the Structure of Society: Selected Research from the Fifth Berkshire Conference on the History of Women,* ed. Barbara J. Harris and JoAnn K. McNamara (Durham, N.C.: Duke Univ. Press, 1984), 140. Jean M. Humez, ed., *Gift of Power: The Writings of Rebecca Jackson, Black Visionary, Shaker Eldress* (Amherst: Univ. of Massachusetts Press, 1981), 311–16.

52. Steward, *Memoirs,* 120, 46.

53. Steward was quick to say that Rebecca "affected no plainness of dress. "Plainness in dress" was a buzz word for the attire worn by holiness preacher women. Amanda Berry Smith indicated that her plain Quaker-styled dress marked her as a proponent of women's ordination. See Smith, *Autobiography,* 200.

54. Steward, *Memoirs,* 45.

55. For a discussion of Dr. Susan Steward, see Seraile, "Susan McKinney Steward," 27–44; Hallie Q. Brown, ed and comp., *Homespun Heroines and Other Women of Distinction* (Xenia, Ohio: Aldine Publishing, 1926; reprint, with an introduction by Randall Burkett, New York: Oxford Univ. Press, 1988), 160–68.

56. See James Melvin Washington, *Frustrated Fellowship: The Black Baptist Quest for Social Power* (Macon, Ga.: Mercer Univ. Press, 1986).

57. Evelyn Brooks Higginbotham, "Religion, Politics, and Gender: The Leadership of Nannie Helen Burroughs," in *This Far by Faith: Readings in African-American Women's Religious Biography,* ed. Judith Weisenfeld and Richard Newman (New York: Routledge, 1996), 142. Also see Higginbotham, *Righteous Discontent.*

58. See Collier-Thomas, *Daughters of Thunder,* 22–25.

59. Quoted in Moss, *American Negro Academy,* 38.

60. For a look at Sarah Garnet's life, see Hallie Q. Brown, *Homespun Heroines,* 110–16. See also sketch of Dr. Steward in M. A. Broadstone, *History of Greene County, Ohio* (Indianapolis: B. F. Bowen, 1918), 2:968–73.

61. Quoted by Maritcha R. Lyons in the introduction to Susan M. Steward, "Woman in Medicine: A Paper Read Before the National Association of Colored Women's Clubs at Wilberforce, Ohio August 6, 1914" (Wilberforce, Ohio), 3, available at Indiana Univ. Libraries, Bloomington. Also see Leslie L. Alexander, "Early Medical Heroes: Susan Smith McKinney-Steward, M.D., 1847–1918," *Crisis* 87, no. 1 (Jan. 1980): 22.

62. See Seraile, "Susan McKinney Steward," 35, and Brown, *Homespun Heroines,* 110.

63. Judith Weisenfeld, *African American Women and Christian Activism: New York's Black YWCA, 1905–1945* (Cambridge: Harvard Univ. Press, 1997), 42–43.

64. James J. Walsh, *Old-time Makers of Medicine: The Story of the Students and Teachers of the Sciences Related to Medicine during the Middle Ages* (New York: Fordham Univ. Press, 1911).
65. Steward, "Woman in Medicine," 20.
66. Susan M. Steward, "Colored American Women," *Crisis* 3, no. 1. (Nov. 1911): 33–34. Seraile, "Susan McKinney Steward," 39, indicated that the paper was reread before a gathering of friends and family in Brooklyn on 9 September 1911. The paper was not listed among the conference papers in *Papers on Inter-Racial Problems.* Excerpts from the paper were published in the *Crisis* magazine. W. E. B. Du Bois, editor of the *Crisis* magazine, also attended and read a paper at this conference.
67. Steward, "Colored American Women," 34.
68. Ibid., 33.
69. Maria Steward was active in the Women's Christian Temperance Union No. 6 and served as its president in 1884. See Seraile, "Susan McKinney Steward," 35. See also Dorothy Salem, *To Better Our World: Black Women in Organized Reform, 1890–1920* (Brooklyn: Carlson Publishing, 1990), 37.
70. Steward, *Our Civilization,* 25.
71. Brown, *Homespun Heroines,* 166.

Chapter 7

1. Steward, *Fifty Years,* 338, 344.
2. Ibid., 149–51. In 1873, after two years of service at Bethel AME Church in Wilmington, Steward responded to a missionary call to Haiti. While he was a pastor in Wilmington he obtained a private tutor in French which helped to prepared him for his Haitian missionary journey. Yet he found himself otherwise ill prepared for the mission to Haiti and left defeated. He returned to the United States and was appointed to Sussex County, Delaware. He later wrote a pamphlet, not extant, outlining his failed mission to Haiti called *African Methodism in Haiti.*
3. Steward was not afraid to use force for self-defense, as seen in the diary note dated 8 March 1869, when he perceived trouble by a group of whites: "Saw a crowd of (white) 'roughs' gathering [outside the] store evidently bent on mischief[,] came home fired off my pistol and reloaded it." Steward Diary, Steward Papers.
4. See Steward, *Army as a Trained Force,* 6–7, where Steward indicated that "[w]e [African Americans] who are here, and the race we represent, owe our deliverance from chattel slavery to the men in arms who conquered the Slaveholders' Rebellion. It is a sad thought, but nevertheless one too true thus far in human history, that liberty, man's greatest earthly boon, can be reached only through a pathway of blood. The army made good our declaration of independence; and upon the army and navy Lincoln relied for the efficacy of his plan of emancipation."

5. Steward, *Army as a Trained Force,* 8, 23.
6. T. G. Steward to John Wanamaker, 8 Oct. 1891, Selected ACP, T. G. Steward, RG 94, NA.
7. See Stover, *Up from Handymen* 3:88–91; Earl F. Stover, "Chaplain Henry V. Plummer, His Ministry and His Court-Martial," *Nebraska History* (Spring 1975): 20–50; Frank N Schubert, "Henry Vinton Plummer," in Logan and Winston, *Dictionary of American Biography,* 498–99.
8. T. G. Steward to John Wanamaker, 8 Oct. 1891, Selected ACP, T. G. Steward, RG 94, NA.
9. See E. F. Tibbott, private secretary to General Benjamin Harrison, to T. G. Steward, 6 Dec. 1894, Monroe Trotter Papers, Boston Univ. Archives.
10. See Steward, *Fifty Years,* 272, 285. Steward served as interim pastor of the Presbyterian Church of Missoula for a number of years. He was recognized for his service via a resolution, dated 13 March 1895, by the local session of the church: "We the session of the Presbyterian Church of Missoula at a regular meeting of said body passed a resolution deeming it our duty to express our high sense of gratitude to you, the Rev.d. T. G. Steward Chaplain at Fort Missoula, for the very considerate and Christian Spirit manifested towards us in your continuing to come and fill our Pulpit, when we were without a Pastor and we can assure our Brother in Christ of our unfeigned appreciation of the grand and doctrinal appeals so ably set before us for the up building of Christian character and growth in grace and we will ever continue to think kindly of you, and bless God that He has so richly endowed a human vessel with such rare gifts, and whenever in the Providence of God you may be called to labour for the Redeemer[']s cause here on earth we would pray that your every effort may be followed with the greatest success, and that your every undertaking may be owned and blessed of the Lord, and you finally crowned with His richest laurels, and our united best wishes are that you may fare-well in time and fare-well in Eternity."
11. Steward, *Fifty Years,* 278–79. He also spoke of these southern transplants in his article "A Glimpse of Montana Life," *Independent,* 22 Aug. 1895, pp. 114–15. Steward, *Fifty Years,* 281–89; Steward, "Colonel George L. Andrews," 437.
12. T. G. Steward, "The Colored American as a Soldier," *United Service* 25 (Jan.–June 1894): 323.
13. Ibid., 323–27. Steward furthered his argument regarding the relative healthiness of the African Americans, in general, and of African American soldiers, in particular, in an article titled "Negro Mortality," *Social Economist,* Oct. 1895. See also the reprint in Steward, *Fifty Years,* 296–302.
14. See Steward, *Colored Regulars.*
15. According to August Meier, *Negro Thought in America, 1880–1915: Racial Ideologies in the Age of Booker T. Washington* (Ann Arbor: Univ. of Michigan Press, 1963), 57, Benjamin Arnett was known to have been the chief advisor to President McKinley on African American appointments. Steward indicated in Steward, *Fifty Years,* 306–7, he was "relieved from duty at Fort Logan

on the special request of Bishop B. W. Arnett and assigned to the honorable task of writing the history of the Colored Regulars, dealing particularly with their work in Cuba."

16. These were two periodicals based in New York and Boston respectively.

17. William H. Ward to T. G. Steward, 10 Dec. 1898; and Paul Tyner to T. G. Steward, 16 Dec. 1898, Selected ACP, T. G. Steward, RG 94, NA.

18. See Colonel A. S. Burt to Adjutant General U.S. Army, 13 February 1899, Selected ACP, T. G. Steward, RG 94, NA. The exact reason for the transfer is not clear, except that Colonel Burt indicated that Steward's services were not needed at Fort Logan due to the presence of "Post Chaplain J. B. McCleery, who, in addition to his regular duties is a valuable officer as Commissary and officer in charge of prisoners and counsel for prisoners before G. C. M. There are so few officers here that Chaplain McCleery's services can be ill spared. . . . Chaplain Steward is of no value whatever beyond his Chaplain's functions and there are many posts in Arizona and New Mexico garrisoned by colored soldiers who have no opportunities of receiving religious attention, particularly from a Chaplain of their own color." It is possible that Burt took advantage of Steward's request for leave to tend to his ill wife, Dr. Susan Steward, in Brooklyn. He was given a one-month leave on 22 December 1898, which was extended on January 16 for two more months as Steward stressed "without any application on my part or real desire for it." See Steward's Efficiency Report, 1 July 1899, Selected ACP, T. G. Steward, RG 94, NA.

19. Seraile, *Voice of Dissent,* 124–25. Seraile noted that Steward, in part, wanted the transfer to West Point in order to be closer to his two older sons, Charles and Frank, who were students at Harvard at the time, and to assist his other sons in entering an eastern university.

20. Benjamin W. Arnett to R. A. Alger, 12 Mar. 1899; and Levi J. Coppin to William McKinley 7 Mar. 1899, Selected ACP, T. G. Steward, RG 94, NA.

21. Benjamin W. Arnett to R. A. Alger, 12 Mar. 1899, Selected ACP, T. G. Steward, RG 94, NA.

22. Levi J. Coppin to William McKinley 7 Mar. 1899, Selected ACP, T. G. Steward, RG 94, NA.

23. Steward, *Colored Regulars,* 12.

24. See Deuteronomy 32:21 and Romans 10:19.

25. Steward, *Colored Regulars,* 14–15.

26. Ibid., 15.

27. Ibid.

28. Ibid., 18–19.

29. Ibid., 59.

30. Ibid., 61.

31. George Washington Williams, *A History of the Negro Troops in the War of the Rebellion, 1861–1865* (New York: Harper & Brothers, 1888).

32. Steward, *Colored Regulars,* 63.

33. This article was first read before the American Negro Academy in 1898.
34. Steward, *Haitian Revolution.* Steward also challenged the United States to move toward a peaceful benevolence as it ruled those countries which it occupied. That he defended their rights to self-determination was evident in *The Haitian Revolution.* His goal was to present a people of color who were respectable in the eyes of whites and who were shown to be more committed to democracy, freedom and independence than white America.
35. Steward, *Colored Regulars,* 82. Also see Theophilus Gould Steward, "How the Black St. Domingo Legion Saved the Patriot Army in the Siege of Savannah, 1779," *American Negro Academy* 5 (1899): 15.
36. Steward, *Colored Regulars,* 88–89, 199, 305–6.
37. Quoted in George P. Mark III, ed. and comp., *The Black Press Views American Imperialism (1898–1900),* with a preface by William Loren Katz (New York: Arno Press and the New York Times, 1971), 33–34.
38. See Mark, *Black Press,* 33–50. Between eight and ten thousand blacks entered as volunteers in the army infantries: the Seventh, Eighth, Ninth, and Tenth United States Volunteer Infantries. These troops came from states such as Alabama, Ohio, Massachusetts, Illinois, Kansas, Indiana, Virginia, and North Carolina. David Trask indicated that only Illinois, Kansas, and North Carolina permitted black commissioned officers. See David F. Trask, *The War with Spain in 1898* (New York: Macmillan, 1981), 156. Frank Steward in his detailing of colored officers concurred with Trask's observation but added that two battalions of black soldiers, one each from Ohio and Indiana, were "entirely under colored officers." See Steward, *Colored Regulars,* 322.
39. Steward, *Colored Regulars,* 92.
40. Ibid. Steward's paternalistic rhetoric regarding the war effort was reflective of a much larger view of the war held by many. Even the social gospel advocate, Washington Gladden articulated his support for the war in similar language. Gladden indicated in a sermon which was later published as *Our Nation and Her Neighbors,* that "[t]o break in pieces the oppressor, to lift from a whole population the heavy hand of the spoiler, to lead in light and liberty, peace and plenty—is there any better work than this for the great nations of the earth?" He further stated that America would fight "not for territory or empire or national honor, but for the redress of wrongs not our own, for the establishment of peace and justice in the earth. . . . Any foreign war which had not for its central purpose the welfare of humanity would curse this nation with a great curse." Quoted in Trask, *War with Spain in 1898,* 58. See also Washington Gladden, *Our Nation and Her Neighbors* (Columbus, Ohio: Quinius and Ridenour, 1898).
41. Ida Wells-Barnett, *On Lynchings: Mob Rule in New Orleans,* 46–47. Wells-Barnett was one of Steward's contemporaries. She wrote three different pamphlets, *Southern Horrors* (1892), *A Red Record* (1895), and *Mob Rule in New Orleans* (1900), outlining the travail of lynchings of African Americans

by whites. (The three volumes were combined into a single volume titled *On Lynchings: Southern Horrors, A Red Record, and Mob Rule in New Orleans,* with a new preface by August Meier [New York: Arno and New York Times Press, 1969].)

42. Theophilus Gould Steward, *Independent,* 28 Apr. 1898, pp. 535–36. Also quoted in the *Nation,* 5 May 1898, 335, and in Herbert Aptheker, ed., *A Documentary History of the Negro People in the United States* with a preface by W. E. B. Du Bois (New York: Citadel Press, 1969), 822–23. For further descriptions of the segregation incident at Chattanooga, see Theophilus Gould Steward, "The New Colored Soldier," *Independent,* 16 June 1898, pp. 781–82.

43. Theophilus Gould Steward, "The Reign of the Mob," *Independent,* 11 May 1899, pp. 1296–97.

44. For a detailed treatment of the events surrounding the resignation of the six black officers of the Sixth Virginia, see Edward A. Johnson, *History of Negro Soldiers in the Spanish-American War and Other Items of Interest* (Raleigh, N.C.: Capital Printing, 1899), 92–112.

45. Theophilus Gould Steward, "No Grounds for Complaint," *Colored American,* 29 Oct. 1898, p. 1. This military equality was elusive at best, as has been borne out in American military history. The Brownsville, Texas, incident of 1906 was a case in point during Steward's own lifetime. The situation involved his own regiment, which was alleged to have shot up the town of Brownsville. The regiment was dishonorably discharged from the Army on less than convincing evidence. Steward placed most of the blame on the racist environment in Texas rather than placing significant weight on the army and President Theodore Roosevelt who discharged the three companies.

46. Ibid., 1, 5.

47. Ibid.

48. Steward, *Fifty Years,* 252–53.

49. Ibid., 254. In response to the protest the army reorganized the volunteer army and included two black regiments. With this the army reinstated some of the black officers who had been discharged. Steward was hopeful that, with the expansion of the standing army, "the American Negro, both as soldier and officer, will receive that full measure of justice of which the formation of the present two regiments is so conspicuous a part." See *Fifty Years,* 255.

50. Steward, "Garrisoning Cuba and Porto Rico," 1927.

51. Ibid., 1928. This remark is noteworthy for the implicit racist tone toward Native Americans, especially given the fact that Steward's family had intermarried with American Indians.

52. Ibid.

53. Bernard C. Nalty, *Strength for the Fight: A History of Black Americans in the Military* (New York: Free Press, 1986), 73.

54. Steward, *Fifty Years,* 317–18.

55. Ibid., 338.

56. Quoted in Willard B. Gatewood Jr., *Black Americans and the White Man's Burden* (Urbana: Univ. of Illinois Press, 1975), 282.

57. For a discussion of the views of white Americans toward race in the Philippines, see Gatewood, *Black Americans and the White Man's Burden,* 281–86.

58. Patrick Mason to the *Cleveland Gazette* in Willard B. Gatewood Jr., *"Smoked Yankees" and the Struggle for Empire: Letters from Negro Soldiers, 1898–1902* (Fayetteville: Univ. of Arkansas Press, 1987), 257.

59. Fragment manuscript, Steward Papers.

60. Ibid.

61. Ibid.

62. Ibid.

63. Steward, *Fifty Years,* 318–19.

64. Theophilus Gould Steward, "Manila," *Christian Recorder,* 4 Oct. 1900, p. 1.

65. Theophilus Gould Steward, "The Race Issue, So-Called, a Social Matter Only," *Competitor* 1, no. 3 (Mar. 1920): 6.

66. Ibid.

67. Ibid., 7.

68. Ibid.

69. Ibid.

70. Ibid.

71. See Lothrop Stoddard, *Rising Tide of Color Against White World Supremacy* (New York: C. Scribner's Son, 1920).

72. For a brief discussion of Stoddard and his involvement in the development of racial theory, see Michael Barkum, *Religion and the Right: The origins of the Christian Identity Movement,* rev. ed. (Chapel Hill: Univ. of North Carolina Press, 1997), 137–38.

73. Theophilus Gould Steward, "The White World Peril Fore=cast and Facts, Lothrop Stoddard's Book," *A.M.E. Church Review* 37 (July 1920): 34–35.

74. Steward, *End of the World,* 78.

Bibliography

Books and Published Pamphlets by Theophilus Gould Steward

Active Service; or, Religious Work Among U.S. Soldiers. Introduction by John B. Ketchum, Cor. Sec'y, etc. New York: United States Army Aid Association, n.d.

The Army as a Trained Force and the Birth of the Republic: Addresses. Cincinnati: By the Author, c. 1904.

A Charleston Love Story; or, Hortense Vanross. New York: F. Tennyson Neely, 1899.

The Colored Regulars in the United States Army: With a Sketch of the History of the Colored American, and an Account of His Services in the Wars of the Country, from the Period of the Revolutionary War to 1899. Introductory Letter from Lieutenant-General Nelson A. Miles. Philadelphia: AME Book Concern, 1904; New York: Arno Press and the New York Times, 1969.

The Divine Attributes: Being an Examination of What Is Said of God, with Relation to Nature and Sentiment, and Rational Creatures, with Special Treatment of Omnipresence, with Analysis and Notes. Tawawa Series in Systematic Divinity, No. 1. Philadelphia: Christian Recorder Print, 1884.

The End of the World; or, Clearing the Way for the Fullness of the Gentiles. With an Exposition of Psalm 68:31 by James A. Handy, D.D. Philadelphia: AME Church Book Rooms, 1888.

Fifty Years in the Gospel Ministry: From 1864 to 1914. Introduction by Rev. Reverdy C. Ransom. Philadelphia: AME Book Concern, n.d.

Genesis Re-Read; or, The Latest Conclusions of Physical Science, Viewed in Their Relation to the Mosaic Record. To which is Annexed an Important Chapter on the Direct Evidences of Christianity by Bishop J. P. Campbell, D.D, LL.D. Philadelphia: AME Book Rooms, 1885.

———, with William Steward. *Gouldtown: A Very Remarkable Settlement of Ancient Date.* Philadelphia: J. B. Lippincott, 1913.

The Haitian Revolution: 1791 to 1804 or Side Lights on the French Revolution. 1971. Reprint, New York: Russell and Russell, 1914.

"How the Black St. Domingo Legion Saved the Patriot Army in the Siege of Savannah, 1799." *American Negro Academy* 5 (1899).

The Incarnation of the Son of God: Annual Sermon Preached at Wilberforce University June 13, 1880. Philadelphia: AME Book Rooms, 1881.

Memoirs of Mrs. Rebecca Steward, Containing a Full Sketch of Her Life, with Various Selections from Her Writings and Letters; Also Contributions from Bishop Campbell, D.D., Prof. B. F Lee of Wilberforce University, B. T. Tanner, D.D., Editor of the Christian Recorder, Rev. T. Gould, Mrs. Elizabeth Lloyd, and Wm. Steward. Philadelphia: Publication Department of the AME Church, 1877.

"Message of San Domingo to the African Race." *Papers of the American Negro Academy,* Dec. 28, 29, 1915, 25–37.

My First Four Years in the Itineracy of the African Methodist Episcopal Church. Brooklyn: By the Author, 1876.

Our Civilization; a Popular Lecture. Wilberforce, Ohio: c. 1919.

Pioneer Echoes: Six Special Sermons. Baltimore: Hoffman, 1889.

Articles by Theophilus Gould Steward

"The Activities of Departed Spirits." *A.M.E. Church Review* 39 (Oct. 1922): 89–94.

"Angels." *A.M.E. Church Review* 38 (Jan. 1922): 118–22.

"The Army as a Trained Force." In *Masterpieces of Negro Eloquence: The Best Speeches Delivered by the Negro from the Days of Slavery to the Present time,* ed. Alice Moore Dunbar, 277–89. New York: Bookery Publishing, 1914; New York: Johnson Reprint, 1970.

"Camp Life at Chickamauga." *Independent,* May 12, 1898, pp. 614.

"Colonel George L. Andrews." *Harpers Weekly,* May 7, 1892, 437.

"The Colored American as a Soldier." *United Service* 25 (Jan.–June 1894): 323–27.

"The Colored Crack Rifle Shot." *Army Magazine,* Oct. 1894, 67–70.

"The Coming of the Prince." Poem. *A.M.E. Church Review* 37 (Oct. 1920): 84–85.

"Communion with Men-Angels." *A.M.E. Church Review* 39 (July 1922): 29–32.

"Cultured Society and the Negro." *Independent,* Apr. 16, 1896, p. 514.

"Distinguished Women of the Bible—Rebecca." *Christian Recorder,* Mar. 30, 1876, p. 8.

"The Doctrine of the Incarnation Stated." *A.M.E. Church Review* 9 (Jan. 1893): 214–23.

"The First Move in the War." *Independent,* Apr. 28, 1898, pp. 535–36.

"Garrisoning Cuba and Porto Rico." *Independent,* Dec. 29, 1898, pp. 1927–28.

"Germany and Hayti." *Independent,* Dec. 2, 1897, pp. 1569–70.

"A Glimpse of Montana Life." *Independent,* Aug. 22, 1895, pp. 114–15.

"The Gospel in the Army." *Independent,* Feb. 20, 1896, p. 249.

"History and the Races—Pernicious School History." *A.M.E. Church Review* 19 (July 1902): 423–26.

"Holy Week in Manila." *Colored American Magazine,* Apr. 1901, 446–55.

"The Influence of Euphony upon the Employment of Language." *A.M.E. Church Review* (Apr. 1884): 41–43.

"In Luzon." *Independent,* Feb. 1, 1900, pp. 312–14.

"Inspiration and Immortality." *A.M.E. Church Review* 10 (Apr. 1894): 499–507.

"Ira Aldridge, a Great American Negro Actor of the Past Century." *A.M.E. Church Review* 29 (Oct. 1912): 113–17.

"The Itinerant." Poem. *A.M.E. Church Review* 32 (July 1915): 39.

"Life in a Negro Republic." *Independent* 56 (Mar. 3, 1904): 477–79.

"The Morals of the Army." *Independent,* Feb. 11, 1892, p. 195.

"Negro Mortality." *Social Economist* 9 (1895): 204–7.

"The New Colored Soldier." *Independent,* June 16, 1898, pp. 781–82.

"A New Reading of an Old Phrase: The End of the World ('Η συνιελεια του αιωνοσ)." *A.M.E. Church Review* 5 (Jan. 1889): 204–5.

"No Grounds for Complaint." *Colored American,* Oct. 29, 1898, pp. 1 and 5.

"The Old and New Commandments; or, Brotherhood in Creation and Brotherhood in Christ Compared." *A.M.E. Church Review* 6, no. 3 (Jan. 1890): 306–8.

"A Plea for Patriotism." *Independent,* Sept. 29, 1898, pp. 887–88.

"The Race Issue, So-Called, a Social Matter Only." *Competitor* (Mar. 1920): 6–7.

"The Reign of the Mob." *Independent,* May 11, 1899, pp. 1296–97.

"Ripeness in the Gospel Ministry." *A.M.E. Church Review* 1 (July 1884): 66–68.

"Robert Purvis, Last Survivor of the American Anti-Slavery Society." *A.M.E. Church Review* 13 (Oct. 1897): 214–18.

"Seeing the Unseen." *A.M.E. Church Review* 38 (July 1921): 6–8.

"Some Glimpses of Ante Bellum Negro Literature." *A.M.E. Church Review* 29 (Jan. 1913): 229–32.

"The Spirit of the Just." *A.M.E. Church Review* 38 (Apr. 1922): 176–78.

"Starving Laborers and the 'Hired Soldier.'" *United Service* 14 (Oct. 1895).

"The Third Witness." *A.M.E. Church Review* 7 (Jan. 1891): 261–63.

"Two Kinds of 'Fogy.'" *Independent,* Sept. 16, 1897, pp. 1198–99.

"Two Years in Luzon. I. Filipino Characteristics." *Colored American Magazine* 4 (Nov. 1901): 4–10.

"Two Years in Luzon. II. Examining Schools, Etc." *Colored American Magazine* 4 (Jan.–Feb. 1902): 166–67.

"Two Years in Luzon. III. Preparations for Civil Government." *Colored American Magazine,* Aug. 1902, 244–49.

"Washington and Crummell." *Colored American,* Oct. 29, 1898, p. 6.

"The White World Peril Fore-casts and Facts, Lothrop Stoddard's Book." *A.M.E. Church Review* 37 (Jan. 1920): 34–35.

Archival Materials

American Missionary Association Collection, Amistad Research Center, Tulane Univ.

American Negro Historical Society Papers, Leon Gardiner Collection, Historical Society of Pennsylvania.

Douglass Papers, Library of Congress. Photocopies.

Historical Society of Delaware, Wilmington, Delaware.

Monroe Trotter/Guardian Papers, Boston Univ.

T. G. Steward Individual Report under G.O. 41, A.G.O. Selected ACP, T. G. Steward, RG 94, National Archives. Photocopies.

Theophilus Gould Steward Papers, Archive Collection, Schomburg Center for Research in Black Culture, New York Public Library.

Newspapers and Journals

American Missionary

Christian Recorder

Cleveland Gazette

Colored American

Daily Commercial

Delaware State Journal

Every Evening

Indianapolis News

Macon American Union

Morning News

National Anti-Slavery Standard

New National Era

New York Times

Philadelphia Press

General Bibliography

Adams, Oscar Fay. *Dictionary of American Authors.* Boston: Houghton, Mifflin and Co., 1897.

African Wesleyan Methodist Episcopal Church. Brooklyn, N.Y.: African Wesleyan Methodist Episcopal Church Known as Bridge Street AME Church, 1980.

Ahlstrom, Sydney E. "The Scottish Philosophy and American Theology." *Church History* 24 (1955): 257–72.

Alexander, Leslie L. "Early Medical Heroes: Susan Smith McKinney-Steward, M.D., 1847–1918." *Crisis* 87, no. 1 (Jan. 1980): 21–23.

Alford, Henry. *The New Testament for English Readers: Containing the Authorized Version, with Marginal Corrections of Readings and Renderings; and a Critical and Explanatory.* Vols. 1 and 2. London: Rivingtons, 1868, 1872.

Allen, Richard. *The Life Experience and Gospel Labors of the Rt. Rev. Richard Allen.* With an introduction by George A. Singleton. Nashville: Abingdon Press, 1960.

Allen, Robert L. *Black Awakening in Capitalist America.* Garden City, N.Y.: Doubleday 1970.

Andrews, William L. "Liberal Religion and Free Love: An Undiscovered Afro-American Novel of the 1890's." *MELUS: The Journal of the Society for the Study of the Multi-Ethnic Literature of the United States* 9, no.1 (Spring 1982): 23–36.

————, ed. *Sisters of the Spirit: Three Black Women's Autobiographies of the Nineteenth Century.* Bloomington: Indiana Univ. Press, 1986.

Angell, Stephen Ward. *Bishop Henry McNeal Turner and the African-American Religion in the South.* Knoxville: Univ. of Tennessee Press, 1992.

————. "The Controversy over Women's Ministry in the African Methodist Episcopal Church during The 1800's: The Case of Sarah Ann Hughes." In *This Far by Faith: Readings in African-American Women's Religious Biography,* ed. Judith Weisenfeld and Richard Newman. 94–109. New York: Routledge, 1996.

Annual Minutes of the Philadelphia Conference of the African Methodist Episcopal Church Held in Smyrna, Delaware, May 11–17, A.D. *1881.* Philadelphia: Christian Recorder Print, 1881.

Aptheker, Herbert, ed. *The Correspondence of W. E. B. Du Bois.* Vol. 1, *Selections, 1877–1934.* Amherst: Univ. of Massachusetts Press, 1973.

————. *A Documentary History of the Negro People in the United States.* With a preface by W. E. B. Du Bois. New York: Citadel Press, 1969.

Arnett, B. W., and S. T. Mitchell, comps. *The Wilberforce Alumnal: A Comprehensive Review of the Origin, Development and Present Status of Wilberforce University.* Xenia, Ohio: Printed at the Gazette Office, 1885.

Arnett, Benjamin W., ed. *Proceedings of the Quarto-Centennial Conference of the African M. E. Church of South Carolina at Charleston, S.C., May 15, 16, and*

17, 1889 (1890). Archives and Special Collections, Rembert E. Stokes Learning Resources Center Library, Wilberforce Univ.

Barkum, Michael. *Religion and the Right: The Origins of the Christian Identity Movement.* Rev. ed. Chapel Hill: Univ. of North Carolina Press, 1997.

Beard, Charles A., and Mary R. Beard. *The American Spirit: A Study of the Idea of Civilization in the United States.* Vol. 4. New York: Macmillan, 1942.

Becker, William H. "The Black Church: Manhood and Mission." *Journal of the American Academy of Religion* 40, no. 3 (Sept. 1972): 316–33.

Bell, Howard H., ed. *Minutes of the Proceedings of the National Negro Conventions, 1830–1864.* New York: Arno Press and the New York Times, 1969.

Berger, Peter L., and Richard John Neuhaus. *To Empower People: The Role of Mediating Structures in Public Policy.* Washington, D.C.: American Enterprise Institute for Public Policy Research, 1977.

Blake, John B. "Mary Gove Nichols, Prophetess of Health." In *Women and Health in America,* ed. Judith Walzer Leavitt, 359–75. Madison: Univ. of Wisconsin Press, 1984.

Boller, Paul F., Jr. *American Transcendentalism, 1830–1860: An Intellectual Inquiry.* New York: G. P. Putnam's Sons, 1974.

Bracey, John H., Jr., August Meier, and Elliot Rudwick, eds. *Black Nationalism in America.* New York: Bobbs-Merrill, 1970.

Brewton, Barry. *Almost White.* Toronto: Collier, 1969.

Broadstone, M. A. *History of Greene County, Ohio.* Vol. 2. Indianapolis: B. F. Bowen, 1918.

———. "Rev. Theophilus Gould Steward and S. Maria Steward, M.D." In Broadstone, *History of Greene County, Ohio,* 968–73.

Brown, Hallie Q., ed. and comp. *Homespun Heroines and Other Women of Distinction.* Xenia, Ohio: Aldine Publishing, 1926; reprint, with an introduction by Randall Burkett, New York: Oxford Univ. Press, 1988.

Bushnell, Horace. *Christian Nurture.* New York: Scribner, Armstrong, 1876.

Butchart, Ronald E. *Northern Schools, Southern Blacks, and Reconstruction: Freedmen's Education, 1862–1875.* Westport, Conn.: Greenwood Press, 1980.

Butler, Joseph. *Ethical Discourses and Essay on Virtue.* Arranged as a Treatise on Moral Philosophy; and edited, with an analysis, by J. T. Champlin, D.D. Boston: John P. Jewett, 1859.

Caleff, Susan E. "Gender, Ideology and the Water-Cure Movement." In *Other Healers: Unorthodox Medicine in America,* ed. Norman Gevitz. 82–98. Baltimore: Johns Hopkins Univ. Press, 1988.

Carter, Paul A. *The Spiritual Crisis of the Gilded Age.* DeKalb: Northern Illinois Univ. Press, 1971.

Cauthen, Kenneth. *The Impact of American Religious Liberalism.* Washington, D.C.: Univ. Press of America, 1983.

Cayleff, Susan E. *Wash and Be Healed: The Water-Cure Movement and Women's Health.* Philadelphia: Temple Univ. Press, 1987.

Collier-Thomas, Bettye, ed. *Daughters of Thunder: Black Women Preachers and Their Sermons, 1850–1979.* San Francisco: Jossey-Bass Publishers, 1998.

Cone, James H. *Black Power and Black Theology.* Twentieth Anniversary Edition. New York: HarperSanFrancisco, 1989.

Conrad, Henry C. *A Glimpse of the Colored Schools of Delaware: A Paper Read before the Annual Meeting of the State Teachers' Association, Held at Rehoboth Beach, Delaware, August 21, 1883.* Wilmington: James and Webb, 1883.

Coppin, L. J. *Unwritten History.* 1919. Reprint, New York: Negro Univ. Press, 1968.

Crummell, Alexander. *Civilization: The Primal Need of the Race.* Occasional Papers, No. 3. Washington, D.C.: American Negro Academy.

De Boer, Clara. "The Role of Afro-Americans in the Origins and Work of the American Missionary Association." Ph.D. diss., Rutgers Univ., 1973.

Deichmann, Wendy Jane. "Josiah Strong: Practical Theologian and Social Crusader for a Global Kingdom." Ph.D. diss., Drew Univ., 1991.

Dodson, Jualynne. "Nineteenth-Century AME Preaching Women." In *Women in New Worlds,* ed. Hilah F. Thomas and Rosemary Skinner Keller. 276–89. Nashville: Abingdon, 1981.

———. "Power and Surrogate Leadership: Black Women and Organized Religion." *Sage,* V, no. 2 (Fall 1988): 37–42.

———. "Women's Ministries and the African Methodist Episcopal Tradition." *Religious Institutions and Women's Leadership: New Roles Inside the Mainstream,* ed. Catherine Wessinger. 125–38. Columbia: Univ. of South Carolina Press, 1996.

Donegan, Jane B. *"Hydropathic Highway to Health": Women and Water-Cure in Antebellum America.* New York: Greenwood Press, 1986.

Drake, Richard B. "Freedman's Aid Societies and Sectional Compromise." *Journal of Southern History* 29, no. 2 (May 1963): 175–86.

Du Bois, W. E. B. *Black Reconstruction.* New York: Harcourt, Brace, 1935; reprint, with introduction by Herbert Aptheker, Millwood, N.Y.: Kraus-Thomson Organization, 1976.

———. *The Philadelphia Negro: A Social Study.* Philadelphia: Univ. of Pennsylvania, 1899.

———. *The Souls of Black Folk.* Greenwich, Conn.: Fawcett Publications, 1961.

Dvorak, Katharine L. *An African-American Exodus: The Segregation of the Southern Churches.* Brooklyn, N.Y.: Carlson Publishing, 1991.

Emilio, Luis F. *A Brave Black Regiment: History of the Fifty-Fourth Regiment of Massachusetts Volunteer Infantry, 1863–1865.* 2d ed. Revised and Corrected, with Appendix upon Treatment of Colored Prisoners of War. Boston: Boston Book, 1894; New York: Arno Press and the New York Times, 1969.

Felts, Alice S. "Women in the Church." *Christian Recorder* 24, no. 7 (Feb. 18, 1886).

Fields, Barbara J. "Ideology and Race in American History." In *Region, Race and Reconstruction: Essays in Honor of C. Vann Woodward,* ed. J. Morgan Kousser and James M. McPherson. 143–77. New York: Oxford Univ. Press, 1982.

Fitchett, E. Horace. "The Free Negro in Charleston, South Carolina." Ph.D. diss., Univ. of Chicago, 1950.

Foner, Eric. *Reconstruction: America's Unfinished Revolution 1863–1877.* New York: Harper and Row, 1988.

Foster, Lawrence. *Religion and Sexuality: The Shakers, the Mormons, and the Oneida Community.* Chicago: Univ. of Illinois Press, 1984.

Frothingham, O. B. "Education and Religion." *Independent* 18 (July 12, 1866): 1–2.

Fulop, Timothy E. "'The Future Golden Day of the Race': Millennialism and Black Americans in the Nadir, 1877–1901." *Harvard Theological Review* 84, no. 1 (1991): 75–99.

Gaines, Wesley J. *African Methodism in the South; or, Twenty-Five Years of Freedom.* With an introduction by W. S. Scarborough. Atlanta, Ga.: Franklin, 1890.

Gatewood, Willard B., Jr. *Aristocrats of Color: The Black Elite, 1880–1920.* Indianapolis: Indiana Univ. Press, 1990.

———. *Black Americans and the White Man's Burden* . Urbana: Univ. of Illinois Press, 1975.

———. *"Smoked Yankees" and the Struggle for Empire: Letters from Negro Soldiers, 1898–1902.* Fayetteville: Univ. of Arkansas Press, 1987.

George, Carol V. R. *Segregated Sabbaths: Richard Allen and the Emergence of Independent Black Churches, 1760–1840.* New York: Oxford Univ. Press, 1973.

Gladden, Washington. *Our Nation and Her Neighbors.* Columbus, Ohio: Quinius and Ridenour, 1898.

Gleason, Philip. "From Free-Love to Catholicism: Dr. and Mrs. Thomas L. Nichols at Yellow Springs." *Ohio Historical Quarterly* 70 (Oct. 1961): 283–307.

Gossett, Thomas F. *Race: The History of an Idea in America.* New York: Schocken Books, 1965.

Grave, A. *The Scottish Philosophy of Common Sense.* Oxford: Oxford Univ. Press, 1960.

Gravely, William B. "African Methodism and the Rise of Black Denominationalism." In *Rethinking Methodist History: A Bicentennial Historical Consultation,* ed. R. Richey and K. Rowe. Nashville: Kingswood Books, 1985.

———. "James Lynch and the Black Christian Mission During Reconstruction." In *Black Apostles at Home and Abroad: Afro-Americans and the Christian Mission from the Revolution to Reconstruction,* ed. David W. Wills and Richard Newman. Boston: G. K. Hall, 1982.

Griffin, Paul. *Black Theology as the Foundation of Three Methodist Colleges.* Washington, D.C.: Univ. of America Press, 1984.

———. "The Theology of Black Rational Orthodoxy, 1863 to 1935." Paper presented at the annual meeting of the American Academy of Religion, Atlanta, Ga., Nov. 22–25, 1986.

Grimké, Francis. "Colored Men as Professors in Colored Institutions." *A.M.E. Church Review* 2, no. 2 (Oct. 1885): 142.

Guizot, François. *The History of Civilization from the Fall of the Roman Empire the French Revolution.* Translated by William Hazlitt. London: Bell and Daldy, 1873.

Habermas, Jürgen. "The Public Sphere: An Encyclopedia Article (1964)." *New German Critique* 1 (Fall 1974): 49–55.

Hancock, Harold B. "The Status of the Negro in Delaware after the Civil War, 1865–75." *Delaware History* 13 (Apr. 1968): 57–66.

Handy, James A. "The Mystery of Man." *A.M.E. Church Review* 2 (July 1885): 20.

Handy, Robert. *A Christian America: Protestant Hopes and Historical Realities.* 2d. ed. New York: Oxford Univ. Press, 1984.

Harding, Vincent. "Religion and Resistance Among Antebellum Negroes, 1800–1860." In *Religion in American History: Interpretive Essays,* ed. John M. Mulder and John F. Wilson, 270–87. Englewood Cliffs, N.J.: Prentice-Hall, 1978.

Hatch, Nathan O. *The Democratization of American Christianity.* New Haven, Conn.: Yale Univ. Press, 1988.

Hegel, G. W. F. *Elements of the Philosophy of Right.* Ed. Allen W. Wood and translated by H. B. Nisbet. Cambridge: Cambridge Univ. Press, 1991.

Hershberg, Theodore, and Henry Williams. "Mulattoes and Blacks: Intra-group Color Differences and Social Stratification in Nineteenth-Century Philadelphia." In *Philadelphia: Work, Space, Family, and Group Experience in the Nineteenth/Century: Essays toward an Interdisciplinary History of the City,* ed. Theodore Hershberg, 392–434. New York: Oxford Univ. Press, 1981.

Higginbotham, Evelyn Brooks. "African-American Women's History and the Metalanguage of Race." *Signs* 17, no. 2 (Winter 1992): 251–74.

———. "Religion, Politics, and Gender: The Leadership of Nannie Helen Burroughs." In *This Far by Faith: Readings in African-American Women's Religious Biography,* ed. Judith Weisenfeld and Richard Newman, 140–57. New York: Routledge, 1996.

————. *Righteous Discontent: The Women's Movement in the Black Baptist Church, 1880–1920.* Cambridge: Harvard Univ. Press, 1993.

Hiller, Amy M. "The Disfranchisement of Delaware Negroes in the Late Nineteenth Century." *Delaware History* 8 (1966): 124–53.

Hoffecker, Carol E. "The Politics of Exclusion: Blacks in Late Nineteenth-Century Wilmington, Delaware." *Delaware History* 16, no. 1 (Apr. 1974): 60–72.

Hofstadter, Richard. *Social Darwinism in American Thought.* New York: George Braziller, 1959.

Holland, Frederick May. *Frederick Douglass: The Colored Orator.* New York: Funk and Wagnals, 1891.

Holmes, Dwight Oliver Wendell. *The Evolution of the Negro College.* New York: Bureau of Publications, Teacher's College, Columbia Univ., 1934.

Hordern, William E. *A Layman's Guide to Protestant Theology.* Rev. ed. New York: Macmillan, 1968.

Horton, James Oliver. "Shades of Color: The Mulatto in Three Antebellum Northern Communities." *Afro-Americans in N. Y. Life and History* 8, no. 2 (July 1984): 37–59.

Howe, Daniel Walker. *The Unitarian Conscience.* Cambridge: Harvard Univ. Press, 1970.

Humez, Jean McMahon. "'My Spirit Eye': Some Functions of Spiritual and Visionary Experience in the Lives of Five Black Women Preachers, 1810–1880." In *Women and the Structure of Society: Selected Research from the Fifth Berkshire Conference on the History of Women,* ed. Barbara J. Harris and JoAnn K. McNamara. 129–43. Durham, N.C.: Duke Univ. Press, 1984.

————, ed. *Gift of Power: The Writings of Rebecca Jackson, Black Visionary, Shaker Eldress.* Amherst: Univ. of Massachusetts Press, 1986.

Hutchison, William R. *The Modernist Impulse in American Protestantism.* New York: Oxford Univ. Press, 1976.

————. *The Transcendentalist Ministers: Church Reform in the New England Renaissance.* New Haven: Yale Univ. Press, 1959.

Interdenominational Theological Center 1988–1991 Catalog.

Johnson, Edward A. *History of Negro Soldiers in the Spanish-American War and Other Items of Interest.* Raleigh, N.C.: Capital Printing, 1899.

Johnson, Michael P., and James L. Roark. *Black Masters: A Free Family of Color in the Old South.* New York: W. W. Norton, 1984.

Joiner, William A. *A Half Century of Freedom of the Negro in Ohio.* Compiled and arranged by W. A. Joiner. Xenia, Ohio: Smith Adv., [1915].

Jordon, Winthrop D. *White Over Black: American Attitudes Towards the Negro, 1550–1812.* Chapel Hill: Univ. of North Carolina Press, 1968.

Kamentz, Jerman. "History of American Spas and Hydrotherapy." In *Medical Hydrology,* ed. Sidney Licht, 160–89. Baltimore: Waverly Press, 1963.

Kern, Alexander. "The Rise of Transcendentism." In *Transitions in American Literary History,* ed. Harry Hayden Clark, 247–314. Durham, N.C.: Duke Univ. Press, 1953.

Killian, Charles. "Daniel A. Payne and the A.M.E. General Conference of 1888: A Display of Contrasts." *Negro History Bulletin* 32, no. 7 (1969): 11–14.

Koster, Donald N. *Transcendentalism in America.* Boston: G. K. Hall, 1975.

Lee, Jarena. *The Life and Religious Experience of Jarena Lee, a Coloured Lady, Giving an Account of Her Call to Preach the Gospel.* In Andrews, *Sisters of the Spirit.*

Lee, M. E. "The Home-Maker." *A.M.E. Church Review* 18, no. 1 (July 1891).

Lewis, Ronald L. "Reverend T. G. Steward and the Education of Blacks in Reconstruction Delaware." *Delaware History* 19, no. 3 (1981): 156–78.

———. "Reverend T. G. Stewart and 'Mixed' Schools in Delaware, 1882." *Delaware History* 19 (Spring–Summer 1980): 53–58.

Lincoln, C. Eric, and Lawrence H. Mamiya. *The Black Church in the African American Experience.* Durham, N.C.: Duke Univ. Press, 1990.

Litwack, Leon F. *Been into the Storm So Long: The Aftermath of Slavery.* New York: Vintage Books, 1980.

———. *North of Slavery: The Negro in the Free States, 1790–1860.* Chicago: Univ. of Chicago Press, 1961.

Litwack, Leon, and August Meier, eds. *Black Leaders of the Nineteenth Century.* Chicago: Univ. of Illinois Press, 1988.

Livesay, Harold C. "Delaware Blacks, 1865–1915." In *Readings in Delaware History,* ed. Carol E. Hoffecker, 121–54. Newark: Univ. of Delaware Press, 1973.

Logan, Rayford W. *The Betrayal of the Negro: From Rutherford B. Hayes to Woodrow Wilson.* London: Collier Books, 1965. Originally published as *The Negro in American Life and Thought: The Nadir, 1877–1901.* New York: Dial, 1954.

Logan, Rayford W., and Michael R. Winston, eds. *Dictionary of American Negro Biography.* New York: W. W. Norton, 1982.

Luker, Ralph E. "The Social Gospel and the Failure of Racial Reform, 1877–1898." *Church History* 46 (Mar. 1977): 80–99.

———. *The Social Gospel in Black and White: American Racial Reform, 1885–1912.* Chapel Hill: Univ. of North Carolina Press, 1991.

Lynch, John Roy. *Reminiscences of an Active Life: The Autobiography of John Roy Lynch,* edited and with an Introduction by John Hope Franklin. Chicago: Univ. of Chicago Press, 1970.

Lyons, Maritcha R. "Susan S. (McKinney) Steward." In Brown, *Homespun Heroines.*

Mark, George P., III, ed. and comp. *The Black Press Views American Imperialism (1898–1900).* With a preface by William Loren Katz. New York: Arno Press and the New York Times, 1971.

Marsden, George M. "Fundamentalism and American Evangelicalism." In *The Variety of American Evangelicalism,* ed. Donald W. Dayton and Robert K. Johnston, 22–35. Knoxville: Univ. of Tennessee Press, 1991.

Martin, Sandy Dwayne. *For God and Race: The Religious and Political Leadership of AMEZ Bishop James Walker Hood.* Columbia: Univ. of South Carolina Press, 1999.

Martin, Waldo E., Jr. *The Mind of Frederick Douglass.* Chapel Hill: Univ. of North Carolina Press, 1984.

Mathews, Donald G. "The Second Great Awakening as an Organizing Process." In *Religion in American History: Interpretive Essays,* ed. John M. Mulder and John F. Wilson. 199–217. Englewood Cliffs, N.J.: Prentice-Hall, 1978.

May, Henry F. *Protestant Churches and Industrial America.* New York: Octagon Books, 1963.

McGinnis, Frederick Alphonso. *A History and an Interpretation of Wilberforce University.* Wilberforce, Ohio: Brown Publishing, 1941.

McPherson, James M. *Battle Cry of Freedom: The Civil War Era.* New York: Oxford Univ. Press, 1988.

———. "Grant or Greeley? The Abolitionist Dilemma in the Election of 1872." *American Historical Review* 71 (Oct. 1965): 43–61.

Meier, August. *Negro Thought in America 1880–1915, 1880–1915: Racial Ideologies in the Age of Booker T. Washington.* Ann Arbor: Univ. of Michigan Press, 1963.

Miller, Albert G. "'Her Children Shall Rise Up and Call Her Blessed': The Use of Rebecca Steward as a Paragon of Female Domesticity." Paper presented at American Academy of Religion, Nov. 21–24, 1992, San Francisco, California.

———. "Striving to Reconcile the World: A Glimpse of the Life and Writings of Theophilus Gould Steward." *A.M.E. Church Review* 111, no. 362 (1996).

Miller, Floyd. *The Search for Black Nationality: Black Emigration and Colonization, 1787–1863.* Chicago: Univ. of Illinois Press, 1975.

Miller, Hugh. *An Autobiography. My Schools and Schoolmasters; or, The Story of My Education.* Boston: Gould and Lincoln, 1857.

———. *The Testimony of the Rocks; or, Geology in Its Bearings on the Two Theologies, Natural and Revealed.* Boston: Gould and Lincoln, 1857.

Miller, Kelly. *Radicals and Conservatives and Other Essays on the Negro in America.* New York: Schocken Books, 1968.

Minutes of the Eighth Session of the North Ohio Annual Conference of the A.M.E. Church: Held at St. James A.M.E. Church in Troy, Ohio from September 18th to 25th 1889. Wilberforce Univ. Library Archives.

Minutes of the National Convention of Colored Citizens: Held at Buffalo on the 15th, 16th, 17th, 18th, and 19th of August 1843 for the Purpose of Considering Their Moral and Political Condition as American Citizens. New York: Piercy and Reed, 1843.

Minutes of the Nineteenth Florida Annual Conference of the African Methodists Episcopal Church. Nov. 1884. Wilberforce Univ. Library Archives.

Minutes of the Twenty-Third Session of the Pittsburgh Conference of the A.M.E. Church: Held at Williamsport, Pa. October 8th to 15th 1890. Wilberforce Univ. Library Archives.

Mitchel, O. M. *Astronomy of the Bible.* New York: Oakley and Mason, 1868.

Moorhead, James H. "James Addison Alexander: Common Sense, Romanticism and Biblical Criticism at Princeton." *Journal of Presbyterian History* 53 (1975): 51–65.

Morris, Robert C. *Reading, 'Riting, and Reconstruction: The Education of Freedmen in the South, 1861–1870.* Chicago: Univ. of Chicago Press, 1981.

Moses, Wilson Jeremiah. *Alexander Crummell: A Study of Civilization and Discontent.* New York: Oxford Univ. Press, 1989.

Moss, Alfred, Jr. *The American Negro Academy: Voice of the Talented Tenth.* Baton Rouge: Univ. of Louisiana Press, 1981.

Muller, Dorothea R. "Josiah Strong and American Nationalism: A Reevaluation." *Journal of American History* 53, no. 3 (Dec. 1966): 487–503.

Murphy, Larry. "Education and Preparation for the Ministry in the African Methodist Episcopal Church, 1787–1900." *A.M.E Church Review* 101, no. 323 (July–Sept. 1986): 19–33.

Nalty, Bernard C. *Strength for the Fight: A History of Black Americans in the Military.* New York: Free Press, 1986.

Nichols, T. L., and M. S. G. Nichols. *Marriage: Its History, Character, and Results; Its Sanctities and Its Profanities; Its Science and Its Facts; Demonstrating Its Influence, as a Civilized Institution, on the Happiness of the Individual, and the Progress of the Race.* Rev. ed. Cincinnati, [1855].

Nissenbaum, Stephen. *Sex, Diet, and Debility in Jacksonian America: Sylvester Graham and Health Reform.* Westport, Conn.: Greenwood Press, 1980.

Noll, Mark A. "Common Sense Traditions and American Evangelical Thought." *American Quarterly* 37 (Summer 1985): 216–38.

Number, Ronald L. *Prophetess of Health: A Study of Ellen G. White.* New York: Harper and Row, 1974.

Otto, Rudolf. *The Idea of the Holy.* Translated by John W. Harvey. New York: Oxford Univ. Press, 1971.

Outlaw, Lucius. "Toward a Critical Theory of 'Race.'" In *Anatomy of Racism,* ed. David Theo Goldberg, 58–82. Minneapolis: Univ. of Minnesota Press, 1990.

Painter, Nell Irvin. *Exodusters: Black Migration to Kansas after Reconstruction.* New York: Alfred A. Knopf, 1977.

———. *Standing at Armageddon: The United States, 1877–1919.* New York: W. W. Norton, 1987.

Paris, Peter J. *The Social Teaching of the Black Churches.* Philadelphia: Fortress Press, 1985.

Payne, Daniel A. *History of African Methodist Episcopal Church.* Nashville: Publishing House of the African Methodist Episcopal Sunday School Union, 1891; reprint, New York: Arno Press, 1969.

———. *Recollections of Seventy Years.* With an introduction by Rev. F. J. Grimké, A.M., D.D. Nashville: Publishing House of the AME Sunday School Union, 1888; reprint, New York: Arno Press and the New York Times, 1968.

———. *A Treatise on Domestic Education.* 1885. Reprint, Freeport, N.Y.: Books for Libraries Press, 1971.

Perkins, Linda Marie. "Fanny Jackson Coppin and the Institute for Colored Youth: A Model of Nineteenth Century Black Female Educational and Community Leadership, 1837–1902." Ph.D. diss., Univ. of Illinois at Urbana-Champaign, 1978.

Perry, Rufus L. *The Cushite; or, The Descendents of Ham as Found in the Sacred Scriptures and in the Writings of Ancient Historians and Poets from Noah to the Christian Era.* Springfield, Mass.: Willey, 1893.

Pope, William B. *Higher Catechism of Theology.* New York: Phillips & Hunt, 1884.

Porter, Lawrence C. "Transcendentalism: A Self-Portrait." *New England Quarterly* (Mar. 1962): 27–47.

Price, Clement Alexander, ed. *Freedom Not Far Distant: A Documentary History of Afro-Americans in New Jersey.* Newark: New Jersey Historical Society, 1980.

Proceedings of the Convention of Colored People. Dover, Delaware, Jan. 9, 1873.

Quarles, Benjamin. *Black Abolitionists.* New York: Oxford Univ. Press, 1975.

Raboteau, Albert J. "The Black Experience in American Evangelicalism: The Meaning of Slavery." In *The Evangelical Tradition in America,* ed. Leonard I. Sweet, 181–98. Macon, Ga.: Mercer Univ. Press, 1984.

———. "'Ethiopia Shall Soon Stretch Forth Her Hands': Black Destiny in Nineteenth-Century America." The University Lecture in Religion at Arizona State Univ., Jan. 27, 1983.

———. *Slave Religion: The "Invisible Institution" in the Antebellum South.* New York: Oxford Univ. Press, 1978.

Ralston, Thomas Neely. *Elements of Divinity.* Cincinnati: Poe & Hitchcock, 1863.

Ransom, Reverdy C. *The Pilgrimage of Harriet Ransom's Son.* Nashville: AME Sunday School Union, n.d.

Redkey, Edwin S. *Black Exodus: Black Nationalist and Back-to-Africa Movements, 1890–1910.* New Haven: Yale Univ. Press, 1969.

Republican Congressional Committee (1871–1873), *Grant or Greeley—Which? Facts and arguments for the consideration of the colored citizens of the United States: being extracts from letters, speeches, and editorials by colored men and their best friends. Sumner's mistake, Greeley's surrender, and Grant's faithfulness. Opinions in brief of Wm. Lloyd Garrison, Wendell Phillips, Prof. J. Mercer, Langston, R. H. Dana, Jr., Judge Hoar, Fred. Douglass, Speaker Blaine, Wm. D. Forten, Prof. Wm. Howard Day.* Washington, D.C.: Our National Progress, 1872.

Richardson, Joe M. *Christian Reconstruction: The American Missionary Association and Southern Blacks, 1861–1890.* Athens: Univ. of Georgia Press, 1986.

Rose, Anne C. *Transcendentalism as A Social Movement, 1830–1850.* New Haven: Yale Univ. Press, 1981.

Salem, Dorothy. *To Better Our World: Black Women in Organized Reform, 1890–1920.* Brooklyn: Carlson Publishing, 1990.

Schor, Joel. *Henry Highland Garnet: A Voice of Black Radicalism in the Nineteenth Century.* Westport, Conn.: Greenwood Press, 1977.

Schwantes, Carlos A. *Coxey's Army: An American Odyssey.* Lincoln: Univ. of Nebraska Press, 1985, 27–44.

Sears, Hal D. "The Sex Radicals: Free Love in High Victorian America." *Virginia Quarterly Review* 48 (Summer 1972): 377–92.

———. *The Sex Radicals: Free Love in High Victorian America.* Lawrence: Regents Press of Kansas, 1977.

Seraile, William. "Susan McKinney Steward: New York State's First African-American Woman Physician." In *Afro-Americans in New York Life and History,* July 9, 1985, 27–44.

———. "Theophilus G. Steward, Intellectual Chaplain, 25th US Colored Infantry." *Nebraska History* 66 (1985): 272–93.

———. *Voice of Dissent: Theophilus Gould Steward (1843–1924) and Black America.* Brooklyn, N.Y.: Carlson Publishing, 1992.

Sernett, Melton. *Black Religion and American Evangelicalism: White Protestants, Plantation Missions and the Flowering of Negro Christianity, 1787–1865.* Metuchen, N.J.: Scarecrow Press, 1975.

Simmons, William J., ed. *Men of Mark: Eminent, Progressive and Rising.* Cleveland: Geo M. Rewell, 1887; New York: Arno Press and the New York Times, 1968.

Singleton, George A. *The Romance of African Methodism: A Study of the African Methodist Episcopal Church.* New York: Exposition Press, 1952.

Sklar, Kathryn Kish. *Catharine Beecher: A Study in American Domesticity.* New York: W. W. Norton, 1976.

Smith, Amanda. *An Autobiography: The Story of the Lord's Dealings with Mrs. Amanda Smith the Colored Evangelist.* With an introduction by Jualynne E. Dodson. Chicago: Meyer, 1893; reprint, New York: Oxford Univ. Press, 1988.

Smith, Charles Spencer. *A History of the African Methodist Episcopal Church.* Philadelphia: AME Book Concern, 1922.

Smith, E. Shelton. *In His Image, But . . . : Racism in Southern Religion, 1780–1910.* Durham, N.C.: Duke Univ. Press, 1972.

Smith, Timothy. "Slavery and Theology: The Emergence of Black Christian Consciousness in Nineteenth Century America." *Church History* 41 (1972): 497–512.

Smith-Rosenberg, Carroll. "Women and Religious Revivals: Anti-Ritualism, Liminality, and the Emergence of the American Bourgeoisie." In *The Evangelical Tradition in America,* ed. Leonard I. Sweet. 199–231. Macon, Ga.: Mercer Univ. Press, 1984.

Sobel, Mechal. *Trabelin' On: The Slave Journey to an Afro-Baptist Faith.* Princeton, N.J.: Princeton Univ. Press, 1988.

Spiller, G., ed. *Papers on Inter-Racial Problems Communicated to the First Universal Races Congress Held at the University of London, July 26–29, 1911.* London: P. S. King and Son, 1911.

Spurlock, John C. *Free Love: Marriage and Middle-Class Radicalism in America, 1825–1860.* New York: New York Univ. Press, 1988.

Stampp, Kenneth M. *The Era of Reconstruction, 1865–1877.* New York: Alfred A. Knopf, 1965.

Starobin, Robert. "Denmark Vesey's Slave Conspiracy of 1822: A Study in Rebellion and Resistance." In *American Slavery: The Question of Resistance,* ed. John Bracey Jr., August Meier, and Elliott Rudwick. 142–57. Belmont, Calif.: Wadsworth, 1970.

Stearns, Bertha-Monica. "The Forgotten New England Reformers." *New England Quarterly* 6 (Mar. 1933): 59–84.

———. "Memnonia; The Launching of a Utopia." *New England Quarterly* 15 (June 1942): 280–95.

Steward, Gustavus Adolphus. "The Church of My Fathers." *Crisis* (July 1932): 220–21, 236.

Steward, Susan M. "Colored American Women." *Crisis* 3, no. 1. (Nov. 1911): 33–34.

———. "Woman in Medicine: A Paper Read Before the National Association of Colored Women's Clubs at Wilberforce, Ohio August 6, 1914." Wilberforce, Ohio. Indiana Univ. Libraries, Bloomington.

Stoddard, Lothrop. *Rising Tide of Color Against White World Supremacy.* New York: Charles Scribner's, Sons, 1920.

Stoehr, Taylor. *Free Love in America: A Documentary History.* New York: AMS Press, 1979.

Stover, Earl F. "Chaplain Henry V. Plummer, His Ministry and His Court-Martial." *Nebraska History* (Spring 1975): 20–50.

———. *Up from Handymen: The United States Army Chaplaincy, 1865–1920.* Vol. 3. Washington, D.C.: Office of the Chief of Chaplains, Department of the Army, 1977.

Strong, Josiah. *The New Era; or, The Coming Kingdom.* New York: Baker and Taylor, 1893.

———. *The Next Great Awakening.* New York: Baker and Taylor, 1902.

———. *Our Country.* 2d ed. New York: Baker and Taylor, 1891; Cambridge: Belknap Press, Harvard Univ. Press, 1963.

———. *Our Country: Its Possible Future and Its Present Crisis.* New York: American Home Missionary Society, 1885.

Stuckey, Sterling. *The Ideological Origins of Black Nationalism.* Boston: Beacon Press, 1972.

Sweet, Leonard I. *Black Images of America, 1784–1870.* New York: W. W. Norton, 1976.

Tanner, Benjamin T. "Book and Pamphlet Table." *A.M.E. Church Review* 4 (May 1887): 461–67.

———. *The Color of Solomon—What?* Philadelphia: AME Book Concern, 1895.

———. *The Descent of the Negro.* N.p.: n.p., 1898.

Tanner, Benjamin T. "Genesis Re-Read." *A.M.E. Church Review* 2 (Jan. 1886): 235–37.

———. *The Negro in Holy Writ.* Philadelphia: n.p., 1902.

———. *The Negro's Origin.* Philadelphia: African Methodist Episcopal Depository, 1869.

Thomas, Bettye C. "Public Education and Black Protest in Baltimore, 1865–1900." *Maryland History Magazine* 71, no. (1976): 381–91.

Thorpe, Earl E. *The Mind of the Negro: An Intellectual History of Afro-Americans.* Baton Rouge, La.: Ortlieb Press, 1961.

Tindall, George Brown. *South Carolina Negroes, 1877–1890.* Columbia: Univ. of South Carolina Press, 1952.

Trask, David F. *The War with Spain in 1898.* New York: Macmillan, 1981.

Trinity A.M.E. Church Gouldtown, NJ, 200th Year Anniversary 1792–1992.

Turner, Henry McNeal. *The Genius and Theory of Methodist Polity; or, The Machinery of Methodism: Practically Illustrated through a Series of Questions and Answers.* Philadelphia: Publishing Department, AME Church, 1885.

United States Congress. *Biographical Dictionary of the United States Congress, 1774–1989.* Washington, D.C.: GPO, 1989.

Van Deburg, William L. "Frederick Douglass: Maryland Slave to Religious Liberal." *Maryland Historical Magazine* 69, no. 1 (Spring 1974): 27–43.

———. "Rejected of Men: The Changing Religious Views of William Lloyd Garrison and Frederick Douglass." Ph.D. diss., Michigan State Univ., 1973.

Walker, Clarence E. *A Rock in a Weary Land: The African Methodist Episcopal Church during the Civil War and Reconstruction.* Baton Rouge: Louisiana State Univ. Press, 1982.

Walsh, James J. *Old-time Makers of Medicine; The Story of the Students and Teachers of the Sciences Related to Medicine during the Middle Ages.* New York: Fordham Univ. Press, 1911.

Ward, T. M. D. "Quadrennial Address of the Board of Bishops of the A.M.E. Church." Delivered at the Nineteenth Session of the General Conference of the AME Church, May 12, 1888. Reprinted in *A.M.E. Church Review* 102 (Apr.–June 1988): 17–33.

Washington, James Melvin. *Frustrated Fellowship: The Black Baptist Quest for Social Power.* Macon, Ga.: Mercer Univ. Press, 1986.

Wears, Isaiah C. "Rev. Theophilus Gould Steward, D.D., Chaplain U.S. Army." *A.M.E. Church Review* 10 (July 1894): 137–40.

Weisenburger, Francis P. "William Sanders Scarborough: Early Life and Years at Wilberforce." *Ohio History* 71, no. 3 (Oct. 1962): 203–26.

———. "William Sanders Scarborough: Scholarship, the Negro, Religion, and Politics." *Ohio History* 72, no. 1 (Jan. 1963): 25–50.

Weisenfeld, Judith. *African American Women and Christian Activism: New York's Black YWCA, 1905–1945.* Cambridge: Harvard Univ. Press, 1997.

Weiss, Harry B., and Howard R. Kemble. *The Great American Water-Cure Craze: A History of Hydropathy in the United States.* Trenton, N.J.: Past Times Press, 1967.

Wellek, René. "Emerson and German Philosophy." *New England Quarterly* 16 (1942): 41–62.

Wells-Barnett, Ida. *On Lynchings: Southern Horrors, A Red Record, and Mob Rule in New Orleans.* With a new preface by August Meier. New York: Arno and New York Times Press, 1969.

West, Cornel. *Prophesy Deliverance! An Afro-American Revolutionary Christianity.* Philadelphia: Westminster Press, 1982.

———. *Prophetic Fragments.* Grand Rapids, Mich., and Trenton, N.J.: William B. Eerdmans Publishing and African World Press, 1988.

Wheeler, Edward J. *Uplifting the Race: The Black Minister in the New South, 1865–1902.* Lanham, Md.: Univ. of America Press, 1986.

White, Ronald C., Jr. *Liberty and Justice for All: Racial Reform and the Social Gospel.* San Francisco: Harper and Row, Publishers, 1990.

Wilberforce Bulletin. Ser. 4., no. 3 (June 1918).

Wilkie, Jacqueline S. "Submerged Sensuality: Technology and Perceptions of Bathing." *Journal of Social History* (Spring 1986): 649–64.

Williams, D. B. "The Harmony between the Bible and Science Concerning Primitive Man." *A.M.E. Church Review* 9 (July 1892): 19–20.

Williams, George Washington. *History of the Negro Race in America from 1619 to 1880, Negroes as Slaves, as Soldiers, and as Citizens; Together with a Preliminary Consideration of the Unity of the Human Family, an Historical Sketch of Africa, and an Account of the Negro Governments of Sierra Leone and Liberia.* Vols. 1 and 2. New York: G. P. Putnam's Sons, 1883.

―――. *A History of the Negro Troops in the War of the Rebellion, 1861–1865.* New York: Harper & Brothers, 1888.

Williamson, Joel. *New People: Miscegenation and Mulattoes in the United States.* New York: Free Press, 1980.

Wills, David W. "Aspects of Social Thought in the African Methodist Church 1884–1910." Ph.D. diss., Harvard Univ., 1975.

―――. "Womanhood and Domesticity in the A.M.E. Tradition: The Influence of Daniel Alexander Payne." In *Black Apostles at Home and Abroad: Afro-Americans and the Christian Mission from the Revolution to Reconstruction,* ed. David W. Wills and Richard Newman, 133–46. Boston: G. K. Hall, 1982.

Wilmore, Gayraud S. *Black Religion and Black Radicalism.* New York: Orbis Books, 1985.

―――. *Black Religion and Black Radicalism: An Interpretation of the Religious History of African Americans.* 3d ed. Maryknoll, N.Y.: Orbis Books, 1998.

Wilson, Jeremiah Moses. *Alexander Crummell: A Study of Civilization and Discontent.* New York: Oxford Univ. Press, 1989.

―――. *The Golden Age of Black Nationalism.* Hamden, Conn.: Archon Books, 1978.

Woodson, Carter G. *The History of the Negro Church.* 3d ed. Washington, D.C.: Associated Publishers, 1985.

Wright, Conrad. *The Beginnings of Unitarianism in America.* Boston: Starr King Press, 1955.

Wright, Richard R., Jr., comp. *Encyclopaedia of African Methodism.* 2d ed. Philadelphia: Book Concern of the AME Church, 1947.

Wrobel, Arthur. "Phrenology as Political Science." In *Pseudo-Science and Society in Nineteenth-Century America,* ed. Arthur Wrobel, 122–43. Lexington: Univ. Press of Kentucky, 1987.

Wuthnow, Robert. *The Struggle for America's Soul: Evangelicals, Liberals, and Secularism.* Grand Rapids, Mich.: William B. Eerdmans, 1989.

Index